THE DOCTRINE
OF THE TRINITY

THE DOCTRINE OF THE TRINITY

CROALL LECTURES, 1942–1943

BY

LEONARD HODGSON

D.D.(Oxon), Hon.D.D.(Edin.)

REGIUS PROFESSOR OF DIVINITY IN THE UNIVERSITY OF OXFORD
CANON OF CHRIST CHURCH

LONDON: NISBET AND CO., LTD.
22 BERNERS STREET, W.1

First Published . . . September 1943
Reprinted . . . . . May 1944
Reprinted . . . . . February 1946

THE TYPOGRAPHY AND BINDING
OF THIS BOOK CONFORM TO THE
AUTHORIZED ECONOMY STANDARDS

MADE IN GREAT BRITAIN
PRINTED BY MORRISON AND GIBB LTD.,
LONDON AND EDINBURGH

PREFACE

THIS book contains the Croall Lectures delivered in Edinburgh in January 1943. They are printed exactly as they were spoken, except that in the speaking some passages in the fourth, fifth and sixth lectures had to be omitted for lack of time. What extra matter I have thought it necessary to provide has been added in the form of appendices and not by expansion of the lectures.

My first duty in writing this Preface is to express to the Croall trustees my deep appreciation of the honour they have done me in appointing me to the lectureship. My gratitude is also due to Principal Curtis and the members of New College whose hospitality provided an ideal setting for the delivery of the lectures.

I must add a very special word of thanks to the Rev. H. K. Archdall, Principal of St. David's College, Lampeter. For two and a half years, as each lecture came from the typewriter, he gave a copy of it sanctuary in his college safe, and thus enabled me to listen to the sound of the sirens with equanimity. Moreover, he has helped me from time to time with comments on what I have written, and, in particular, I am indebted to him for a catena of Scripture passages of which I made considerable use in writing Appendix III.

I am also greatly indebted to the Rev. John Marsh of Mansfield College. When my *Towards a Christian Philosophy* was being published, he very kindly read the final proofs at too late a stage for me to be able to express my thanks in the preface, and saved that book from a number of errors. Now he has not only promised to give the same help again, but also to see this book through the press during my absence in America in the coming months. Its appearance will be the token of my gratitude to him and to the publishers for their combined assistance.

In some footnotes references to my books, *Essays in*

Christian Philosophy and *The Grace of God in Faith and Philosophy*, are followed by a reference to *Towards a Christian Philosophy*. This is because all remaining stocks of the two first named were destroyed by enemy action in 1941 and parts of them have been re-issued under the fresh title.

L. H.

CHRIST CHURCH,
OXFORD,
May 1943.

NOTE TO SECOND EDITION

To avoid a possible misunderstanding I should like to add a further word about the criticism on p. 134 of certain passages in the Archbishop of Canterbury's Gifford Lectures. His conclusion on the point at issue seems to me to involve what I have called the idealist metaphysic, and that metaphysic to involve the subordination of the personal to the impersonal. But I should, perhaps, have made it clearer that the Archbishop would himself repudiate any such subordination, or the surrender of the witness of revelation to any metaphysic. His aim was to provide a rational means of subordinating the demands of metaphysic to the witness of revelation, and he thought that this might be done by a scheme which calls in question the antithesis between moral and metaphysical and insists that in this realm the only metaphysical connections are moral connections. For the reasons given in the text, I think myself that he was attempting the impossible. But the attempt was well worth while, and besides containing so much of permanent value in other parts of the book, on this point *Nature, Man and God* will always have its place in the history of English theological thought as marking a stage in its emancipation from the idealist indifference to revelation.

L. H.

January 1944.

CONTENTS

LECTURE II

THE REVELATION IN THE NEW TESTAMENT

LECTURE III

THE REVELATION IN THE NEW TESTAMENT
(continued)

(i) Jesus of Nazareth was born of the Jews and ultimately accepted by His followers as fulfilling the Messianic prophecies. When the gospel spread to the Gentile world the Church had to

LECTURE IV

TRINITARIAN THEOLOGY

LECTURE V

THE DOCTRINE AND PHILOSOPHY

LECTURE VI

THREE CLASSICAL EXPOSITIONS: AUGUSTINE, AQUINAS, CALVIN

LECTURE VII
TRINITARIAN RELIGION

APPENDICES

THE
DOCTRINE OF THE TRINITY

LECTURE I

REVELATION AS THE SOURCE OF DOCTRINE

(i)

THE subject of these lectures is to be the Christian doctrine of God, and in speaking to this audience I need not labour the point that this means the doctrine of the Trinity. For has not John Calvin himself asserted, in the first book of his *Institutes*, that unless we think of the unity of God as trinitarian we have no true knowledge of God at all, only the word "God" flutters through our brain, naked and void of meaning ? [1]

My subject, then, is the doctrine of the Trinity, and it will be my aim to try to give an exposition of this doctrine in terms of the thought of the present day. I shall not, therefore, follow the plan familiar to us in many courses of lectures, whereby there is first given a history of the doctrine to which the lecturer's own exposition of it is appended as a conclusion. But neither can I simply reverse this order, and begin straight away with my own exposition, afterwards testing it by reference to its past history in order to see whether what is expounded is indeed the historic Christian doctrine. For it is necessary first to explain what I mean by the " terms of the thought of

---

[1] Ita se praedicat unicum esse, ut distincte in tribus personis considerandum proponat, quas nisi tenemus, nudum et inane duntaxat Dei nomen sine vero Deo in cerebro nostro volitat.

the present day." It may help to avoid confusion if I preface what I have to say by a brief statement of the plan which I propose to follow.

There is general agreement that the doctrine of the Trinity is a revealed doctrine. It is, for example, for St. Thomas Aquinas the classic example of the kind of doctrine which can only be made known to man by divine revelation,[1] and Calvin's exposition of it[2] is an exposition of what he accepts as biblical revelation. But what do we mean by "revelation" or "revealed doctrine"? This is a question on which there is much discussion in the theological world of to-day, as is evidenced by the valuable book which Professor John Baillie helped to edit in 1937.[3] Again, the doctrine of the Trinity, even if it be a revealed doctrine, is a form of theism, and theism, as Professor Sorley has pointed out, is one possible answer to a definitely philosophical question.[4] I shall therefore devote this first lecture to a consideration of the sense in which we may regard this doctrine both as a matter of revelation and as a matter of philosophy. Having dealt with these necessary prolegomena, I shall be free to consider the doctrine itself, and the second, third and fourth lectures will contain an exposition of its biblical basis, its formulation in the creeds of the early Church, and the statement of it which I wish to submit to your judgment. In the fifth lecture I shall consider these conclusions in relation to certain trends in modern philosophical thinking, and in the sixth I shall try to test them by comparing them with the expositions of the doctrine by St. Augustine, St. Thomas Aquinas and John Calvin. In this way I shall hope to show that they are true to the historic faith of Christendom. I shall then conclude the course with a seventh lecture in which I shall draw out some practical corollaries of the doctrine for Christian life and worship.

[1] S.T. I. 12, xiii ad. 1.   [2] *Institutes*, I. xiii.
[3] *Revelation*, edited by John Baillie and Hugh Martin. London, Faber & Faber.
[4] *Moral Values and the Idea of God*. Cambridge, 1921, p. 305.

(ii)

"The dominant problem of contemporary religious thought is the problem of revelation." So wrote Dr. Temple, then Archbishop of York, in 1937.[1] It is tiresome that it should be so, for the problem of revelation is part of the curse of Adam, a recurrent weed in the garden of thought which has to be cleared out of the way before we can attend to the proper object of our care and interest. We must examine afresh the relations between revelation and reason, between theology and philosophy, before we can consider the doctrine of the Trinity.

The emergence of this problem to be at least one of the main themes of present-day theological discussion is connected with the rise in catholicism and protestantism respectively of neo-thomist and neo-calvinist schools of thought. However they may differ in other respects, both these schools are at one in repudiating their immediate predecessors whose liberalism and idealism, they say, led them to subordinate revelation to reason and theology to philosophy, and thus to obliterate the true character of the Christian religion. As usually happens in such reactions, the first impulse of the new movement was towards a wholesale condemnation of what had gone before. But the time has now come when it should be possible to try to reach a more balanced judgment on the question at issue, and this we must try to do.

The first thing that is necessary is to distinguish between that philosophical movement of nineteenth-century thought which was dominated by post-Kantian idealism, and the contemporary theological movement which was dominated by the literary and historical criticism of the Bible. However closely they may have been interconnected, however deeply they may have influenced one another, they were distinct movements and must be considered separately. One thing, indeed, they had in common, and that was a belief in the unity and objectivity of truth, and of its

[1] Baillie and Martin: *Revelation*, p. 83.

paramount claim on the allegiance of the human mind. In this they were surely right, for however true it may be that men or groups of men can only approach the truth along the several perspectives open to them in their different historical situations, it is surely better that they should think of themselves as seeking to apprehend the one objective truth and to correct one another's misapprehensions, than that they should be content with a chaos of "existential judgments" in which victory must go to the one which can be shouted loudest or enforced with the most powerful armaments.[1] Such a pluralism, if it were accepted as the last word about the nature of things, would be inconsistent with Christian belief in the unity of God, and though we must face the question whether apart from divine revelation man is shut up within such a chaotic conflict of existential judgments, we must not acquiesce in that scepticism as to the unity and objectivity of God's truth which would make might to be right in the spheres both of action and of thought.

Anything I may have to say about the alleged iniquities of idealistic philosophy must be left until the fifth lecture. I must confine myself now to the effect of literary and historical criticism on our reading of the Bible.

No one can read the literature of the controversies of the last century without realising that a hundred or so years ago Christian believers regarded any statement contained in the Bible as a statement of fact to be accepted as true because uttered by God. This applied to statements concerning matters of historical and scientific inquiry as well as to those pronouncing God's moral judgments or bearing witness to His justice and mercy. The divine revelation was given in the form of a collection of statements or propositions to be accepted and believed on the authority of the Giver. The Bible was this collection of divinely

[1] From its original technical use by Kierkegaard the phrase "existential judgment" has come to be used more generally to denote the fact that human judgments must inevitably be those of finite creatures viewing the world from the standpoint of their own existences. On this see my *Essays in Christian Philosophy*, XII = *Towards a Christian Philosophy*, Ch. II.

guaranteed propositions; it was the Word of God because it contained the words of God.

It was this view of the Bible which was rudely shaken by the scientific discoveries and historical researches of the last century. There is no need here to retrace the history of that difficult period, that to us rather dreary period when the conclusions of criticism seemed so largely negative, when the devout believer had to choose between scholarly commentaries which provided no nourishment for his soul and devotional commentaries which rode rough shod over the doubts and questionings in his head. Those were days of mental agony for thinking Christians, days when reading the Bible seemed like walking among quicksands. We owe a debt of gratitude to our fathers whose perseverance in honesty has brought us through that perilous passage to the firm ground of to-day. We owe it to them that for us, as for our earlier ancestors of a century ago, scholarship and piety can again unite to expound the Bible as God's Word addressed to us for our salvation. Those earlier ancestors could take for granted the belief that the Bible was a collection of propositions expressing words of God on which they were to meditate for their souls' good. We can take for granted a post-critical approach to the Bible and make the first aim of our study the discernment of whatever God wills to reveal to us through its pages.

What have we gained at the cost of this agonising transition from the pre-critical to the post-critical approach? A clearer apprehension than was given to any previous age that the revelation of God is not given in words but in deeds; that the reason why "the holy Scriptures contain sufficiently all Doctrine required of necessity for eternal salvation through faith in Jesus Christ" is because they bear witness to the activity in history of God our Creator, Redeemer and Sanctifier. This is not, indeed, a new idea. But in earlier ages it was entangled with the thought of the Bible as containing the divine revelation given in the form of propositions; it is only of recent years that we have een able to see it standing clear, so that we can more fully

appreciate its significance. It was certainly so entangled
both in St. Thomas Aquinas and in Calvin. St. Thomas
and Calvin differed from one another at two points. St.
Thomas acknowledged the power of human reason apart
from revelation to discover truth in the field of natural
knowledge and regarded the Church as the authoritative
interpreter of the Bible. Calvin rejected both these positions.
But they were agreed in holding that the divine revelation,
acceptance of which by faith was necessary to salvation,
was given in the form of propositions contained in the Bible.
This profoundly affected their views both of the relation
between revelation and reason and of that between theology
and philosophy. If, therefore, in this important respect we
of the post-critical era cannot see eye to eye with St. Thomas
or Calvin, we must ask whether what was essential and enduring in their thought can be disentangled from what has perished
in such a way as to justify the neo-Thomist and neo-Calvinist
insistence on revelation as the basis of Christian theology.

The traditional distinction between philosophy and
theology, such as we find in St. Thomas Aquinas, is not
itself derived from the Bible, nor is it exclusively of Christian
or Jewish origin. Wherever else it may also be found, it is
part of the common stock of the Greek tradition, in which
rational philosophical thought and mythology were regarded
as parallel sources (either rival or complementary) of human
knowledge.[1] In the commonly accepted Christian tradition
represented by St. Thomas, the Biblical revelation succeeds
to the position previously held by mythology, the difference
being that the myth-element in Christianity claims to be
true history. Philosophical doctrines are derived from the
exercise of pure rational thinking; theological doctrines
are the exposition of the content of the myth or the alleged
history. These two sources of information are thought of
as giving it in the form of propositions. The contrast between
philosophy and theology is made, so to speak, at the level
of propositions. The basic philosophical proposition is one

---

[1] I owe recognition of this to a paper read to an Oxford Society by Mr.
M. B. Foster in 1939 which, so far as I know, has not been published.

which is rationally coherent and intelligible; the basic theological proposition is one which is accepted on faith as divine revelation, a word of God.

I wish now to argue that this distinction drawn in this way cannot be maintained, that it does not accurately describe the actual procedure of either philosophy or theology, and that the distinction between the two needs to be redrawn on other lines.

Consider first philosophy. To summarise what I have argued at greater length elsewhere,[1] philosophy is essentially a questioning activity, an attempt to understand the given universe of our experience, an attempt which goes beyond the scientific attempt to discover how particular things fit in with one another, and asks why the whole should exist at all and in the way it does exist.[2] In its development the philosophical quest gives birth to particular philosophies or philosophical systems. Each such system comes to birth through some element in the totality of our experience being regarded as of supreme significance for the interpretation of the whole. This element becomes, so to speak, the " key-feature" of the universe, and the adherents of each philosophy are seeking by the aid of its key-feature to unlock the door which will give us insight into the nature of things. We can all of us think of philosophies in which respectively the key-features are logical consistency, moral goodness, the physical order, mathematics, or the interplay of economic forces.

The Christian faith maintains that a certain sequence of events in the history of this world is the key-feature in the light of which everything in heaven and earth is to be

[1] In *The Grace of God in Faith and Philosophy* (London. 1936), pp. 48–55 = *Towards a Christian Philosophy* (London. 1943), pp. 38–50.

[2] Cp. W. R. Sorley in *Moral Values and the Idea of God* (Cambridge, 1921), p. 305: "We are seeking to understand reality, if possible, as a whole; and our beginning must be made from reality as it is known to us. We have found that the parts of reality are all connected together; there is no absolutely independent unit among the objects of experience; in this sense, therefore, reality is known to us as a whole. The problem is, how are we to understand this whole? This is definitely a philosophical question, to which theism is one possible answer."

understood. That sequence of events is regarded as having this supreme significance because it is believed to embody the action of God at work within history rescuing His world from evil and restoring its possibility of perfection. The "Word of God" for Christian faith is not a proposition or series of propositions prescribing what we are to believe or think. It is a series of divine acts to which the Bible bears witness. These acts give rise to propositions when they are reflected on by the mind as it seeks to grasp their significance. The revelation of God is given in deeds; the doctrines of the faith are formulated by reflection on the significance of those deeds.

The biblical record of these events which embody God's redemptive activity is one element among all the given material which we try to understand when we are philosophising. It is *there*—like the ideals of logical consistency and moral goodness, like the physical order, like the mathematical and economic factors in our experience.[1] In making it central, in using it as the key with which to unlock the mysteries of all being, the Christian thinker is behaving in a manner parallel to the idealist, the materialist, and the disciples of Sir James Jeans or Karl Marx. If there can be said to be an idealist philosophy, a positivist philosophy, a mathematico-physicist philosophy and a Marxian philosophy, in precisely the same sense there must be said to be a Christian philosophy.

In this Christian philosophy, as in all other philosophies (*i.e.* philosophical systems) and in philosophy in general (*i.e.* the quest) it is possible to distinguish the formal and the empirical elements. In philosophy in general the empirical element is the given universe of experience about

---

[1] There may be in some quarters a tendency to criticise such a statement as this on the ground that it classes together the objectively given revelation of God and ideals, etc., which are the subjective product of our own minds. This criticism is based on a post-Kantian type of idealistic philosophy which I believe to be false. I here assume a position in which all the things mentioned are equally regarded as objectively presented to the mind for its consideration. See my *Grace of God*, pp. 7, 38, 137, 149 = *Towards a Christian Philosophy*, pp. 14, 119, 181, 191 and below, Lecture V.

which we are thinking, which we are seeking to understand. The formal element is provided by the rational principles of thought[1] in accordance with which the mind seeks to order its experience. In particular philosophical systems a distinction is drawn within the empirical element, between that feature which is regarded as of supreme significance for the interpretation of the whole, and the rest. But the philosophical method by which it is sought to maintain the distinction, and to investigate the relation between the key-feature and the rest, remains the same. The validity of the system as a philosophical system depends on the fidelity with which the relations within the empirical element can be ordered in accordance with the rational principles of thought.

It follows that within each system we may distinguish the study of the key-feature itself from its use as an instrument of philosophical systematising. We can distinguish logic and ethics from idealism, the natural sciences from positivism, mathematics from the philosophy of Jeans and economics from Marxism. What, then, I wish to suggest is that theology should be defined as the study of the key-feature of Christian philosophy, and I would state my thesis in the following seven propositions:

1. Philosophy in general is the attempt to understand the whole of our experience as a whole, asking both what it is and why it should be so.

2. The special sciences are attempts to observe and describe different elements in that experience.

3. Among these elements is the series of events composing Christian history, as recorded in the Old and New Testaments and the history of the Church.

4. Philosophical systems arise through different elements being taken as key-features for the interpretation of the whole.

---

[1] This phrase must not be taken to imply that the human mind is the generative source of these principles. I believe that any genuinely rational principles of thought are as objectively *presented to* our minds as any of the objects of our sense experience. They can only be true laws of thinking because of their prior reality as laws of being.

5. In each case the philosophical use of the key-feature may be distinguished from the scientific study of it.

6. Christian philosophy is the attempt to interpret the whole on the hypothesis that Christian history is the key-feature.

7. Theology is the study of that history with a view to determining the exact nature and meaning of its content.

In support of this thesis I would urge three considerations.

In the first place, this definition of theology as the study of Christian history corresponds to the actual use of the term in current practice. At first sight it is somewhat difficult to see why in my own and (so far as I know) in all other universities and theological colleges "theology" should be held to cover such diverse topics as Hebrew grammar, Hellenistic Greek, textual criticism, biblical exegesis, dogmatics, ecclesiastical history, liturgics and ethics. This becomes intelligible when we think of the subject as the events composing a certain historical series, including the beliefs and teachings of the persons concerned in it.

Secondly, it is found impossible in practice to draw the boundary between theology and philosophy in such a way as to prevent overlapping. The two fields of study are like intersecting circles with an intermediate area which is not no-man's-land but both-men's-land. Philosophical thought is involved in the theologian's formulation of Christian doctrines; philosophers have to consider questions of theological scholarship, as, for example, the evidence for miracles. Now this is parallel to what occurs in the other cases I have mentioned, where a similar both-men's-land is shared by systematising philosophers on the one hand and by logicians, ethicists, natural scientists, mathematicians or economists on the other.

Thirdly, I would test this thesis by applying it to that teaching of St. Thomas Aquinas to which I have already referred and which is so directly relevant to my main subject—the teaching that while we can know by reason that God is, we can only know of His trinitarian nature by

revelation. From what I have said it follows that I believe
St. Thomas here to be calling attention to a real distinction,
but that the distinction is wrongly drawn if it is regarded
as contrasting two classes of propositions of which one is
the discovery of rational thinking and the other a revealed
doctrine presented by God ready-made in propositional
form.

St. Thomas himself refutes the notion that the work of
reason is to formulate formally self-consistent propositions
free from any empirical element. Reason arrives at the
conclusion that God is by reflecting upon the empirically
given created universe; the given existence of creatures is
the material for the argument which concludes to the
existence of God as their cause.[1] Now it is as true to-day
as it was when St. Thomas was writing that the doctrine
of the Trinity is not the product of rational reflection on
the existence of creatures in our general experience. But
it is the product of rational reflection on those particular
manifestations of the divine activity which centre in the
birth, ministry, crucifixion, resurrection and ascension of
Jesus Christ and the gift of the Holy Spirit to the Church.
It is as true to-day as it was then that the doctrine of the
Trinity is a theological doctrine derived from the special
self-revelation of God, a doctrine which, so far as we can
see, could not have been discovered by reason apart from
that revelation. But this is because it could not have been
discovered without the occurrence of those events which
drove human reason to see that they required a trinitarian
God for their cause. Considered logically, the rational
process by which one argues from the existence of creatures
in general to the existence of God is identical with that
by which one argues from the events of the New Testament
to His trinitarian character. The difference in the conclusions
is due to the difference in the empirical elements which
the reason is seeking to account for and to understand.
There is also, however, this difference, that whereas the
argument to a first cause seems to belong to that part of

[1] *S.T.* I. 2, iii.

the philosopher's field which is indisputably the province of philosophy, the argument to the Trinity belongs to that both-men's-land where the circles intersect, where theology and philosophy overlap. I must therefore attempt, in the following lectures, both to expound the theological signific-ance of those events and to consider their philosophical implications.

(iii)

This substitution of revelation in act for revelation in propositions by no means removes all the difficulties of the subject. It does little more than clear a way of approach to the more difficult of them, those concerned with the reception of revelation on the human side.

The phenomena which to some minds are self-evident instances of revelation make no such appeal to others, but, so to speak, "leave them cold." This is so, whether we think of these phenomena as propositions or as acts. It is as true of the events which compose the Christian history as of the sentences which compose the Bible that they speak home to some men as the authentic utterance of the Living God, and for others have no such meaning. Why are these things accepted as revelation by A and B but not by X and Y? And among them, why are some accepted by A and not by B, and others *vice versa*? Why, for example, do some Christians seem to accept the evidence which bears witness to God's mercy and love but to exclude that which tells of His wrath and judgment, while others do the opposite? In such a welter of opinions, how can we be sure where any true revelation is to be found? And if we cannot escape from this uncertainty, how can we continue to believe in revelation at all? Is it credible that God should will to reveal Himself to man in a way which leaves man in such doubt and uncertainty about what He wills to reveal?

The dispassionate consideration of these questions as an intellectual problem is rendered more difficult by the fact that the situations which give rise to them are never exclusively intellectual. When a man is confronted by either a proposition or an event which claims to be divine revelation, the claim which it makes upon him involves moral and emotional factors; it is not a demand merely for intellectual assent but for the response of the whole man. It is the recognition of this truth which gives their importance to the writings of Kierkegaard, Karl Barth and Emil Brunner, and we must always be grateful to them and others like them, who have recalled it to our attention, for it was in danger of being overlooked in the rationalistic liberalism of the preceding era. A man who has been stirred to the depths of his being by the realisation of his condition as the object of God's wrath and mercy cannot, and should not, regard the message which has pierced him to the quick as though it were a mathematical or scientific proposition calling for nothing more than the cool judgment of his reason. It is difficult for such a man dispassionately to examine the credentials of the revelation which comes to him as an imperious and authoritative claim upon him. His theological utterances can only be prophetic in character, as he seeks to find human language in which to express the message he has received.

If there were unanimity among prophetic theologians in the content of these messages, nothing more might be needed. But since there is not, there must clearly be room in God's sight for another class of theologians, those who are called to examine and compare the utterances of the prophets. Their difficulty is this. Unless they can in some measure share in the prophet's *feeling*, they cannot really understand what he is trying to say, but they must not share it so fully as to be rendered incapable of a dispassionate consideration of the total experience. Those of us who are called to this particular work may take comfort from the thought that the work is necessary if theology is not to degenerate into a shouting match between rival prophets. God commissions scholars and theologians as well as prophets.[1] But in the doing of it we must always strive to maintain and keep sensitive this tension in our thinking,

[1] S. Matt. xxiii. 34.

lest we fail either on the one hand to understand what we are thinking about or on the other to think about it clearly. We must bear this continually in mind as we proceed with the present inquiry.

From the fact that the same material—be it propositions or events—produces different effects on different people, we may justly conclude that the difference is due to predisposing causes in the persons concerned. Here Fr. D'Arcy, in the volume to which I have already referred, rightly points out that this phenomenon is not peculiar to the field of divine revelation:

". . . the human mind will have to be illuminated so as to perceive the divine character in the good news. This illumination is by what theologians call grace, and without it there will be lacking that intuitive sympathy which in other fields, as we know, makes all the difference between a successful and unsuccessful interpreter of a manuscript or work of art or novel work of philosophy. What happens in human relations is that something clicks in our minds, the pieces fall into pattern, and our sympathetic efforts are rewarded by possession of the mind of the author."[1]

In the ordinary language of every day we speak of men having different gifts or talents which give, for example, special powers of insight into mathematical, aesthetic or mechanical phenomena. To what extent it is possible to trace the history and origins of these psychological endowments, I do not know. But something of the same kind would seem to be operative in the cases with which we are directly concerned. If this be so, then we have to face the question whether a man's psychological predisposition is such as to give him a clearer insight into truth or to distort his vision. It is possible, for example, that an exaggerated emphasis on God's wrath and judgment, or a one-sided concentration on His benevolence may both have their roots in psychological causes which can be discovered and so discounted. But to pursue this matter further would lead us too far away from our main subject. For our present purpose we must content ourselves with saying that if there

[1] Baillie and Martin, op. cit. p. 212 f.

is to be revelation there must be both the divinely given *revelatum* and also the psychological predisposition to appreciate it on the part of the human recipient.

Now whatever may be the psychological history of this predisposition, the Christian believes that in so far as it gives a man genuine insight into revealed truth, it is ultimately a gift of God. Thus in classical theology it is ascribed to the grace of God, is regarded as the *testimonium Spiritus Sancti internum* and is called faith. "The essential condition of effectual revelation," writes the Archbishop of Canterbury, "is the coincidence of divinely controlled event and minds divinely illumined to read it aright."[1]

Let us now try to imagine ourselves in the position of a man who is conscious of being the recipient of divine revelation. I am not, to begin with, thinking of Amos as he followed his flock, of Isaiah in the year that King Uzziah died, of Ezekiel by the river Chebar, of St. Paul on the road to Damascus or of St. John in the Isle of Patmos. I am thinking of some quite ordinary man of to-day to whom the word of God in the gospel of Jesus Christ comes home in a way which grips him and takes hold upon his whole self. It may come through the actual reading of the Bible, or through the presentation of the gospel story in a sermon or book, or through some experience by which the gospel story which is already well known to him is made to "come alive" as it has never done before, or it may be that on reflection he realises what he has been imperceptibly growing to believe more and more firmly as the years have gone by. Whatever the occasion, the result is the same. He has a subjective certainty concerning both the gospel events and their significance. His eyes have been opened to see that the birth, life, death and resurrection of Jesus Christ were God in action rescuing His world from evil and bringing a message of forgiveness and hope to penitent sinners. This inner, subjective certainty may extend beyond the events of the gospel story, to include the whole of the Bible, the content of creeds or confessions of faith, or such things

---

[1] Baillie and Martin, *op. cit.* p. 107. See also Appendix II, p. 207.

as miracles in the lives of the saints, but for the moment this is irrelevant.

The believing Christian humbly acknowledges that by God's grace his eyes have been opened by the Holy Spirit to see the significance of the biblical record. If this be so, there is reproduced in him the same subjective activity of response to the divine *revelatum* which inspired the prophets and the writers of the Bible itself. The eyes of the prophets were opened to see the significance of the historical events of their time; the eyes of the apostles and of other New Testament writers were opened to see the significance of the life and death and resurrection of Jesus Christ. These all bore witness to what they saw, and their testimony remains in the written word. But it only becomes revelation to those who are inspired in a similar manner to see the significance of what is written.

This inspiration, this opening of the eyes, brings with it both the sense of obligation to respond by the surrender of the whole self, and also a sense of certainty of the truth of what is revealed. This sense, or rather this conviction, of certainty shares in the "givenness" of the whole experience; it comes upon the man as something which is bound up with the reception of the revelation. He knows within himself that his salvation depends upon his acceptance of and response to that which has been given him. From this he might justifiably generalise and argue that a similar obligation would rest upon anyone whose eyes were similarly opened.

Can we go further? I think we can. But the result is to diverge somewhat widely from a commonly accepted tradition in Christian writings. The conclusion that seems to me to be justified is that a man is under obligation to accept and respond to whatever he honestly believes to be true. Whether the field be that of mathematics, medicine, politics, economics, or any other, if it seem to a man that his eyes have been opened to see some truth, then there lies upon him the obligation to accept that truth and to direct his life accordingly, and his salvation depends on his response to that obligation. This would even be so if in the field of religious belief it seemed that his eyes had been opened to see the falsity of the Christian faith, and the required response were apostasy.

The very different conclusion, which is so commonly accepted in Christian writings, is that there are certain truths, those revealed to the prophets, apostles and other writers of the Bible, acceptance of and response to which is necessary to salvation. That is to say, the obligation is transferred a stage further back. It is no longer merely an obligation consequent upon the opening of the eyes. It is an obligation to have the eyes opened so as to see particular things and to see them in a particular light.

How has this transference come about? We are dealing with revelation on the subjective side, where psychologically emotional and intellectual activities are intertwined. Now considered intellectually, two things would seem clear. The first is that truth matters; it is absurd to think that a man is equally well off whether he believes truth or falsehood. The second is that if anything were to be directly revealed by God its truth would be guaranteed absolutely, it would have a certainty superior to anything apprehended otherwise. Emotionally the recipient of the revelation feels that he has learned what it is most important for him to know, and has learned it in a way which absolutely guarantees its truth. He naturally and rightly concludes that this apprehension of truth was never meant to be a private benefit for himself alone; if it is good for him to have it, it will be good for others to have it too. It is an experience in which for their own good all men ought to share.

What precisely is the meaning of the word "ought" in this last sentence? Accurately interpreted it expresses an obligation incumbent not on the persons who lack the experience but on the universe which fails to provide them with it. It is equivalent to the hypothetical judgment, "If the universe were all that it should be, all men would share this experience." But somehow or other the obligation has got transferred from the universe to certain of its

members and they are held responsible for the state of
affairs of which they are the victims. "This is an experience
in which for their own good all men ought to share" is
taken to mean "There is incumbent upon all men an
obligation to have this experience."

It is probably impossible to determine accurately the
source of this confusion. There may be other factors
involved beside the fact that a complex intellectual and
emotional experience finds its natural expression in an
ambiguous form of words. However that may be, it results
in a contradiction in classical Christian theology which
seems to go beyond the limits of what can be endured as
a tension between counterbalancing truths. On the one
hand, it is maintained, a man must be faithful to the truth
as he sees it; on the other that he must, on pain of damnation,
accept the truth as it is taught by the Christian revelation.

I see no way of resolving this contradiction except by
drawing a distinction between the faith which is necessary
to avoid damnation and the faith which is necessary for
ultimate salvation or beatitude. By insisting that for ultimate
salvation it is necessary to believe the Christian revelation
we safeguard the importance of objective truth. It does
matter what we believe. Surrender to the truth of the
Christian faith is an integral element in human blessedness;
it is an experience in which for their own good all men
ought to share. Some of us, by God's grace, may be privileged
to enter upon it during this life, and all who are to be saved
will be given it either here or hereafter. Meanwhile, the
condition of avoiding damnation, the justifying faith which
is necessary, so to speak, in order to be in the running for
the higher privilege of saving faith, is of another kind. It
consists in the surrender of a man's whole self in devotion
to whatever claims he honestly believes to be made upon
him by truth.

One great obstacle to the acceptance of this conclusion
is provided by that conviction of certainty which I have
described as an integral element in the experience of receiving revelation. We all have a natural desire to know

the truth. Human endeavour in philosophy, in the sciences, and in other departments of study, is nerved by the desire to pass from inadequate subjective impressions to a fuller grasp of objective truth. It seems to the recipient of revelation that his dearest wish has been fulfilled, and his subjective conviction of certainty is rationalised by the argument that what God reveals must self-evidently be absolutely guaranteed, and thus take precedence of whatever man may otherwise think to have discovered. This produces the thesis that there is a body of truth which God has made so clear and certain that acceptance of it can be required on pain of damnation.

This wish for certainty, and this rationalisation of its achieved fulfilment, are to be found both in St. Thomas Aquinas and in Calvin.[1] But what is the ground for believing that God wills to give mankind a *revelatum* so clear and self-evident that anyone who fails to grasp its truth and its significance stands self-condemned? This is the premiss which underlies the whole argument, and the more I think about it, the more it appears to be an *a priori* notion of the less reputable sort, to be derived from our own ideas of what we would do if we were God, not from reflection on the revelation which God has given of Himself in what He has actually done.[2] What He has done is to enter personally into the history of this world in order to rescue it from the evil with which it had become infected, and to illuminate the minds of certain men so that they see and understand this. In the course of this redemptive activity He has revealed Himself as essentially righteous and loving, and as one whose fundamental demand on man is for

---

[1] Aliae scientiae certitudinem habent ex naturali lumine rationis humanae, quae potest errare; haec autem certitudinem habet ex lumine divinae scientiae, quae decipi non potest. *S.T.* I. i. v.

Si naturaliter tantum edocti sunt homines, nihil certum vel solidum, vel distinctum tenere: sed confusis tantum principiis esse affixos, ut Deum incognitum adorent. . . . Semper enim Deus indubiam fecit verbo suo fidem, quae omni opinione superior esset. *Inst.* I. v. 12, vi. 2.

[2] I have dealt with this point rather more fully in *Essays in Christian Philosophy*, Essay X. = *Towards a Christian Philosophy*, chap. IV.

inward sincerity. The only possible conclusion to be drawn
from the actual revelation which God has given us is that
while for His own good purposes He enables some people
and not others to grasp that revelation, what He demands
of all men as the condition of their justification is the
sincerity which is true to what it honestly believes and will
not pretend to believe what it does not.

Can we go further and hazard any guess about the purposes for which this illumination is given to those to whom
it comes? Or rather, the reason why it is in this way given
to some and not to others? The more I reflect upon the
nature of this universe and the history of mankind, on the
revelation which God gives of Himself through His handi-
work in creation and that redemptive activity to which
the Bible bears witness, the more clear it seems to become
that God is not seeking simply to collect out of this world
a sufficient number of souls, characterised by the negative
virtue of sinlessness, to be the human population of Heaven.
His aim is to produce a community of creatures each of
which shall be, in his individualised personality, a self-
conscious, intelligent, purposive, free being. If this be
indeed God's purpose, it does render intelligible the actual
mode in which revelation is given. For the fulfilment of
this purpose we need to be given conditions in which we
can grow intellectually, æsthetically and morally as well
as devotionally. The actual result of God's refusal to make
His revelation so clear and self-evident that no one can
fail to grasp it is that our minds are kept on the stretch,
our wits sharpened, our tastes trained, our characters
strengthened. No one, for example, can study the history
of Christian doctrine without discovering how greatly
our insight into its significance has grown through the
interchange of thought between theology and philosophy,
between Christian and pagan, between orthodox and
heretic. All this would have been impossible had God made
clear His mind in the manner suggested by some passages
in St. Thomas and Calvin, and often taken for granted
in traditional Christian theology. But God has chosen the

more excellent way, and when we see this, we see that the apparent arbitrariness in His disposal of revelation plays an intelligible part in His purpose for His world, and is in no way inconsistent with the divine justice. The reason why a particular revelation is given to one man and not to another is that the interplay of their differing minds is for the mutual benefit of both, and it is this mutual benefit that of His love for both God wills with impartial justice to bestow upon them.

(iv)

We have now reached the following conclusions. The divine revelation is given in acts rather than in words, and is received by those whose eyes God opens to see the significance of what He does. The eyes of the biblical writers were opened to see the significance of certain events as the key-feature for the understanding of the universe. They proclaim that these events manifest God's redemptive activity, and by surveying the universe from this standpoint they are enabled to recognise elsewhere His creative and preservative activity. The Bible comes to us in the form of propositions because only by statements in the form of propositions could those whose eyes were opened bear record to future generations of what they saw. It is not these propositions as such which are the *revelatum*. They bear record to the *revelatum*, but as the ages go by they can only continue to mediate the revelation in so far as in each generation men's eyes are opened to see for themselves the significance of the revelatory acts of God to which they bear witness.

One further point needs here to be noticed. It is not sufficient to say simply that each generation must see for itself what was seen by the original recipients of the revelation; as the years go by God enables successive generations to see both what their fathers saw and more. By that interplay of thought between theology and philosophy, between Christian and pagan, between orthodox and heretic, of which I have just spoken, God gives us new insights into and a fuller appreciation of the richness of the significance of the revelation which, just because it is given in unique particular historical events, remains itself one and the same, a once-for-all *depositum fidei*, as the centuries roll on. It is therefore the duty of theologians in every age to soak themselves so far as they can in the thought of their own times and thus imbued to approach again the record of those events, seeking whatever fresh light God will wills to break forth upon them and has been training them to see.

The obligation which lies upon all of us, whether we be Christians or not, is to strive to grasp the truth as we can see it, and to surrender ourselves to what we are given to see. Those of us who are Christians are so because God has opened our eyes to see certain truths. It is not for us to dictate to Him His method of governing His universe; it is not for us to blame those who cannot see things as we see them or to think that they are therefore less well-pleasing in His sight. It may be that in the day of judgment we shall be put to shame by their fidelity to their vocation, and stand aside to see them pass on ahead into the celestial kingdom. Our task is to seek to be faithful to the vocation which God has given to us. He has opened our eyes to see in the events to which the Bible bears witness the key-feature with the aid of which we are to press forward towards a fuller knowledge of God. That is the path in which our Lord bids us Christian theologians to follow Him; if He wills that others should tarry till He come, what is that to us?

In this central assertion that the events which form the substance of the biblical revelation are the key-feature for our knowledge of God and our understanding of all things we are at one with St. Thomas and with Calvin. It can be disentangled from the theory that God's *revelatum* is given in the form of propositions, from mistaken methods of distinguishing between theology and philosophy, and from the belief that to have one's eyes opened to see its truth is the faith which is required of man on earth for justification. This disentangling is one of those fuller insights which

God bestows upon us in this generation, and we give him most high praise and hearty thanks for those of our fore-runners through whose agony in the birth-pangs of modern biblical criticism He has shed this light upon us. Whether we be neo-Thomists or neo-Calvinists, our vocation is not to repeat uncriticised in the twentieth century whatever St. Thomas and Calvin said in the thirteenth and sixteenth, but to try to do for our age and generation what they did for theirs. With them we may believe that the doctrine of the Trinity is in the fullest sense of the words a revealed doctrine, for it is a doctrine which as a matter of historical fact has come to man through the biblical revelation and which, so far as we can see, man had and has no means of discovering for himself apart from that revelation. It is with this understanding of the nature of revelation, of the origin of the doctrine of the Trinity, and of the task and duty of the Christian theologian, that I shall approach this doctrine in the lectures which are to follow.

THE REVELATION IN THE NEW TESTAMENT

(i)

IN his essay on "The Evolution of the Doctrine of the Trinity,"[1] the Bishop of Oxford has called attention to the distinction between two modes of relationship between man and God which may be called respectively "communion" and "possession." In communion with God there is never lost the awareness of a duality; of participation in intercourse between the self and another. But in possession by God, this disappears. "In such conditions," to quote Dr. Kirk,[2] "the human spirit was thought of as temporarily eliminated from personality, its place being taken by another Spirit which assumed control of the human lips and limbs, and produced utterances and actions sometimes indeed intelligible enough, but at other times merely terrible and marvellous." It is to be noticed that this experience of "possession" has not always been confined to relations between man and God. The New Testament contains many instances of alleged possession by evil spirits, and it must be remembered that this was the background against which the Christian doctrine of the Holy Spirit grew up. In a world where men and women were thought to fall from time to time under the influence of alien spirits so as to be "possessed" by them, One was singled out for recognition in all its manifestations as the Spirit of God.

This thought of being possessed by God, as distinct from enjoying communion with God, is at first glance

[1] In Rawlinson: *Essays on the Trinity and the Incarnation* (London. 1928).
[2] *Op. cit.* p. 185.

something distasteful, if not actually repugnant, to many of us. It seems to suggest a relapse into primitive, superstitious ways of religion, which we should like to think we had outgrown. It seems to be undoing the work of the Old Testament, that record of God's education of man to find in true religion the demand for a human moral response to the divine initiative. But second thoughts prevent our dismissing it without further consideration. Is there not in the life of every Christian among us something which needs for its description just this term "possession" rather than "communion," if "communion" always connotes the awareness of intercourse with another? I speak of those times when it is our bounden duty to be entirely concentrated on the work which lies before us, when to let our mind's eye flicker from its task, even to become aware of God's presence with us, would be a dereliction from the duty to which He has called us. It may be a mathematician, a scientist, or some other scholar at work on a problem; it may be a doctor engaged in diagnosis or in the performance of an intricate operation; it may be a preacher preaching a sermon, or a parent or a tutor wrestling with some difficult child or pupil. In these, and countless similar situations, it is our duty to be, as we say, "lost in" them. But is there one of us who has not known what it is, looking back on such a time, to be aware that he has been lifted above himself to perform the task in a manner which he could never have anticipated, or planned to do, from his knowledge of his own powers? Somehow or other light broke on the problem and he grasped its solution; somehow or other the right words came into his mouth, and he was given the power to utter them with convincing conviction. There are also, of course, times when we find ourselves in the grip of less desirable powers. We may be carried away by anger, hatred, jealousy, or lust, so that we describe the matter afterwards by saying that we "forgot ourselves."

These two types of experience cannot simply be equated as similar instances of loss of self-control, differing only in the respective directions in which we are carried away. In the former case, the power which comes upon us enables us more truly to become our real selves. When we think it out, we find it to be not a diminution but an increase of our self-control. For by "self-control" we mean the capacity to gather up all our being and exert it in the achievement of those ends towards which we will our life as a whole to be directed, and what we have received is an increase of the power at our disposal for the execution of our will. But in the other case, what happens is that the progress of our life as a whole is temporarily subordinated to the pursuit of some end contradictory to its true purpose. There is, so to speak, ground lost, which must be recovered before we can move forward again on the true path. We have surrendered to a disintegrating influence, which has caused what is really and truly a loss of self-control.

These unfortunate surrenders I have mentioned here only in order that we may put them aside for later consideration.[1] Our immediate subject is the experience of being lifted above ourselves so as to be more truly ourselves in the performance of the work that God has given us to do. The next point we have to notice is that this does not usually happen in a haphazard and irrational manner, it is not a chaotic irruption into an otherwise ordered universe. On the contrary, there is what we may perhaps call a technique of preparation for the reception of this power, which we neglect at our peril. Think, for example, of the doctor confronted by some difficult problem of diagnosis. He has behind him years of training in the medical schools, enriched by subsequent experience in clinical practice, together with the continued study of the literature of his science and discussion with fellow-physicians. All these together, working it may be upon the basis of a certain natural gift, have gone to make him the man he is, the kind of man prepared in a crisis to receive the flash of illumination whereby he sees the true explanation of the patient's unfamiliar condition.

[1] See below, p. 54.

The Christian interpretation of this widespread element in human experience is that in every such occurrence we have an instance of the working of the Spirit of God, taking the self which man offers in God's service, and raising it to a higher power than was antecedently predictable. The Christian views all such occurrences in the light of our Lord's words recorded in Mark xiii. 11[1]: "And when they lead you to judgement, and deliver you up, be not anxious beforehand what ye shall speak: but whatsoever shall be given you in that hour, that speak ye: for it is not ye that speak, but the Holy Ghost."

(ii)

In order to understand the application of this saying, we must remember the principles which underlie all right exegesis of the words of our Lord. As I have argued elsewhere,[2] the Gospels give us the picture of Christ in the days when He was living as man, and to live as man means to live as one who thinks and speaks on the basis of a particular bodily experience in space and time. The recognition of this empirical element in our Lord's sayings gives them a wider application than might be supposed. For remarks concerning the particular topic of the moment are found upon reflection to have far-reaching implications. Thus, in the present instance, the particular form of the saying was dictated by the fact that at the time when He said it He was thinking about the persecutions which His disciples would have to endure. Among their trials would be arrest and the consequent examination before the authorities. It would be no use trying to make up in advance set speeches, for no one could tell in advance on what lines the questions would be put. They must trust to being the kind of people who could meet the crisis when it comes. To be this kind of person is, in our Lord's language, to

[1] Cp. parallels in Matt. x. 19, Luke xii. 11, 12, and the interesting variant in Luke xxi. 14, 15.
[2] See *And Was Made Man* (Longmans, 1928).

be one who speaks what is given him in that hour, for the
Holy Spirit teaches him what he ought to say. It is clear
that this implies a principle which cannot be confined to
those occasions on which a man is called upon to answer
the questions of a magistrate or prosecuting counsel. The
Christian is to be the kind of person who can see his way
through problems for which it is impossible to prepare
in advance seeing that until they come upon him no one
can foretell what particular response they will require.
The Christian is to be the man who is equal to the novel
and unprecedented situation. And he is to be this because
he can rely upon the Spirit of God to possess him and raise
him up to meet the emergency.

So much, at least, is clearly implied in our Lord's words.
The meaning is not read into them but read out of them.
But there is still more to be found in them. We have asked
what is the sphere of the saying's application; we must also
ask what were the grounds on which it was asserted.

There can be little doubt, I think, that we must regard
our Lord as speaking out of His own experience of human
life. That life was a life of daily and hourly waiting upon
the Father in order to find and do the Father's will in the
circumstances of life as they came to Him. Those circumstances, unpredictable and often unexpected, provided
the given material on which His mind had to work, in
response to which He had to speak and act, and thus fulfil
His vocation and fashion His life on earth. The entire
consecration of mind and body to the doing of the Father's
will was what He brought with Him to the task. And what
was the result? Often in the Gospels we read of Him being
met by clearly unexpected situations. More than once,
for example, the failure of His disciples to understand Him
brings a note of surprise into His voice. But there is no
occasion on which He does not appear as master of the
situation, entirely adequate to meet its challenge. Alone
in the Garden of Gethsemane He may have to wrestle in
prayer until the way becomes clear; but when the soldiers
arrive, and when He is brought before High Priest or

Roman Governor, He dominates the scene with a calm strength which St. Peter's very natural human weakness serves only to throw into higher relief. He predicts for His disciples, in the saying from which we started, that they should follow in His steps and share the way of life which was His own. And what was for Him the secret of that way of life appears in the passage where He is accused of casting out evil spirits through Baalzebub the prince of evil spirits.[1] The power that works in Him is not Baalzebub but τὸ πνεῦμα τὸ ἅγιον, the Holy Spirit.

It follows that the earthly life of our Lord may be described as the continual seeking to find and do the Father's will in the guidance and strength of the Spirit. His own actual references to the Spirit in the Synoptic Gospels are, indeed, few in number: but I am convinced that it is justifiable to regard these references as of great significance. The revelation of God in Christ is not to be estimated by the unintelligent canon of numerical addition. These few sayings are to be read in the light of all human experience of the spiritual life, in the light of Socrates' references to his δαιμόνιον as well as of Elijah's "still small voice," of the "spirit" or "Word" of the Lord as received by the Hebrew prophets, and of the "Life in the Spirit" as lived by St. Paul and countless other Christian men and women. If I am right, throughout the history of man's religious life on its inner side there are interwoven the experiences of communion with and possession by God. In His life on earth our Lord held communion with the Father, and referred to the Spirit the insight whereby He saw things with the Father's eyes and the power whereby He did the Father's will. But throughout that life He was discovering more and more clearly how little this way of life was known and understood by His fellow-men. Here I would like to quote my earlier comment on the saying "I thank thee, O Father, Lord of heaven and earth, that thou didst hide these things from the wise and understanding, and didst reveal them unto babes: yea, Father, for so it was well

[1] Mark iii. 22–30.

pleasing in thy sight. All things have been delivered unto
me of my Father: and no one knoweth the Son, save
the Father; neither doth any know the Father, save the
Son, and he to whomsoever the Son willeth to reveal
him."[1]

"Assuming the authority of this saying as recorded, how are we
to think of our Lord as having come on earth to the knowledge of
His unique relationship to the Father? I would suggest that here as
elsewhere there is involved that empirical element in the knowledge
of Christ of which we have been thinking. All His life He has known
what it is to live in communion with the Father, to 'know' the Father.
Again and again He has been astonished to find how little this
experience is shared by His fellow men and women, how little He
can take it for granted that they will understand Him when He
speaks of what He knows. He has preached to the crowds, but they
have not understood. He has chosen those who showed some glimmer
of a capacity for learning, He has made them His disciples, and
devoted Himself to their training. Even they are continually failing
Him, and asking Him to explain. Even after the flash of inspired
insight which won for Peter his blessing at Caesarea Philippi, that
disciple falls back almost at once into such lack of sympathy with
his master's outlook that he becomes the mouthpiece of his master's
tempter.[2] It is hardly too much to say that the uniqueness of His
relationship to the Father was forced upon our Lord's attention
at every stage of His life on earth."[3]

We are now in a position to consider another most
significant saying. This time it is a saying from the Fourth
Gospel; but it is one of those sayings which so clearly give
us the inner thought of the Synoptic Christ that I believe
it to have all the authority of an *ipsissimum verbum* of our
Lord Himself,[4] "Nevertheless, I tell you the truth; it is
expedient for you that I go away: for if I go not away, the
Paraclete will not come unto you; but if I go, I will send
him unto you."[5] Why, we may ask, did our Lord come to
the conclusion that it was expedient for His disciples that

---

[1] Matt. xi. 25–27; Luke x. 21, 22.   [2] Matt. xvi. 13–23.
[3] *And Was Made Man*, p. 40.
[4] See *And Was Made Man*, pp. 189–208.   [5] John xvi. 7.

He should leave them? Surely, it was because of this very fact that we have been considering. It was His ambition for them that they should come to share the outlook and way of life which was His own. But just as He had found his works of healing to be a hindrance rather than a help towards opening the ears of the multitudes to His message, so now He found His presence in the flesh a hindrance rather than a help to the opening of the eyes of the disciples to the true way of life. Anyone who has had much experience of university and post-graduate teaching knows something of the desire to initiate pupils into the scholar's way of life, and something of the despair one feels over the too docile pupil, the pupil who will do nothing but receive and repeat at second hand what he is told, who, at an age when he should be entering in to share in first-hand experience of the adult scholar's life, asks only to have his open mouth fed further from the same spoon. Just so did our Lord find the disciples unable to grow up from a second-hand religion, dependent upon their partially understood memory of His spoken words, into a full sharing of His relationship to the Father and to the world around. This was to be their adult way of life, when His education of them bore its fruit; this must be its fruit if they were to carry on His work in His name when He was gone. So now He sees still further light upon His Father's will for Him and them. The death, through which He is to be a "ransom for many," and to pass into the full glory of the Son of Man, is also to set Him free to share His life with His followers in a manner as yet impossible. Only so can they be raised from the status of "servants" to that of "friends."[1]

Our attention now turns to those disciples. We have seen what was their Master's ambition for them, and now we must try to trace the working out of its fulfilment. For convenience, we may divide their discipleship into four periods. The first, from their calling to the Crucifixion of their Lord, we have already dealt with. It was the period

[1] Cp. John xv. 15.

of their "second-hand" dependence on His presence in the flesh, with fluctuations of faith and insight which rose to their highest in St. Peter's flash of divine inspiration at Caesarea Philippi, only to fall at once to the low level of his subsequent remark.[1] Our second period is what is known as "The Great Forty Days," the period between the Resurrection and the Ascension. During that period, so far as our present interest is concerned, there was no essential change in their outlook. The Resurrection had indeed restored and confirmed their faith in their Lord's messiahship. There had been no mistake. This *had* been "He that should come." But still there was that same attitude of "second-hand" dependence; they waited about from one appearance to the next to be told some more. In the very last of such recorded instances[2] they are still asking the same kind of uninspired question which had so often been on their lips before: "Lord, dost thou at this time restore the kingdom to Israel?" His reply points to His realisation that it was no use trying to explain things to them until they had ceased to be dependent on such methods of intercourse, and had come instead to share with Him in possession by the Spirit. This must have been still His unfulfilled ambition for them, and it was a true insight which led the Church to use the sixteenth chapter of the Fourth Gospel for the Sundays preceding Ascension Day. Whether or no it contains *ipsissima verba*, and whenever such as it contains, if any, were spoken, there can be no doubt that it reveals our Lord's thoughts about His disciples both in the latter part of His earthly ministry and in the days after His resurrection.

There is no need for us to enter into the question of the precise nature of the Ascension. It is enough for our present purpose to think of it as our Lord leaving His disciples in such a manner as to make clear that this was the last of the appearances on which they were coming to depend. In this way He initiated the third period of their discipleship, a short period of ten days in which, again, there was

---

[1] Mark viii. 27–33; Matt. xvi. 13–23.   [2] Acts i. 6–8

no essential change in their outlook. They are still just waiting about for something to happen, without any real insight into the Lord's mind, and without any initiative to drive them into action unless He should appear again and give them instructions and the word of command.

Then came the Day of Pentecost, ushering in the fourth and final stage of their discipleship. As with the Ascension, we need not pause to consider the exact nature of the phenomena which accompanied their receiving this completion of their education. What is of importance for us now is the permanent change wrought in them, and this is a fact written in flaming letters upon the pages of history. Those men who had been waiting about for something to happen, with no insight and no initiative, now have a gospel to proclaim and burning zeal to proclaim it. It is not long before Christians are spoken of as men who are turning the world upside down.[1]

The change that was wrought by the coming of the Spirit at Pentecost was nothing less than the taking of the disciples within the mind of their Master, the making of them the "friends" who "know what their Lord doeth." I do not mean to imply, of course, that they passed immediately to a full understanding of His mind. There was much that they did not know; after nearly twenty centuries there is still much that we, with the aid of all who have followed in their footsteps and built upon their foundations, do not know. It is probable, for example, that at first they did not think of our Lord as actually present among them "in the Spirit." They thought of Him rather as the Messiah who, risen and ascended, was dwelling in Heaven, and sending down the Spirit upon them from above. They did not yet realise that to be a member of the Christian Church was to be able to say "I live; yet not I, but Christ liveth in me,"[2] that they "had" the Son, and having Him had "eternal life." No; but the change which had taken place was that first step which made all the others possible. It was a change of status and consequently of outlook. They

---

[1] Acts xvii. 6.　　　　[2] Gal. ii. 20.

had been standing outside, peering in at the life of Christ
and trying to make out just what it was all about. Now they
looked out at the world around from within His life and
mind. They have, as I said, a gospel to preach and initiative
to act, and this gospel and this initiative are those which
had been the Lord's in His earthly life. As He had spoken,
so they speak—in His name. As He had acted, so they act
—in His name. "And Peter said unto them Repent ye,
and be baptized every one of you in the name of Jesus
Christ unto the remission of your sins; and ye shall receive
the gift of the Holy Ghost." "In the name of Jesus Christ
of Nazareth, walk."[1]

Here, then, began the fulfilment of what I have called
our Lord's ambition for His disciples, His ambition that
they should share in His relationship to the Father and His
outlook on the world, that for them, as for Him, life in the
flesh should be the seeking, finding and doing of the Father's
will in the guidance and power of the Spirit. This was to
be the characteristic way of life for the Christian, and at
Pentecost it began. Some years later St. Paul, when he
had been caught up into the current of that life, described
it as an adopted sonship. "Ye received," he writes, "the
spirit of adoption, whereby we cry, Abba, Father," and
again, "God sent forth his son . . . that we might receive
the adoption of sons. And because ye are sons, God sent
forth the Spirit of his Son into our hearts, crying, Abba,
Father."[2] It will be worth our while to spend a little time
in thinking out what is implied in this language.

When a child is adopted, it is taken to share in a social
life which is already going on before he comes into it. In
a typical instance there might be a father and a mother
and one or two children. Between them flows the current
of family love, and into this life an orphan child is taken

---

[1] Acts ii. 38, iii. 6. In all this I must not be thought to be trying to expound
what the disciples then thought about their status and their activity, but
to be interpreting them in the light of what later reflection showed to be
implied by them.

[2] Rom. viii. 15; Gal. iv. 4–6.

to share in it, and as a member of it to look out from within it upon the world around. St. Paul's language, if taken seriously and not regarded as a mere illustrative metaphor, suggests that there is a social life in the godhead, into the current of which life the Christian is taken up, so that his life is that of a member of the divine society, looking out on the world from within it.

That this language is to be taken seriously appears from the many passages in which St. Paul shows clearly that he thinks of the Christian life as a life of a definite, distinct kind. The Christian is "in Christ," and in Christ he is a "new creature" whose "citizenship is in Heaven."[1] Moreover, this thought is not peculiar to St. Paul. Whilst the forms of its expression differ in different writers, the underlying idea is the same. It is, so to speak, common stock of the Christian consciousness. In the Johannine literature the Christian is "born again," hath the Son, hath the Father also, and hath the Paraclete, all this giving him a new quality of life called "eternal." The tradition of Christian worship is that we offer our Eucharist to the Father "in the Son," His presence making us "bold to say, 'Our Father'," and in the Catechism we learn to speak of our baptism as making us "members of Christ, children of God, and inheritors of the Kingdom of Heaven." This last phrase carries our thought back again to St. Paul, for it is based on his words, "Now ye are the body of Christ, and members in particular."[2]

(iii)

We can now begin to see whither our argument is tending, and it will help towards a clear understanding if I here anticipate its conclusion and state briefly the position which these lectures are written to maintain. The Christian life is life "in the Spirit," and as such reproduces in each Christian the same way of life as was that of Christ on earth.

---

[1] *E.g.* Gal. ii. 20, vi. 15; Phil. iii. 20.
[2] 1 Cor. xii. 27. Cp. Rom. xii. 4, 5.

D

As He sought, found and did the Father's will through the Spirit, so does the Christian. He seeks to find and do the will of the Father with the companionship of the Son through the guidance and strength of the Spirit. But this reproduction of Christ's life in the life of each Christian is not simply a matter of copying a pattern or example; it is made possible by an initial act of God "adopting" the Christian to share in the sonship of Christ. Thus he shares His Lord's relationship to the Father and the Spirit. Hence the doctrine of the Trinity is the formal statement of the divine setting of the Christian life, arrived at by an analysis of the implications of that life as it has come into existence and continued to exist in the history of this world. The Blessed Trinity is not some incomprehensible mystery which we dimly worship from without; it is the revealed nature of the God "in whom we live and move and have our being," as well-known and familiar to the Christian, and as often unnoticed, as the air he breathes.

This is the thesis which I am now proposing to examine and to maintain. It is clear that its establishment requires at least four distinct lines of inquiry, if our theology is to be interpretation of the actual and not baseless imagination. We have to assure ourselves that we have rightly grasped the true historical origin and nature of the Christian life. Assured of this, we have to trace out the ramifications of the implied theology, in an attempt to discover just what doctrine of God it is to which we are committed. Thirdly, we have to consider the general philosophical question of the nature of the universe, asking how far the doctrine of God arrived at by reflection upon the historical facts of the Christian life is harmonious with all else that we gather about the universe from other sources. And, fourthly, we cannot avoid the responsibility to review the development of trinitarian thought in the Christian tradition, to see whether our conclusions are consonant with those expressions of its belief which from age to age the Church has found acceptable. It will also not be out of place in these lectures to give some attention to yet a fifth topic:

the practical effect upon the direction of Christian life and devotion which issues from a right apprehension of the revealed nature of God.

In regard to the first of these tasks, the inquiry into the actual nature of the Christian life as historically manifested, it is necessary to distinguish carefully between what I am and what I am not trying to do. I am not trying to write a history of the ideas which at different times Christians have held about the life they were living, and of which they have left record in their writings. That kind of inquiry —the study of the exegesis of documents with its concomitant study of the filiation of ideas—is of the greatest importance as the foundation of our work here; but it must be taken for granted in these lectures precisely as itself it takes for granted the critical textual study which establishes the material on which it is to work. Our task is to reflect upon the life about which they held these opinions, with a view to grasping what its nature must have been. We are trying to state the underlying logic of it which worked itself out in its various manifestations, including these opinions. Thus it is no necessarily valid criticism of the earlier part of this lecture to say that the interpretation there given of the gift of the Spirit at Pentecost ignores the fact that the disciples probably thought of it as the pouring into them from above by the absent Messiah of a quasi-physical something, the chief result of which was to cause in them extraordinary and ecstatic behaviour. Neither need we be perturbed if it appears from various passages in *Acts* and *Epistles* that the common conception of the Spirit in the primitive Church was that of an influence which made people jump and shout. Our ultimate interest is not in what they thought about it, but in what it really was; and our next step is to pay some more attention to the activity of the Spirit as it may be understood by reflection upon the New Testament documents.

What I have urged so far is that our primary notion of the Spirit is that of God working in and through us without our being aware of the fact at the moment, and that this element in human life is a reproduction of an element in the human life of our Lord, which first made its appearance on the Day of Pentecost.[1] Undoubtedly its coming was accompanied by emotional excitement so intense as to drive those "on whom the Spirit came" to extraordinary behaviour, and undoubtedly this behaviour so took hold on their minds and the minds of those around them that they thought it the chief mark of the Spirit's activity. But their actions bore witness to the fact that they had now an insight and an initiative which had not been theirs before, and in reflecting upon their experience the more clear-sighted thought of later days came to see that this was the essential permanent change wrought upon them, while the other was an impermanent and, in the strict sense of the word, an accidental accompaniment of it.

We do not have to go beyond the New Testament to see that this was the considered judgment of the Christian consciousness upon that event. It is true that glossolaly and other ecstatic phenomena were for some time regarded as the clearest evidence of the Spirit's presence. I do not wish in any way to minimise the evidence for this, or to deny the probability of the view that the association of the gift of the Spirit with baptism was largely due to the ecstatic behaviour of converts as they emerged from the baptismal water. But when time enough had gone by for Christian thought to reflect on Christian experience, and considered discrimination of the relative importance of the different activities which had been taken to be working of the Spirit became possible, the issue is not in doubt. The passages in which St. Paul sets out his mature thought on the subject[2] definitely estimate the ecstatic gifts of the Spirit as of lower importance than the quickening of men's natural gifts

---

[1] Consideration of the obvious objection that we cannot confine the activity of the Spirit in human life within the bounds of the post-pentecostal Christian Church is deferred to its proper place in the discussion where it rightly belongs. See below, Lecture VII. pp. 181 ff. At the present stage all statements are rough-hewn, and require more accurate definition as the argument proceeds.

[2] E.g. 1 Cor. xii.–xiv. ; 2 Cor. iii. ; Gal. v. 22, 23.

and talents, and the "fruit" of the Spirit is pre-eminently
the perfection, not the negation, of the virtues to which
human life may aspire. Moreover, both St. Paul and the
author of the first Johannine Epistle regard the claim to
divine inspiration as one which must submit to rational
criticism.[1] The ecstasy as such is not its own guarantee
of its origin; only those are to be accepted as true manifestations of the Spirit which are consonant with the
acceptance of Jesus Christ as the revelation of God and
(we may add) bear fruit in a life which is a recognisable
imitation of His character. The truest indications of the
Spirit's presence, that is, are depth of insight, especially
of insight into the significance of the coming of Jesus Christ,
and strengthening of character. It only needs the application of this principle to the events of the Day of Pentecost
to see that its ecstatic phenomena, whatever they were,
were secondary accompaniments of those gifts of insight
and initiative, the evidence for which is to be found written
upon the pages of history by the lives of those in whom
the change was wrought. And this considered judgment,
once reached by Christian thought and given expression
in such writings as those of St. Paul and the Johannine
author, established itself as the enduring view of the Church.
Undue respect for the ecstatic as such might live on for
a while and only die a lingering death; from time to time
(as in the Montanist movement) attempts might be made
to revive it; but the underlying logic of the facts proved
too strong, making its death certain and its resurrection
impossible.

There follows from this a further point, of importance
both for our present discussion and of one to follow in a
later lecture.[2] We have thought of the Holy Spirit working
in human life by "possession" as distinguished from "communion." Our initial repugnance to this notion we met
by calling attention to those occasions which we find, on
reflection, to have been at one and the same time both

[1] I Cor. xii. 3, 10, xiv. 29 ; I John iv. 1–3.
[2] See below, Lecture VII, pp. 180 ff.

experiences of possession and of our most effective exercise
of self-control.[1] Now if, as argued above, this is due to
the fact that such possession enables us to affirm our own
true will, and thus differs *toto coelo* from being carried
away in the opposite direction, we may expect to find in
the New Testament a corresponding difference between
the phenomena ascribed to the Holy Spirit and evil spirits
respectively. And this is just what we do find. The "evil
spirit" takes possession of a human being in such a way
as to render futile his own efforts to live his life to the best
of his ability. It drives him out to prowl like a naked wild
beast among the desert tombs of Gadara, or casts him
willy-nilly into the fire and the water. It does not affirm
his own true self, but sets it aside and acts as substitute.
But the Holy Spirit takes possession in order to promote
the growth of that true self in its own true freedom. The
result is that their intense belief in the activity of the Holy
Spirit did not lead the writers of the New Testament, taken
as a whole, to disparage the strenuous pursuit of either
intellectual or moral perfection. It is possible that so long
as the thought of the Holy Spirit's activity as mainly
manifested in ecstatic phenomena was uppermost in their
minds, there may have been a surface contradiction between
the moral exhortation of an early Christian teacher and his
references to the work of the Spirit; but so long as this
was so, the two elements were affirmed in turn, and no
attempt was made to solve the problem by withdrawing
either line of teaching. There is no encouragement in
the New Testament for the preacher who excuses his lack
of work in the preparation of his sermon on the ground
that he is leaving the way open for the operation of the Holy
Spirit, or for the man who substitutes what he calls "waiting
upon divine guidance" for the rational planning of his daily
life. The Spirit may be the ground of our unity in the
Christian brotherhood, but we have to "endeavour" to
keep it.[2] It is God who worketh in us, both to will and to
work; nevertheless we have to work out our own salvation.[3]

---

[1] Above, p. 40.   [2] Eph. iv. 3.   [3] Phil. ii. 12.

Here again what I have called the underlying logic of the facts controlled the development of the thought, forbade the desertion of either side of the truth because of its apparent disharmony with the other, and drove the Church onward to a deeper conception both of human nature and of the Spirit's activity in which both were reconcilable. Perhaps on this point the practical teaching of the New Testament may be summed up by saying that, since it is the work of the Holy Spirit to take, quicken, intensify and work through what is best in human nature, it is our part to see that what we offer Him for the purpose is the best that we can achieve.

I spoke earlier of there being in the Christian's reliance on the guidance and strength of the Spirit something corresponding to the background of study and experience which makes the doctor the man he is when confronted with a problem of diagnosis or the work of an operation. It will be well here to say more of what that something is. I have spoken of the Christian as one who shares by adoption in the sonship of Christ, and thus looks out on the world from within the divine social life of the Blessed Trinity. This way of life is maintained on earth by faithful and regular habits of prayer, meditation and sacramental communion. It is as the product of these habits, which make him the kind of man he is, that the Christian comes to face any particular problem for the mind or task for the will. When confronted by problem or task, his duty is to concentrate all his powers of mind or will upon it; to what extent at such a moment his mind will be spirit-guided intelligence, or his will Spirit-strengthened energy, depends not so much upon his then and there subjective feeling of God's presence as upon the extent to which his whole life is such as to make him that kind of man.

(iv)

We have come back to the central thesis of these lectures, that the Doctrine of the Trinity represents the conception of God involved in the Christian life of adopted sonship in Christ. A *prima facie* objection which might be felt to this statement would perhaps take the form of asking how many Christians actually believe this of themselves. "It is all very well for you to tell me that in virtue of my baptism I am looking out on the world from within the divine life of the godhead," a man might say, "but I have never felt anything of the sort. Is not your statement the product of your imagination, and, strictly speaking, nonsense?"

To this I would say three things in reply.

First, it does not necessarily follow that something is not true of us because we are not aware of it. The baby who lies on his back and plays with his toes does not at first know that they are *his* toes, part of his body. From that stage onwards the history of the conscious life of every human being is in large part the story of his waking up to what he already is. The full truth about him is always more extensive than that portion of it of which he is aware. Sometimes what he learns is so far from what he has previously thought or felt that at first it appears incredible. But this *prima facie* incredibility is not in itself sufficient ground for rejecting the new idea. If it is true, then what he needs to do is to practise himself in letting his imagination play about it, and in acting as though it were true, until it grips him as a reasoned conviction about himself. Whether or no it be true must be established by a wider examination than the consideration of what he is at the moment able to feel.

Secondly, I would call attention to certain facts which seem to show that the idea before us is perhaps not so difficult of assimilation by men and women as we may have imagined. There is a way of thinking which in many ages, and not least in our own, has shown itself capable of exercising a powerful influence over the human mind. I refer to the teaching that human beings are all to a greater or less degree sharers in divinity, that there is, as it is sometimes said, a "spark of the divine essence" in them which is constitutive of their true self, and that the right way of life is for a man to realise that truth about himself, and encourage that divine spark to grow by acting upon the assumption of its reality. So far from being found difficult, this way of thinking is indeed found by many to be so easy as to be taken for granted and made the basis of further speculation, for example in the field of christology. The divinity of Christ, it is argued, means the perfection of his humanity; He was the shower of the way in that He lived out to the full the possibilities of life which are inherent in every one of us. Now it has been said with considerable insight that no heresy has ever made widespread popular appeal except by emphasising some element in the truth to which the orthodoxy of the day paid insufficient attention. In the present case I would suggest that the true issue between the orthodox Christian tradition and the teaching I have just mentioned does not lie in the question whether or no there be in men and women a "divine spark," so that all that is necessary for their perfection is to realise the fact and act upon it. It lies in the question whether this sharing in divinity is an inherent natural element in man by virtue of his creation, or a gift of God in Christ through redemption and adoption.[1] Undoubtedly the orthodox Christian tradition teaches the latter view; but given this account of its origin, the practical exhortation arising out of it need differ little from that based on the heretical view of its source. It is the exhortation to realise and act upon the truth of the divine life which is already ours in Christ. I venture to suggest that if we heard

---

[1] In this paragraph I use the words "orthodox" and "heretical" to describe respectively the view which is in accord with the main catholic tradition of Christendom and that which is not. The question of their truth and falsehood is not raised, but reserved for discussion later. See below, Lecture V, pp. 130 ff.

The phrase "sharing in divinity" must not be taken as necessarily implying substantial deification. All that is necessary for my argument is that here on earth the Christian is adopted to share the status and outlook of Christ incarnate. From this some theologians deduce a doctrine of beatification by deification, which others repudiate, but that question is irrelevant to these lectures.

more of this strain of teaching in orthodox Christian pulpits, we should hear less complaints of congregations going elsewhere in order to find it; and meanwhile the fact that people do find it elsewhere and, finding it, adopt it with enthusiasm, shows that the notion cannot be rejected on the ground of its insuperable repugnance to human credibility.

But, when all is said and done, neither the fact that some people cannot recall any experience which feels like sharing in the life of God, nor the fact that others say they do so, is of avail to establish or to disprove the thesis that the Christian life claims to be such a sharing and is justified in the claim. The ultimate question is not what the Christian life feels like, but what it is. But on what grounds can that be determined, except by analysis of what it feels like? This raises the much-debated question in what sense "experience," is, must be, or should be the basis of theology.

I do not wish to add much to this debate, but there are one or two things that must be said. Why, we may ask, should theology so often be singled out to be the subject of this debate? The real question is whether the taint of subjectivism necessarily infects human inquiry in all departments. Nevertheless, in spite of such analysis of scientific inquiry as one finds, for example, in the first chapter of Wolfgang Köhler's *Gestalt Psychology*, we do commonly think that the experience of a physicist reading a galvanometer has a more obvious claim to be genuine perception of an objective fact than the so-called "religious experience" of God's presence or of the forgiveness of sins. I suppose this is because the former seems to have been patient of more thoroughgoing verification than the latter, through its being an implication of the everyday life of everyone of us, without which that life would not be what it is. The "religious experience" can be discounted as being the peculiarity of certain people of "religious temperament," and the question at issue is whether or no their experience should not be regarded as comparable to that of an intoxicated man who sees two galvanometers where other men see one. To treat it on all fours with our ordinary perception of the external world would be parallel to regarding intoxication as the normal state of mankind. This, indeed, seems to be the view of those who claim that it can be disregarded on the ground that it can be equally well reproduced by means of drugs.[1]

But, if I have been right in my previous lecture, and in the earlier part of this one, it is the specific claim of the Christian faith that it does not represent simply the schematised exposition of the content of some emotional religious experience. No doubt there was such experience at its inception, and there has been ever since; but the intellectual content of the faith has grown through critical reflection upon it in the light of all that we know of the universe through historical, scientific, and philosophical studies. The Christian conviction that as members of the body of Christ we share His relationship to the Father and the Spirit is not a schematised exposition of what the disciples felt on the Day of Pentecost, or afterwards. It is an interpretation of the historical facts of their changed lives, an interpretation arrived at by critical reflection which traced the historical connection between that change in them and its antecedents in the earthly life of their Lord. In the last resort, the truth of Christianity rests upon the impossibility of giving any adequate account of the appearance of the figure of Jesus Christ in the pages of history except upon the recognition of Him as God incarnate, living and dying to redeem mankind and usher in the Kingdom of God.

Thus it has always been the position of Catholic Christianity that the manward movement of God is prior to the godward movement of man. We claim to be sharers in the divine life of the Blessed Trinity not because we are capable of realising what it means, but because we believe that in the Incarnation God entered into the course of this world's history in order to initiate us into this way of life. Our conviction that this is our status is not based on what we have experienced or do experience, but on our belief

[1] See *e.g.* Leuba: *The Psychology of Religious Mysticism.*

about what He has done. Nevertheless this belief, when
accepted, is found most valuable both to interpret and to
control such "religious experiences" as may be given to
Christians during their life on earth. It interprets them
because it sets them in the context of a view of the universe
in which they have a right and proper place; it controls
them because it is a perpetual reminder that only those
experiences which are harmonious with the historical
revelation of God in Christ may safely be accepted as of
divine origin. The humble and contrite heart, the life of
obedience modelled on the obedience of the Son of God,
are the true fruits of the Spirit's working; and all claims
to be sharing the divine life which cannot meet such tests
as these need purging by the most rigid discipline of
critical Christian thought.

THE REVELATION IN THE NEW TESTAMENT
(*continued*)

(i)

THE last lecture was devoted to expounding the thesis that the doctrine of the Trinity expresses the conception of God implied in the Christian life as historically manifested. We saw that that life is a reproduction by Christ in His followers of what had been His own way of life on earth, and that they can thus be spoken of as adopted to share His sonship to the Father in the Spirit. Our attention was mainly directed to considering that way of life and establishing its true nature, as the basis of our further inquiry. We must now carry on that inquiry by attempting to examine more closely the conception of God to which it gives rise.

Our starting-point will be the Christ of the Gospels as viewed in the light of later Christian reflection, and we must begin by reviewing what it means to look at Him from this standpoint. It means that we shall be looking at Him in the same way that we looked at the primitive Christian community in the last lecture, asking, that is, not what He felt, thought or said about Himself, but what must have been the truth about Him to account for His having said and done what He did.

The underlying logic of the situation, which drove the thought of Christendom onwards from Galilee to Nicaea and Chalcedon, may be summarised briefly as follows. Jesus of Nazareth was born of the Jews, at a time when that people was expecting the establishment of the Kingdom of God by a Divine act which should cut across the course of history and initiate a new epoch. By some God was expected to work by redirecting the stream of earthly events, raising up as Messiah a second David who should restore the lost glories of Israel's golden age. By others the coming of the Messiah was looked for as the appearance of a supernatural, celestial Being who should not redirect but put an end to history; and some held that this would be done by the direct action of God Himself, acting as His own Messiah. Of the idea of the Kingdom of God held by these Dr. Easton has written: "The Jewish sense of 'Kingdom of God' is not open to doubt; it describes that purely supernatural state of affairs when God—and God alone—shall rule over men. Hence, we may be pardoned if we repeat, the beginning of the Kingdom has no true continuity with human history. When the Kingdom is inaugurated, human history ceases; the new age is almost anything rather than the result of evolutionary progress. This was a basic belief of Jewish eschatology everywhere, whether apocalyptic or not; apocalyptists differed from non-apocalyptists only in believing that visible signs proved the advent of the kingdom in the very near future. Consequently the phrase 'The Kingdom of God is at hand' meant to everyone who heard it 'The end of the world is at hand,' and could not possibly have had any other significance. And that the overwhelming mass of Kingdom passages in the Synoptists contain this eschatological force is notorious."[1]

And some, perhaps, attempted to combine both standpoints by a millenarianism which expected the restored Davidic era to precede and be closed by the final cataclysm.

These expectations, in their setting of the Jewish theistic interpretation of the universe and its history, formed the framework of our Lord's thought in His earthly life. That He claimed for Himself the position of the expected Messiah, and that as the supernatural "Son of Man," I have no doubt. It seems equally clear that He regarded deliverance from sin and the knowledge of God as the two chief needs of

[1] *Christ in the Gospels*, p. 160.

His people which He had come to meet, and that the mark
of the advent with Him of the Kingdom of God was the
presence of the power of God at work on earth overpowering
the forces of evil.[1] His followers took Him at His word, and
Christianity began as the faith of those Jews who believed
that their Messiah had come in the person of Jesus of
Nazareth. The horizon of their thought was bounded by
the limits of that Jewish view of the universe of which I
have spoken; their creed, before the coming of Jesus, had
in it a place for the Messiah which He had filled. But with
the transformation of Christianity from being the religion
of a sect of Judaism into a universal faith, there came the
necessity of universalising the creed. What if the whole
Jewish faith were of the tissue of mythology, if it were
only in the Jewish imagination that Jehovah had chosen
His people, rescued them from Egypt, nurtured them with
prophets, priests and kings, and fulfilled His promise to
send their Saviour? The Christians based their answer to
this question on their conviction that through Christ they
were set free from their sins, had entered upon a new
knowledge of God, and were possessed of a new power
through which they could meet and overcome the forces of
evil. Contact with the philosophical thought of the Gentile
world forced them to ask what must be the status in reality
of Him through whom these gifts, and especially the first,
had come. In the end, the notion of a supernatural being
of a semi-divine order, intermediate between God and man,
was ruled out as indeed belonging to the realm of mythological imagination, and it was concluded that He who
had done such things must have been none other than
God Himself.

So in the long run it was found that Jesus Christ had
actually confounded historical expectations by fulfilling the
requirements of all the different theories held in advance
about what Messiah would be and do. They had appeared
as inconsistent alternatives between which men must
choose; but He united them all in Himself. He was the

---

[1] Cp. Matt. xii. 28 = Luke xi. 20.

supernatural Son of Man that had been hid from the beginning and was now revealed, but He was revealed incarnate and born of the Davidic line. "For us men and for our salvation He came down from Heaven," cutting across the course of history; but He brought to a close one era of human earthly history only by beginning another.

This is a point which requires careful attention. Devotion to the historical study which aims at accurately determining the teaching intended by men of past ages may lead us to shrink overmuch from expounding their views in the light of later knowledge. Such study (let me say it once again) is the necessary foundation of all further work; we must begin by refusing resolutely to read into the minds of any men the ideas of later ages. But it is quite another thing to conclude that, in the light of later events, the truths they were seeking to express were, as a matter of fact, greater than they ever surmised. Thus, in the present instance, it is only too easy to argue that because to the minds of those first-century Jews who looked for an apocalyptic appearing of a Son-of-Man Messiah "when the Kingdom of God is inaugurated, human history ceases," therefore if Christ claimed to be that kind of Messiah, He must have claimed to bring with Him the end of this world's history, and, moreover, that if in the event it turned out that He had not done this, His claim must have been false: if He had been Messiah at all, He had been some other kind of Messiah. But the reasoning is fallacious. It assumes that the apocalyptic expectations of the Jews were evidence not only for the notions they held about what Messiah would be and do but also for the actual nature of messiahship itself, which is absurd.

The Christian faith implies that the antithesis on which rest the distinctions between the different messianic expectations was in Jesus Christ reconciled and rendered meaningless for all later thought. God was His own Messiah; He came into history from without; yet He did come *within*, and having come within worked from within outwards, initiating a new era of history in which we have been

living ever since, and thus rendering unnecessary any
further expectations of a millennium to come.

"Think not that I came to destroy the law and the
prophets; I came not to destroy but to fulfil." It was not
the cessation but the fulfilment of history that He brought;
the Eternal came into the temporal "not to destroy, but
to fulfil." This essential implication of Christianity seems
curiously to be overlooked in some schools of theological
thought to-day. I refer in particular to some exponents
of the Barthian movement, and of Rudolf Otto's theory
of the numinous. These represent a reaction against a
position we briefly considered in the last lecture, that which
regards godhead as no more than the perfection of the best
natural potentialities of manhood. They emphasise the
gulf between Creator and created, between God and man,
between Eternal and temporal. The practical conclusion
which they draw for religion is that man should acknowledge the utter worthlessness of his earthly life, and bow
himself in uncomprehending awe before the *mysterium
fascinosum tremendum*. But such religion is emphatically
not historic Christianity. Historic Christianity, as we have
seen, is the acceptance of the adopted sonship of God in
Christ, the realisation of a vocation to the status of co-
worker in creation. The depth of the richness of the Divine
Being may be such that He will always be to us *mysterium
fascinosum tremendum*, but it need never again be the utterly
impenetrable mystery of a *wholly* other. The godhead
may be that to men who stand and gaze upon it, so to
speak, from without; but we have been taken within, to
look out upon the world around us with "the mind of
Christ." Hence the Christian doctrine of God contains
the corrective both of human arrogance and of its obscurantist antidote.

(ii)

So we come back to the Christ of the Gospels and see
Him in a new light. Our historical survey began by seeing
in Him a man who went through life seeking to find and

E

do His heavenly Father's will in the guidance and strength
of the Holy Spirit. There was nothing in His life which
could not be brought within that picture;[1] and yet the more
one looked into the picture, the more one saw in it depths
of content far beyond anything known to us in our other
experience of humanity.[2] Those who first reflected upon
the mystery He presented, being Jews, naturally used the
dramatic language of time and space to express their
convictions about Him, and spoke of Him as having *pre-
existed* before His birth at Bethlehem. Thus St. Paul speaks
of Him as One who, "being in the form of God . . . emptied
himself, taking the form of a servant,"[3] and the author of
the Fourth Gospel, speaking of the Word which in the
beginning was with God, says of Him that He "became
flesh and dwelt among us," and makes Him say of Himself
in His earthly life "Before Abraham was, I am," and "O
Father, glorify thou me with thine own self with the glory
which I had with thee before the world was."[4] In all probability religion will never be able on earth to dispense with
this language of pre-existence; religion demands the use
of the imaginative, dramatic terms of personal relationship,
and within this field there seems to be no other way in
which we can hold together our faith in the heavenly and
the earthly lives of our Saviour as belonging both to Him
as one Person. But while religion rightly continues so to
think and speak, theology sees clearly the inadequacy both
of the language and the thought. Eternity and time are not
so related that a life can be thought of as extending for so
long in the one sphere, then coming down and continuing
for some thirty years in the other, and finally returning
to go on henceforward in the first; as a man might spend
his youth and old age in his own country and his middle
years abroad. What is sometimes called the doctrine of

[1] See my *And Was Made Man, passim.*

[2] See C. E. Raven, *The Creator Spirit* (Harvard University Press, 1927),
pp. 234–6; G. Kittel in Bell and Deissmann, *Mysterium Christi* (Longmans,
1930); Hoskyns and Davey, *The Riddle of the New Testament* (Faber and
Faber, 1931).

[3] Phil. ii. 6, 7.   [4] John i. 1, 14, viii. 58, xvii. 5.

the pre-existence of Christ is a doctrine which, strictly speaking, has no meaning unless it means something other than it says. Only in meaning this something other, it means not less than it says, but more. It means that the life about which we read in the Gospels as having been lived in Palestine in the days of Herod and Pontius Pilate was not a life of which the whole story was told between the earthly birth and death, as it is with each of us. It expresses the recognition that it was the earthly life of One who was somehow essentially different from every one of us. How great that difference was the Christian Church came clearly to state when at Nicaea the words ὁμοούσιον τῷ πατρί were written into the Creed, and this formulation of the faith we now see to involve yet a further universalising of the primitive Jewish belief than that we were considering a few moments ago. It substituted the statement of a timeless truth for the recitation of an impossible bit of history. Instead of trying to extend the true history fore and aft into eternity, it directed attention to the essential qualitative difference between one historic Figure and all others.

Our starting-point, then, is that historic Figure, and in its first stages the development of the Christian doctrine of God proceeds by making use of imaginative pictorial language which cannot, as it stands, be pressed too far. Still within the limits of true history we have seen that Figure as the source of a new life, a life of communion with the Father in the Spirit which His followers share through their relationship to Him. When we pass into the stage of imaginative elaboration, we may develop the language of pre-existence used in the New Testament by an extension of that Pauline use of the metaphor of adoption about which we were thinking in the last lecture. That suggested that the Christian is taken up by adoption to share in the eternal "family life," so to speak, of the godhead. Now it often happens in a family that one member, it may be a son, goes to live and work abroad. While there, he still retains his essential relationships to his family as at home, but exercises them under different conditions. He is still the son of his parents, the brother of his brothers and sisters, but letters and messages take the place of the daily intercourse of home life. It is in some such way as this that, at the first stage of development in his thought, the Christian thinks about the Incarnation. Jesus of Nazareth, though living to the full the human life of this planet, is a sojourner whose true home is in another sphere. He retains on earth those relationships to the Father and the Spirit which are His eternally, but He exercises them under the conditions of human life on earth.

How, then, are we to think about that godhead which has thus revealed itself through one of its Persons in history? What must be the nature of the divine life if this is how it appears when lived under human conditions? This is the question presented by the historical facts which form the basis of Christianity. Analysed in more detail it asks: What in the Gospel story can be predicated of Christ in His eternal being, and what is incidental to His incarnate life?

In the last lecture we described His incarnate life as essentially a seeking to find and do the Father's will through the guidance and power of the Spirit. As the writer of the Epistle to the Hebrews put it, "through the Eternal Spirit He offered Himself," or (according to St. John) His meat was to do the will of Him that sent Him.[1] It was a life of self-giving in response to the Father's love, through the Spirit. The Doctrine of the Trinity is the projection into eternity of this essential relationship, the assertion that eternally the Divine Life is a life of mutual self-giving to one another of Father and Son through the Spirit who is the *vinculum* or bond of love between them.

But as lived on earth that life was subject to the limitations of human experience. In mind and in body He was circum-scribed in ways which cannot be predicated of His eternal being. The question arises, therefore, how much of the observed limitations are we to think away in trying to form our conception of the Divine Being? A further question

---

[1] Heb. ix. 14; John iv. 34.

also arises: In what sense can we think of the Spirit, the *vinculum* or bond of love, as a third "Person"? To these two questions we must now address ourselves.

(iii)

Under human conditions, the life of self-giving in response to the Father's love was a life of suffering ending on the Cross. This was the inevitable consequence of living the divine life in a world where evil is entrenched in power and has to be challenged and overcome—as Plato had seen long before.[1] Such sufferings, then, as were due to the evil in the world He came to save must clearly be regarded as incidental to the Incarnation and thought away from our conception of the Divine Life. They may even, perhaps, be considered as non-essential to human life *in se*, as conceivably absent from a perfect human life lived in a perfect world. But more difficult problems remain. We may next consider those limitations which are involved in being human at all, those limitations in body and mind which come from bodily membership in the physical world, and from being in mind, both passively and actively, the subject of experiences mediated through a physical body at a particular time and place in the history and geography of this world. Here again, I suppose, we may regard these limitations as incidental to the Incarnation and to be thought away from our conception of the Divine Life. In Heaven, so to speak, the knowledge wherewith the Son knoweth the Father and what the Father doeth is not mediated through the consciousness of the body born at Bethlehem. But there is yet a third type of limitation, and it is here that the real difficulties begin. I refer to the limitations imposed upon our Lord in His relationship to surrounding creation through the existence in it of freedom and contingency.

There is a noticeable difference in the Gospels between the attitude of Christ to inanimate objects and to men.

---

[1] *Republic*, ii. 361e.

Stones, loaves, trees, waves of the sea, and mountains are regarded as things to be used freely for the furtherance of His purposes. It is assumed that they can be manipulated at will, and that there is no need to obtain in advance their consent. But with human beings it is otherwise. Their freedom has to be respected. They have to be won before they can be used, and won to a free open-eyed choice of His way. Thus in the Temptation both the physical force of arms and the spiritual compulsion of miracle are rejected as methods of bringing in the Kingdom of God. Thus He waits upon His hearers till "those who have ears to hear" shall respond to His message. No attempt is made to conceal the disadvantages of following Him: it may entail the plucking out of an eye or cutting off of hand or foot, the loss of wealth, friends and relations, and life itself, and it is not to be enterprised unadvisedly, lightly or wantonly after the manner of a man who should set out to build a tower or go to war without having given sufficient thought to what it was going to cost. To the end He prays earnestly for Peter and the other disciples that they may not fail; they cannot be coerced into faithfulness, and in the end Judas must be allowed to go his own way to his own place.

This acknowledgment of the relative independence of at least one element in creation is the acknowledgment of a limitation which can by no means so easily be thought away from our conception of the Divine Life as those we have hitherto considered. To begin with, we notice that Judas apparently fell away in spite of our Lord's prayers.[1] This shows that for Christ intercession on behalf of mankind is not the wielding of an instrument of spiritual influence which disregards human freedom of choice. There is a limitation to the exercise of God's power in the fulfilment of His will which is not confined to, and therefore not dependent upon, the Incarnation, but springs from

[1] The alternative would be to think of our Lord as having cast Judas for the part of traitor in the drama of salvation, in order to secure His own sacrificial death.

the relationship of God to His world which we describe as creation.

The doctrine of creation contains within it an unsolved problem, the fundamental problem for human thought. We have to think both of God-in-Himself as unlimited and as impassible, and of God-in-relation-to-creation as self-limited, and by His own self-limiting activity in the true sense of the word passible. We shall see later on that the attempt to use the doctrine of the Trinity to solve this problem breaks down, and that to regard the so-called "Logos Doctrine" as a valuable Christian contribution to its solution has been the source of undesirable confusion of thought which is still too prevalent among us.[1] The case of Judas shows that the Divine self-limitation which respects the freedom that God gives His creation is a form of limitation which applies to the whole godhead, and thus to the Second Person of the Trinity both unincarnate and incarnate. Nor can we get round this conclusion by the hypothesis that this limitation was part of the "straitening" to which our Lord was subject until his work in the flesh was accomplished,[2] and was removed by the pentecostal adoption of His followers of which we were thinking in the last lecture. For whatever increase in our Incarnate Lord's power of influence over human lives came into history at Pentecost, there are no reasonable grounds for holding that it cancelled the divine respect for human freedom and selfhood. The empirical evidence (as we have seen) tells the other way. So in our attempt to think away the "straitening" involved in His life in the flesh, in order to form some conception of His eternal being, we must not divest Him of limitations involved in His participation in the divine creative activity.

That this must include respect for human freedom is clear. When this is taken as an established starting-point, further questions arise. How far is this relative independence given to creation by its Creator to be thought of as extending downwards into sub-human existence? And to

[1] See below, Lecture V, pp. 113 ff.   [2] Luke xii. 50.

what extent is the divine omniscience limited by the element of contingency in the created universe? To discuss these questions properly would take us beyond the scope of these lectures. But we may well spare a moment to ask what light may possibly be thrown on them by the empirical evidence of the Gospels. On the first question, the Gospels seem at first to suggest that as our gaze travels downward from man into the sub-human, we see the degree of freedom and independence progressively decreasing. As I have already pointed out, our Lord assumes a control over inanimate nature which He disclaims in the case of man. To a certain extent, of course, acceptance of this conclusion depends on one's attitude to the miraculous element in the Gospels; but only to a certain and a limited extent. For if the question be simply to determine what human limitations to think away from our conception of our Lord's divine being, the more we think of those limitations as being due to the absoluteness of the divine control as exercised through the regularity of what we call "laws of nature," the more we think of them as incidental to the Incarnation. If as Man He had control, we need not think of Him as having less as God: if as Man His control is limited owing to the limits imposed by God on man's interference with His ordering of the physical world, that limitation applies only to His incarnate activity. In either case the result is the same.

But the matter is complicated by the fact that we cannot treat the question as though it simply concerned the ordering of nature by God and man. There is a third possibility, that of an independence of nature's own, relative both to God and man. In the New Testament this complication appears through acceptance of the belief in dæmonic influence. It was the common assumption that this world is the sphere of activity of various spirits, some of whom, at any rate, were equally as free as man to oppose God's will. Stated in its extreme form, the assumption produces such statements as the references in the Johannine literature to "The Prince of this world" and to the "Evil One" in

whom "this whole world lieth."[1] Our Lord seems to have
shared this belief in the activity of spirits and to have dealt
with the dæmons as hostile powers to be met and overcome
by the power of moral authority. They were rebuked and
overawed, as a good man of strong character may rebuke
and overawe a bad, not manipulated as a potter deals with
his clay. And in the end their power was broken not by a
simple word of command, but by His death upon the Cross.
The world had to be redeemed from their clutches, the
divine control reasserted by divine self-sacrifice.[2]

The first impression produced by this belief is of something wholly alien to our present ways of thinking, a relic
of a bygone age. We feel, perhaps, a little disturbed to
think that we have discovered something as irremovable
from our incarnate Lord's outlook as it is irrecoverable by
our own. But second thoughts suggest that when we attend,
not to forms of thought, but to the underlying realities with
which they attempt to deal, there may be more in it than
at first appeared.

I do not lay much stress upon the conviction of some
biologists that freedom, such as we know it in man, is the
developed form of a spontaneity which has its beginnings
much earlier in the history of living creatures, a notion
which is now even adopted by some physicists as applicable
to the behaviour of the constituent elements in atoms.
Such theories are of great interest in their own sphere,
but the independence of the creature which they involve
is not necessarily such as to interfere with the fulfilment
of God's will in His creation. It may well be that the choices
open to amœbæ or quanta are equally well adapted to their
fulfilling the divine purpose of their existence, and that
their exercise of their spontaneity is the divinely appointed
method of their co-operation in creative activity. It is only
at the developed stage of a conscious, intelligent and purposive choice of ends which may be in opposition to God's
will that the question arises of any significant limitation

---

[1] John xvi. 11; 1 John v. 19. Cp. Rom. viii. 20–23.
[2] On all this see G. Aulén: *Christus Victor* (Tr. Hebert, S.P.C.K., 1931).

of divine control, and in the evolution of living species
on earth this kind of freedom seems first to appear as
characteristic of man.

The real question is whether this evolution, culminating
in human freedom, is the only creation there is of spirits
capable of disobedience to God's will; and in spite of the
impatience which such a suggestion tends to produce in our
minds, it is a question which must be seriously asked. For
to assume a negative answer has very serious consequences
for our thought. It implies that God's will is more certainly
revealed in nature apart from man's manipulation of it than
in human activity, leading us, for example to see the divine
activity in an earthquake rather than in the labours of those
who give of their wealth and service to relieve the suffering
it has caused.

The notion that sub-human nature, if left untouched
by human control, reveals the will of God, is very ancient
and still widely prevalent. But the more one thinks about
it, the more impossible it becomes to rest content with
the view that man dwells in a universe in which everything
works harmoniously together for good apart from the
exceptions introduced by human sin. It is surely the common
experience of men and women who try to work together
corporately for the promotion of some good end, that
frequently they are baffled by what can only be described
as a "cussedness" in things. Their best efforts seem to
be rendered fruitless by the remorseless play of circumstances beyond their control. Now when this happens,
there are four possible attitudes to adopt. (a) The different
parties to the undertaking may attempt to fasten the blame
for the disasters upon one another, each attempting to
convince the rest of the world that one or more of the
others has been at fault. Or (b) they may agree that the
failure is due to their common sharing in human sinfulness,
and unite in penitence for it. Thirdly, (c) they may agree
that the great evil deity, Circumstance, is paramount, and
that all attempts to circumvent it are in the end hopeless
and rather a waste of time. Lastly, (d) while agreeing that

they have been baffled by circumstances which are too much for them, they may refuse to accept these circumstances as expressing the will of the ultimate power behind the universe, but regard them as evidence of a hostile power at work in the universe, to be challenged and overcome by the servants of the true God, and their set-back as bidding them only *reculer pour mieux sauter*.

Now when we think it out we find, I believe, that it is this last view which really underlies our best actual practice. If we say, for example, that what is needed is fresh application to scientific study in order more adequately to control our universe, we are making a call to scientists "to shun delights and live laborious days," in order that nature may be rendered subservient to our purposes. This is a call to self-sacrifice, and implies that the world as it stands is not, so to speak, ready-made as God's perfected creation. It is raw material for the making of God's world, and raw material which can only be worked up into God's world by self-sacrifice on the part of the workers. But what kind of a world is it which can only be conquered by such methods? Is it lapsing into superstitious mythology to regard it as embodying a principle of hostility to God's purposes, which nevertheless can be overcome by the method of the cross?[1]

I do not wish here to carry this argument further, or to enter into any speculations as to the origin or nature of the evil which has this power in creation.[2] All that is relevant

[1] If this argument be sound, then the old saying that nature is conquered by being obeyed is a half-truth. It is true if it be taken to mean simply that we must understand the workings of nature in order to control them. But it is a dangerous error if it is held to mean also that our aim in seeking to understand these workings should be to conform our ways to them rather than to enlist them in the service of our own purposes. This error is a constant form of confusion, for example, in the discussion of such subjects as the ethics of birth-control.

[2] A good instance of the kind of speculation I mean is to be found in the last two of Dr. N. P. Williams' Bampton Lectures (*The Ideas of the Fall and of Original Sin*, Longmans, 1927). While, like many others, I hesitate to accept his theory of a pre-mundane Fall of a World-Soul, I should like to protest against a common habit of treating the highly speculative character

here is to call attention to the fact which such speculations attempt to explain, the fact that, quite apart from man, nature as it stands cannot be taken as infallibly expressing or revealing the will of God.

The conclusion we seem to be justified in drawing is this: God, through His activity in creation, gives to His created universe a relative independence and accepts the self-limitation involved in the fulfilment of His own will. We can distinguish in the created universe two modes of existence: (a) that of "matter," the characteristic of which is that it conforms passively to the divine will, and (b) that of "mind," the characteristic of which is that it is given freedom to co-operate with God consciously of set purpose, or to withhold such co-operation. Where this co-operation is withheld, the divine control is not exercised by force applied *ab extra*, but by winning an inward response to divine self-sacrifice. We know that there is such with-holding of co-operation among men, and that God meets it in this way. We cannot prove that human wills are the only created wills endowed with such freedom, and the hypothesis that there are other such wills at work in creation solves on the whole more difficulties than it creates.[1]

We can now see the relevance of this discussion to our main argument. In asking what limitations consequent upon incarnation we are to think away from our conception of the heavenly life of our Lord (we are still at the stage of pictorial imagining) we cannot think away any which are involved in God's gift of freedom to His creation. If this includes, as we have seen some reason to believe may be the case, a limitation of control over the universe due to the activity of wills other than human, as well as of mankind, we must allow for this in our thought.

of his theory as an excuse for ignoring the problem it is intended to meet.

[1] They are the kind of difficulties which *solvuntur ambulando*, where action is a necessary preliminary to explanation. This happens, for example, whenever social or international problems yield to those who tackle them by the method of the cross. Cp. my *Essays in Christian Philosophy*, pp. 37–8, 55 = *Towards a Christian Philosophy*, pp. 87–8, 106.

The eternal Son, in other words, shares with the Father in that limitation of divine ἀπάθεια which is involved in the activity of creation. But (if I may use the phrase without irreverence), the Father and the Son know what they are doing. It is part of the divine omniscience to know in detail its own limitations, and that intuitively. In their celestial converse with One Another, the Father and the Son know precisely what manner of contingency they have implanted in creation, just where it implies a freedom that must be respected and where it does not. They know, for example, that moral evil cannot be cured by the external application of force, that it is a misdirection of created will such as can only be righted by making the sin an occasion of loving the sinner so intensely that he will be won back to penitence and a new life. The incarnate life of Jesus Christ is the application of this method to this one planet of the created universe. In the incarnate life the knowledge in detail of His limitations is mediated to His human mind through the combination of His communion with the Father and His experience of the world around. The Incarnation is the carrying out in history of the divine plan wherein God manifests His omnipotence by triumphing over the limitations prescribed by Himself in His creation of finite centres of freedom. It involves the Son's entry upon the experience of life under human conditions, in which as man He has to learn anew what eternally as God He knows. What we have to think away, in trying to picture His eternal being by the aid of His historic self-manifestation, is the method of arriving at the knowledge of His powers and limitations, and not the knowledge itself.

(iv)

We have arrived at the picture of the incarnate Lord as One who exercised on earth the divine power as it was at the disposal of the mind and will of a perfect human being, that is to say, of a human being completely consecrated to finding and doing the Father's will, and limited only

by the essential conditions of human existence, and by
those elements in creation which are controllable only by
the winning of their free response. In our last lecture we saw
reason to think that He regarded His sharing in the Father's
mind and power as mediated to Him through the Spirit
We have now to ask to what extent, and in what sense, we
should think of the Spirit in this context as "personal."

It will be well at this point to attend to one of those many
ambiguities in the word "personal" which are often a source
of confusion. When we ask whether in any context the
Spirit is "personal" or "impersonal," we may mean one
of two things. We may be contrasting an activity which
is expressive of a conscious purposive will with a blind
force conceived of after a mechanistic manner. Coming
across a man lying on the road, for example, we might ask
whether he had been knocked down by a robber or by a
tile blown off a roof in a gale. In our ordinary language
we should regard the former event as a personal act, the
latter as an impersonal accident. But we may also be contrasting a force which is expressive of a conscious, purposive
will with such a will itself, considered as the originating
source of the activity, and our terminology (based on the
theological reference of the English word "person" to the
Greek ὑπόστασις) may use "impersonal" for the former
and "personal" for the latter case. Now the question as
to the "personality" of the Spirit in the Bible, Old Testament or New, has no meaning except in respect of the second
of these two contrasts. We must not allow the etymological
affinities of the Hebrew and Greek words for Spirit to
delude us into believing that any Jew ever thought of the
Spirit of God as a something physical and therefore impersonal in the mechanistic sense which the word suggest
to modern ears. Whatever else the Spirit of God may have
been for the Jew, it was always at least the manifestation
of the power of the God whose conscious purposive will
was expressed in its activity. The Spirit through which
Jesus Christ on earth knew and did His Father's will, and
through which by His gift His followers had and have

insight and initiative, was and is "personal" in the sense
that it expresses the Father's conscious, intelligent, purposive will. Though it might be thought of as "poured,"
and its course be as incalculable by human beings as that
of the wind which "bloweth where it listeth,"[1] this latter
phrase would convey to Jewish ears no such suggestion
of mechanistic impersonality as is suggested to us by the
thought of a man knocked down by a tile blown off a roof.
The Spirit could be likened to the wind because the wind
was regarded as controlled by and executing the will of
its Creator.

The real question, then, is of the sense in which the Spirit
can be thought of as "personal" or "a Person" as distinct
from and parallel to the Father and the Son, and is to be
spoken of in His own right as "He," not as "It." That
He should be so regarded and spoken of is undoubtedly
the tradition of Christian orthodoxy. But there is probably
nothing in the traditional doctrine which has caused greater
difficulty to the understanding, and the problem is indeed
one of such difficulty that I can hardly hope in these lectures
to supply its solution. Nevertheless, if I am not to be justly
accused of evading the central crux of my chosen theme,
I must try to say something about it.

The first thing to be done is to notice that there are two
questions involved which must be distinguished from each
other. In the classical formulation of the doctrine the
Greek and Latin words ὑπόστασις and *persona* do not
necessarily involve the notion of a distinct centre of consciousness which is suggested by the modern English use
of the word "person";[2] they denote something which is
real in its own right but might be an "it" rather than a "he."
Thus, if we take the familiar statement whereby the Spirit
is the Love which unites the Father and the Son, the hypostatisation of the Spirit might be taken to be the assertion
that the Love is not an adjectival quality of the Father and

---

[1] Acts ii. 17, x. 45, John iii. 8.
[2] On this see *Essays on the Trinity and the Incarnation* (Ed. Rawlinson,
London, 1928), p. 392.

the Son, but an element as inherently essential to the being of the godhead as the other two Persons, without resembling them in being a third "He."[1] We have thus to consider both whether the Spirit is a distinct hypostasis, and also whether, if so, that hypostasis is an "It" or a "He."

It will be convenient to take the second of these questions first. In this lecture we are primarily concerned with the teaching of the New Testament, and often the New Testament undoubtedly speaks of the Spirit as a "He." There are indeed many ambiguous passages. This is not surprising. Even the most superficial study of apparent personifications of divine attributes and agencies in Jewish writers of the time is enough to show that the distinction which we now have in mind, and which seems so clear to us, was by no means so clear to them. In this matter of "He" or "It" they could apparently use without qualm varieties of language which to us suggest intolerable confusion of thought.[2] There are also passages in which it is difficult to say whether πνεῦμα is intended to mean the Spirit of God or the spirit of man. Is the πνεῦμα υἱοθεσίας of Rom. viii. 15 the divine Spirit of Gal. iv. 6 or the spirit of the Christian as transformed by the coming of the divine Spirit?

This latter ambiguity we can ignore. It is there all the same, whether the divine Spirit is thought of as "He" or "It." The question we have to ask is this. Granted that the New Testament contains both "He" passages and "It" passages, which are we to regard as fundamental for our doctrine of the Spirit?

It seems to me clear that the "He" passages have this right. We have to remember that the Christian belief in the Holy Spirit arose against the background of a belief in many spirits, good and bad.[3] These other spirits were undoubtedly thought of as personal in the "He" sense.

[1] On this see C. C. J. Webb: *God and Personality* (London, 1918), p. 274.

[2] Many alumni of the General Theological Seminary in New York will remember how Dr. Easton, after lecturing on this subject, would ask, "Have you got that clear?" and if anyone answered "Yes" would say "Then you've got it wrong."

[3] Above, Lecture II, p. 38.

Angels and demons had names, and conversations could be carried on with them. In my last lecture I was arguing that the Spirit promised by our Lord to His disciples and received by them at Pentecost was the Spirit which He regarded in His earthly life as inspiring Him and uniting Him to the Father. In the crucial passage to which I then referred, St. Mark iii. 20–30, the Holy Spirit is opposed to Baalzeboul, the prince of evil spirits. Baalzeboul was undoubtedly a "he" spirit, and the implication is that his Opponent was equally a "He." The question "Can Satan cast out Satan?" implies this, as does also the statement that the Holy Spirit can be the object of blasphemy. The Paraclete passages in the Fourth Gospel do not go beyond this synoptic utterance in their personification of the Spirit. Against this evidence the fact that there are also "It" passages, and that in previous literature the Hebrew and Aramaic words for spirit were "it" words, do not prevail. We have seen that we cannot limit our interpretation of our Lord's conception of His messiahship by those conceptions of it which were current at the time of His coming; the fulfilment was more than the expectations.[1] Neither can we constrain the revelation of the Spirit through Christ by researches in Hebrew and Aramaic etymology.[2]

If we accept the "He" passages as expressing the authentic New Testament teaching, we can account for and interpret the "It" passages in accordance with them. It would seem that at the pentecostal coming of the Spirit the minds of the disciples were still mainly coloured by their pre-Christian conceptions. Interpreting their experience by the light of these preconceptions they pictured their risen and ascended Lord as the triumphant Messiah who, during His temporary absence from earth, was keeping in touch with His followers by sending down upon them His "It" Spirit. It took some time for them to learn that the Lord

---

[1] Above, pp. 63–4.
[2] On this subject, see the important contribution by Dr. Edwyn Bevan in *Symbolism and Belief* (London, 1938), Lectures VII, VIII.

was Himself present with them, and that as adopted to share His sonship and to be members of His body they came to share with Him in knowing the Spirit as Him through whom they were united to the Father and enabled to find and do His will. Moreover, the outcome of the Spirit's activity is a χάρισμα or spiritual gift. For example, the activity of the Holy Spirit exercised in our adoption to divine sonship induces in us a filial spirit. When we approach the subject from the human end, it makes no difference whether the immediate cause of the χάρισμα is a "He" or an "It." The effect might have been produced equally well by the Father or the Son by an output of love or power which would be "It" in the same sense as a man's love or power is "It" as contrasted with the man himself. This being so, with the New Testament emerging from the background of thought which I have attempted to describe, it is not surprising that in many passages which approach the subject from the human end, the Holy Spirit is not explicitly and unambiguously described as "He." Thus from the point of view of the "He" passages the "It" passages can be regarded as expressing an apprehension which is partial and incomplete but true as far as it goes and historically explicable. But if the "It" passages are held to express the whole truth, then the "He" passages must be regarded as mythological personifications which for two thousand years have had a sadly misleading influence on the thought and language of Christendom.

So far, then, as exegesis is concerned, I would maintain that the "He" passages are an integral element in the thought of the writers of the New Testament and of our Lord Himself. Can the doctrine they express be maintained when we are asking the further question, whether the truth about God's self-revelation in action was in every detail what they thought it was?

The answer to this question must be left for a later lecture. What I have to say now is that if the "He" character of the Spirit may be taken as revealed in the New Testament experience of God's redeeming activity this is not an element which would have to be thought away when we try to project into eternity God's revelation of Himself in space and time. Whatever may be said on philosophical grounds against the notion of the Spirit as a third "He" in the eternal being of God may be said with equal force in relation to the Spirit's activity in human experience. The "he-ness" was not an attribute incidental to the revelation, for if the Spirit were eternally "It," then "it-ness" would have served the revelatory purpose equally well.

There remains our second question. Granted that in the New Testament the Spirit is "He," is He perhaps to be identified with the risen and ascended Lord, and not regarded as a third "He?" I am not going to spend any time discussing this. There is really no evidence at all for the identification, except what can be manufactured by assuming the certainty of a possible exegesis of an obscure phrase in 2 Cor. iii. 17 and using it to control the interpretation of certain other possibly ambiguous passages. The careful and thoroughgoing examination of this whole subject by Fr. Lionel Thornton in Chapter XII of *The Incarnate Lord* should have effectively killed this theory for all time, so that there is no need for me to go over that ground again.[1]

(v)

I must now briefly summarise the conclusions to which we have been led. We have found the doctrine of the Trinity to be the doctrine of God implied by the earthly life of Christ, when that life was reflected upon by Christians in the light of their experience of being adopted to share His sonship. We thus find ourselves in agreement with the assertion of St. Thomas Aquinas that the doctrine is a revealed doctrine, but we think of it as having been revealed in deeds which required to be reflected upon by human reason in order that it might be put into words. It did not begin as a theological doctrine, but as a religious outlook, the outlook of One who thought of Himself as

[1] See Appendix IV, p. 216.

finding and doing His heavenly Father's will through the indwelling Spirit by whom He was one with the Father. When his disciples came to think of themselves as sharing with their Lord in that way of life which had been His upon earth, they committed their successors to the task of thinking out the doctrine of God implied by their religious practice. This required two things. First it required the attempt to think away from the Son the accidents incidental to His revelation as incarnate, and to think away from the Spirit the accidents incidental to his revelation as inspiring incarnate beings. Secondly, it required the attempt to determine whether the resulting doctrine of God could reasonably be held by any sane man. We have so far only been able to attend to the former of these requirements, and have seen that the New Testament presents us with a God in whose eternal being the Son gives Himself in mutually responsive love to the Father through the Spirit, the Spirit being equally personal with the Father and the Son in every sense in which the word is used of them. Such is the God of the Christian revelation, and if it be true that God has revealed Himself in this way in the history of this world, then that is an empirical fact with implications for philosophy no less than for religion.

LECTURE IV

TRINITARIAN THEOLOGY

(i)

IN the year 1914 a course of Shaw Lectures was delivered
in this University of Edinburgh by Dr. John Laird,
who was then Professor of Logic and Metaphysics in
the Queen's University of Belfast and is now Regius Professor of Moral Philosophy at Aberdeen. Those lectures
formed the basis of Professor Laird's book entitled *Problems
of the Self*, which was published in 1917, and it is no over-
statement to say that these lectures which I am now giving
had their origin in my reading of that book twenty-five
years ago. If there be anything of value in what I am now
able to bring to Edinburgh, it is the value of what came
to me from Edinburgh as its source.

When I began to read that book I had no idea of where
it was going to lead me. I read it out of interest in its own
subject, and if it had led me no further I should still have
been grateful for its contribution to that study. But at the
time when I read it I was a theological tutor engaged in
lecturing upon the history of Christian doctrine in the first
five centuries of our era, and the more I read the more
impressed I became by the closeness of the parallel between
the history of the doctrine of the Trinity in the days of
the Early Church and the history of the doctrine of the
Self as presented by Professor Laird. I am now going to
begin this lecture by trying to exhibit this parallelism.

Professor Laird begins by showing how the human self
is known to us in the three activities of thinking, feeling
and willing. Each of these is only known to us in its active
exercise, when it is always concerned with some object

which gives it content. Each of these activities is distinct
from the other two: thinking is a distinct activity, not to
be identified or confused with feeling or willing, and each
of the others is equally distinct. Yet they interpermeate
one another in such a way that in human life no one exists
except as conditioned by the others: the way in which we
think is coloured by what we feel and will, and so on.
This interpermeation shows them to be elements in a more
or less unified whole, and in spite of the fact that they are
only observably existent when active, there is a continuity
as well as a unity in each interpermeating group, that unity
and continuity which is to be found in the individual life
of each human being. What, then, is the principle that
unites and continues? What is it that is one and continuous?
What is the self or soul that expresses itself in these three
activities? It has sometimes been thought that the self or
soul is a fourth entity to which these activities belong.
But unless the activities are to be regarded as functions
of the body, no such fourth entity is observably existent.
Just as each activity is only observably existent when
exercised about some particular object, so the individual
self or soul is only observably existent when engaged in
its activities; at other times there is at most a hypothetical
potentiality of such activity. And there are insuperable
objections to regarding the body as the principle of unity
and continuity and the activities as its functions. If, then,
there is no fourth entity, can we find the unity by identi-
fying the self with one of the three activities themselves
and reducing the others to terms of it? Attempts have been
made to solve the problem in this way, and each activity
in turn has been tried out as being at bottom the real self.
There have been thinkers for whom man is fundamentally
a rational being, his unity maintained by the subordination
of his feelings and his will to his reason. There have been
thinkers for whom the core of man's personality has been
found in his will, for which his feelings are the material
and his reason the instrument. There have been thinkers
for whom all our activities are the fulfilment of the desires

which form our true selfhood, for whom all our thinking is "rationalising" these same desires. But none of these theories is adequate to account for all the observed facts of our experience, and we are left with a mysterious unity in trinity, a unity which is an object of faith postulated by our reason in order to account for the observed trinity of activities.

I have not attempted to do more than to summarise, and to summarise in my own way, some of the subjects discussed in Professor Laird's book. I have given no indication either of the wealth of material contained in it or of the learning and acumen employed in its detailed investigation or of Professor Laird's views on the problems raised. The relevance of his book to the Christian doctrine of the Trinity lies in its directing attention to the nature of the problem presented by the fact that human beings are what we experience them to be.

Nevertheless, although I have not attempted to state Professor Laird's views or to reproduce his thought, but simply to avail myself of his guidance, my second and third lectures have been evidence of the fact that his book has influenced my whole approach to the subject. He did not begin with any *a priori* notion of the self as a unified whole, but with a description of our experienced and observable activities. Then, after a prolonged study of these activities directed towards securing that they should be accurately observed and described, he asked what kind of a unified and continuous being it must be which manifests itself in these ways. Similarly, I have not started from any *a priori* notion of God as the ultimate unity underlying all the multiplicity of our experience, or anything of that sort, but from the biblical record of God's activities as observable and observed in the history of the world. Hitherto we have been engaged in studying that record with a view to making sure that they have been accurately observed and described. We are now nearing the point where we shall go on to ask the further question, what kind of unity must we postulate of the God who has manifested Himself in these activities?

There are at least three respects in which those who are familiar with the Christian doctrine of the Trinity will have noticed similarities in the account which I have given of the human self.

First, in describing the interrelations of the activities of the self, I have used the word "interpermeation." This word does not occur, so far as I remember, in Professor Laird's book, but it comes naturally to the mind of a theologian when he tries to state what he has learned from that book, because it is the usual English translation of περιχώρησις and *circuminsessio* in the doctrine of the Trinity. There is here in the human self an illuminating analogy to that in the Godhead which this technical term is used to denote. We see that it is not a term artificially invented by theologians for the purpose of concealing a self-contradiction in an irrational theological doctrine; it is an apt and most convenient term for describing a relationship with which in our own experience we are quite familiar.

Secondly, in studying the history of the doctrine of the Trinity the theologian has to deal with what he is accustomed to call "subordinationism." That term is used to describe theories current in the monarchian controversies of the third and fourth centuries. Those theories were attempts to secure the unity of the Godhead by regarding one Person as ultimately God in His own right and the others as divine in a secondary or subordinate sense. There is this difference, that in the history of theology only one of the three Persons, the Father, was in patristic times regarded in this way as the real God, whereas in the history of psychology each of the three activities has in turn been regarded as the real self. But this is immaterial. The underlying principle of the theories is the same in both cases: they are attempts to find the unity by treating one of the elements as ultimate and reducing the others to terms of it. The impossibility of accounting by this method for the facts of our own experience should lead us to surmise that the Church was right in rejecting similar methods of solving its theological problem. There are also in the history of the theological doctrine parallels to those theories which attempt to find the unity of the self's activities in some fourth entity. But these are less obvious because they are less close, and there is no need for us to consider them.

Thirdly, whilst the three activities of the self are observable facts of experience which postulate for it some kind of unity and continuity, the nature of that unity and continuity is mysterious. To put it somewhat crudely, the reader of such a book as *Problems of the Self* is apt to feel, as he comes to its end, that no such incredibly mysterious creature as a man could possibly exist. But as he lays the book down and goes out of his study, he finds no difficulty in resuming his social intercourse with his fellow creatures. Just so does the theologian continue to find pardon, peace and joy in communion with God. While in both cases we are right to acknowledge the mystery as mysterious, there is possibly less justification for the feeling that it is incredible. That is the possibility which we have now to explore.

(ii)

It is clear, I think, that the underlying question concerns the nature of unity. If there be any true analogy between the constitution of the Godhead and of the human self, it is due to their being instances of the same type of unity. To avoid misunderstanding, it should be noted that I am not now attempting to press this analogy beyond this one point. I am not, for example, suggesting any distributive parallelism between the three Persons of the Godhead and the three human activities, each to each. Such suggestions have been made; I only mention them now in order to make it plain that at present I am talking about something else, about the nature of unity itself. We are not for the moment concerned with the nature of the content either of the human self or of the Godhead; it may be that there are many other things, quite different as to the kind of things they are in respect of their content, which are analogous to the God-

head and the human self in the one point which we are now
to discuss, the form of their unity.

Philosophers have long been familiar with what is known
as the problem of the one and the many, of unity and
multiplicity. But too often it seems to have been assumed
that the two terms of the problem when considered apart,
are simple and easily intelligible, that the whole problem lies in their relation to one another. This has been
the case especially with unity. For many a thinker it has been
the multiplicity in the world of our experience which has
caused him perplexity; it has been tacitly assumed that
unity is self-explanatory and intelligible.

Thought of this kind is undoubtedly seeking to give
expression to a truth, the truth that unless every event in
our multiple and varied experience can be seen to fit into
its place in a universe which is a systematic whole, both
the events and the universe remain unintelligible. All
thinking, in the sense of the attempt to understand our
experience, is a futile waste of time if the universe be not
a *uni*verse, a unified whole, a unity. But in the attempt
to understand our experience, we tend to start by assuming
that we know what unity means, and that we shall readily
be able to recognise it when we come across it. We feel that
we know quite well what we mean when we say that a thing
is one. But do we? That is the question.

The idea of unity in our minds is primarily an arithmetical
idea: the criterion of unity is the absence of multiplicity.
Here one is one and three are three; what is one is not three
and what are three are not one. But we have long been
acquainted with unities which are not so simple. There
is, for example, æsthetic unity, the unity of a work of art.
And there is organic unity, the unity of a living creature.
In both of these the unity is far from being simple. It does
indeed exclude certain kinds of multiplicity, such as a
distracting multiplicity of interests in a work of art, or a lack
of co-ordination in the activities of a living creature. But
it can only exist at all by virtue of the presence of another
kind of multiplicity, the multiplicity of the varied elements

which constitute the work of art or the living creature. We are here more directly concerned with organic than with æsthetic unity, and therefore for purposes of convenience I shall for the moment use the terms "organic unity" and "mathematical unity" for the two types which I now wish to contract.

Whilst a mathematical unity just is an arithmetical unity and nothing else, an organic unity is in one respect an arithmetical unity but in another respect is something more. Each organism is an arithmetical unity in respect of being a single member of the world of organisms in general. But it only exists as unifying in a single life history the various elements of which it is composed, elements which can only play their part in that life if they are different from and complementary to one another. Moreover, on the usually accepted scale of values, the higher we go in the world of living creatures, the more complex does the organisation become. The creature which most nearly approximates to the ideal of arithmetical unity is the unicellular amoeba; in the human being there is not only the complex organisation of his physical body, but that body exists as the substratum and instrument of the feeling, willing and thinking self.

A point to be noticed here is that when we speak of the unity of a human being, we are speaking of a unity which may exist in a greater or lesser degree. There may be a want of unity in the body itself, as in the heroine of E. F. Benson's novel *Sheaves* whose lungs required for their health a climate that was fatal to her heart. There may be, so to speak, a state of civil war between the mind and the body, the spirit willing and the flesh weak. There may be a conflict within the mind itself, what some psychologists would call an inadequate integration of personality. The man who is really a unity is the man whose bodily organ and threefold activities of selfhood are unified in one consistent exercise of personal life.

For our immediate purpose the value of Professor Laird's book lies in its exposition of the fact that in the case of at least one instance of organic unity, the human self, the seat of the unity is not to be found in any one of its constituent elements, or in some further entity of the same order of being. What I now wish to suggest is that the historical attempts to do one or other of these things are at bottom attempts to reduce the organic type of unity to the mathematical. The unrealised and therefore uncriticised presupposition of the thought is that an entity which is simple, which approximates to that arithmetical type of unity whose criterion is absence of multiplicity, is more intelligible than an entity which exists as a complex of differing constituents. It is assumed that the hypothetically independent self, or the will, or the reason, or the feeling is in this way more simple and intelligible than the complex life in which they all participate. Human beings would be more intelligible creatures if it could be shown that a man is at bottom one or other of these simpler objects of thought.

But when this presupposition is dragged out into the daylight of reflection it is seen to involve unsuspected difficulties of its own. A few minutes ago we were remembering that in this world the living creature most nearly approximating to the mathematical type of unity is the unicellular amœba. Now we are all familiar with that crux in the philosophical theory of evolution which appears when we ask in what sense the later and more complicated developments can be said to have evolved from the earlier and simpler.[1] If the amœba contains within it in some unobservably embryonic form the germs of what is to appear, it is not the simple thing we thought it was. If, on the other hand, the development from amœba to man is due to contributions from other elements in the universe according to some specific plan, and neither those elements nor the plan are contained within the simplicity of the amœba's constitution, then for all its simplicity the amœba can in no way be the key to the understanding of the man. The same dilemma confronts those who suppose that we

---

[1] See, e.g., the paper on " The Concept of Evolution," by H. W. B. Joseph in *Essays on Ancient and Modern Philosophy* (Oxford, 1935).

can better understand the human self by thinking of it as being really at bottom one or other of its constituent elements. Either the favoured element is too simple to account for the complexities of the whole self, or the problem of the unity of those complexities reappears in the constitution of the element.

We see, then, that it is a fallacy to suppose that we should find the unity of the self less mysterious if we were to find its seat in one of its constituent elements. To do so would not render its unity any more simple in the sense of free from internal multiplicity. What we need to do is to emancipate ourselves from the obsession that the nearer anything approaches that limit, the more intelligible it is. Here we need to distinguish between intelligible *in se* and intelligible *quoad nos*. It may be that a simple unity seems more intelligible *quoad nos* because our minds are incapable of understanding a more complex one, but this may be due to the weakness of our minds and not to any intrinsic irrationality in the complex unity. In every department of knowledge education develops our ability to understand complexity. In mathematics the tyro can see that two and two make four and that two straight lines cannot enclose a space; it is the mark of the trained mind to be able to grasp simultaneously the factors of a complicated problem and to see their implications. In ethics, any one of us who sees a man drop a purse knows that he ought to pick it up and give it back to its owner, but we may also find ourselves in situations where we need the advice of men whose experience and power of moral insight will help us to see the issues involved in their right proportions. There is all the difference in the world between a mystery which is alleged to exist in spite of admitted irrationality, and a mystery which is acknowledged because it is believed to embody a rationality which we are not yet sufficiently experienced and educated to comprehend. I believe the mysteries involved in both the human self and the Divine Trinity to be of this latter kind, and I shall have more to say about this later on. For the moment I will content myself with suggesting that the too common assumption that the mystery of the Divine Trinity is of the former kind rests upon the fallacious argument that because a simpler type of unity seems more intelligible *quoad nos*, a more complex type is *per se* irrational and unintelligible.

This assumption is so widespread that one often meets people who seem to think that the doctrine of the Trinity is an encumbrance to the simple faith of the Christian believer, thinking this because they assume that the unities of our experience are of the simple type and the complex unity of the Trinity a figment of the ecclesiastical imagination. But unless I have misunderstood what I have heard of the researches of physicists, we have no actual experience of any existing unity in this world of space and time which is not of the organic type. The observable unit of matter, the hydrogen atom, is, I understand, composed of two related components and would be destroyed by their collision. If either of the two types of unity is to be called a figment of human imagination, the absolutely simple and undifferentiated unity of the mathematician has the greater claim to that status.

We may then acknowledge the reality of this other type of unity, the unity of a being whose unity consists in nothing else than the unifying activity which unifies the component elements. It follows that the degree of unity achieved by such a being is to be measured by a different scale from that which would be used for the abstract mathematical type. Approximation to the ideal of mathematical unity is measured by a scale of degrees of absence of multiplicity; but approximation to the ideal of organic unity is measured by a scale of intensity of unifying power. We have seen that in the case of the human self the unity is by no means always perfect. Indeed, so long as we are on this earth we are no more likely to be perfect in this respect than in others; though we may escape the disunity of Sally Beauchamp and Miss Bishop, we have to confess that there is in us something of Mr. Hyde as well as of Dr. Jekyll. Perfect unity is our aim, not our present achievement.

But in whatever measure it is achieved, this is not effected by the cancellation of factors until nothing is left but an undifferentiated unity. Each element in our being must, it is true, be purged of whatever in it is evil, and it may be that the limitations of finite life on earth may require us to inhibit development in one direction in order to fulfil our vocation by concentrating on another.[1] All such limitation is an impoverishment of personality, and this statement is only another way of putting the truth that in the Christian religion asceticism is not the renunciation of what is evil but of what is good. It is one of the marks of our human impotence that we are deficient in the dynamic power of unifying more than a very few of the potentialities of our selfhood.

If the degree of unity is thus to be measured by a scale of intensity of unifying power, it is not by decreasing the number or the variety of the elements that the unity will be heightened, but rather the reverse. The man who can only achieve selfhood by concentrating on a narrow selection of interests is one who is weak in unifying power; far more intense is the unity manifested in a life which unifies a wider range.

In the life of an ideal human self there would be unified the three activities which together constitute a human person. According to the revelation of Himself which God has given to us men in history there are three elements perfectly unified in the Divine life, and each of these elements is itself a Person. It is the main thesis of these lectures that the act of faith required for acceptance of the doctrine of the Trinity is faith in this unification, faith that the Divine unity is a dynamic unity actively unifying in the one Divine life the lives of the three Divine persons. It is a mystery, but not an irrational mystery. It is a mystery, because on earth we have no experience of any unity which so perfectly unifies so wide and rich a diversity of content: our experience does not go beyond the imperfect unification of activities in single personal selves, and we by no means

[1] On this, see below, Lecture VII, p. 183.

fully understand that. But it is not an irrational mystery. Mysterious as the unity may be, it is the kind of unity postulated by our reason to account for the observed and recorded evidence. The essence of our faith is that there is in the Godhead the perfect instance of the kind of unity of which we have imperfect analogues on earth. When we have learned to measure by a scale of intensity of unifying power we no longer think that because the elements in the Godhead are not sub-personal activities, but complete persons, the degree of unity must be less than in the human self and that consequently the doctrine is tritheistic. Seeing that the degree of unification demanded so far exceeds anything within our experience, how mysterious, tremendous and fascinating, we argue, must be the intensity of that unifying power which constitutes the unity of the Blessed Trinity.

The Christian doctrine of God thus contains an assertion about the nature of unity. It asserts that all the actual unities of our earthly experience, from the unity of the hydrogen atom to the unity of a work of art, of the human self, or of a human society, are imperfect instances of what unity truly is. We may find in them analogies to that true unity, and learn from them something of what perfect unity must be. But perfect unity itself is to be found only in God, and it is through the revelation of God in Christ that we find the unity of God to be of such a kind as to cast light upon all our lesser unities. Thus the Christian revelation brings with it a contribution to human thought on the subject of unity, a contribution which theologians and philosophers have not always rightly appreciated either as a matter of historical fact or as a source of enlightenment.

(iii)

We may now return to the point at which the third lecture ended and consider this contribution as a matter of historical fact, that is to say, as an episode in the history of human thought. I said then that in coming to think of themselves as adopted to share with our Lord the way of life which had been His upon earth the disciples of Christ committed their successors to the task of thinking out the doctrine of God implied by their religious practice, and that this task included the attempt to determine whether the resulting doctrine could be held by any sane man.[1] We are not for the moment concerned with the question whether or no they were successful in this attempt. That would be considering the doctrine as a source of enlightenment, and will be dealt with later. Our immediate interest is to reflect upon the actual historical development of thought in the first four centuries of our era and to try to understand its implications. Here again, as in our study of the New Testament, I am not directly concerned to provide an exegesis of the relevant texts. We are only concerned to know what the Fathers believed in order that we may deduce from their beliefs their implications for our own thought.

I must, however, say this much on the subject of patristic exegesis. It is now a commonplace of biblical study that sound exposition must rest upon sound exegesis, that sound exegesis issues from the attempt to discover what the original author thought and meant, and that this can only be discovered if his words are interpreted as relevant to the circumstances of his day, the questions to which they gave rise in his mind, and the universe of discourse within which moved his own thought and that of his contemporaries. The application of these principles of interpretation to the study of the Fathers is more recent, and some text-books still in current use are content to treat the patristic writings as though they were theses presented for post-graduate degrees in modern universities. I am not now going to expound *seriatim* what the various Fathers thought and said on the subject of the Trinity. I am going to assume that this is known to you, that I may take it as common ground between us as I offer my reflections upon it; and that you will understand me as having tried to base these

[1] Above, p. 84.

reflections on an exegesis of the same type as that which underlay what I have said about the New Testament.

The Divine revelation had been given in the Divine action, in the life, death, resurrection and ascension of Christ, in the coming of the Spirit and the adoption of Christians to share in the sonship of their Lord. What the Church had to do was to grasp the significance of this revelation for the doctrine of God. The revelation demanded not only a revision of the theological idea of God but also a revision of the philosophical idea of unity. The history of Christian thought in the first four centuries of our era is the history of the way in which the empirical facts of the revelation of God in Christ were enforcing this twofold revision upon the minds of men, often against their will and without their realising what was happening.

It was inconceivable that the Christian Church should ever be other than monotheistic in its faith. On the one hand it was so deeply rooted in Judaism that the blasphemy of a departure from monotheism would have been a psychological impossibility. On the other hand, it learned as part of its heritage from Greek philosophy that monotheism is an intellectual necessity. But both in Hebrew religious thought and Greek philosophical thought it was commonly assumed that the only real kind of unity is of what I have called the mathematical type, unity which is free from internal complexity. To this fact are due on the Jewish side the unending equivocations about the status of intermediary beings to which I have already referred.[1] No matter how convinced a devout Jew might have been that Jahweh Himself was active in His angel or His word, he must always draw back before the blasphemy of seeming to impair the simplicity of the Divine unity. On the other side, the religious faith which embodied the logical outcome of Greek philosophical thought untouched by the Christian revelation was neo-Platonism, a faith in which the ultimate object of devotion was adored as undifferentiated unity.

Reverence and reason combined to insist that God

[1] Above, p. 80.

should be thought of and worshipped as One. But the idea of unity was such as to make this impossible if full weight was to be given to the empirical evidence of the Christian revelation. Hence one or the other, the idea of unity or the revelation, had to give way. To see this is the key to understanding the trinitarian controversies of the patristic age. The views which came ultimately to be rejected as heretical were those which surrendered the revelation to the idea of unity. Orthodoxy clung to the revelation even at the cost of apparent self-contradiction which was eased, but never completely resolved, by the adoption of an agreed terminology.

The intellectual difficulties inherent in the Christian faith came to light in the monarchian controversies of the second and third centuries. Both kinds of monarchianism, adoptionist and modalistic, sprang from the same root. They were attempts to account for the historical facts of the Christian revelation with perfect loyalty to the unrevised conception of unity. The adoptionist kept this unity by denying essential godhead to the Son, the modalist by reducing the incarnation to a theophany. The adoptionist tradition persisted in Arius, the modalistic in Sabellius and Marcellus. Meanwhile the orthodox were in a quandary. They realised that in their attempts to explain the Christian revelation both forms of monarchianism explained it away. The Christ of their faith was their Redeemer and the object of their worship; for this He must be essentially God and not the deified man of adoptionism. To follow the modalists, on the other hand, was to deprive of all meaning the Gospel record of communion between the incarnate Son and His Father in Heaven. These were not revised editions of the revelation, they were denials of it. But, without a thorough-going revision of the idea of unity, what could be put in their place?

What they did was to work out a terminology which involved this revision of the idea of unity, though it is doubtful whether they realised that it has this effect. They needed a formula which should preserve the distinctness

of the Persons required by the revelation and yet unite
them in a truly monotheistic unity. The relation of each
Person to the substance of godhead must be different from
that of each man to the substance of manhood; otherwise
the doctrine would be tritheistic. As everyone knows, the
formula finally accepted was τρεῖς ὑποστάσεις ἐν μιᾷ οὐσίᾳ
tres Personae in una Substantia, three Persons in one Substance. Of itself, of course, the formula could not solve
the problem. It could equally well be used of the relation
of men to manhood as of the Divine Persons to Godhead.
The difference lies in the difference between the substances,
between manhood and Godhead, between the unity
characteristic of the one and of the other.

The Fathers realised this truth and strove to express it.
But for the most part, because their unrevised conception
of unity prevented them from doing otherwise, those who
tried to give an intelligible account of the divine unity
never shook themselves free from subordinationism.

Subordinationism, as I have indicated earlier, attempts
to preserve the unity by making one Person ultimately the
real God and the others divine because of their relation to
Him. Hippolytus of Rome was notorious for the subordinationism into which he was driven in his efforts to refute
Sabellius. Although in this connection Origen is chiefly
memorable for the doctrine of eternal generation by which
he freed trinitarian theology from one element in subordinationism, i.e. temporal secondariness, yet other elements
remained, and the neo-platonic affinities of the doctrine
of eternal generation show how Origen's mind was still
governed by the idea of untidifferenated unity.[1] The

---

[1] Cp. the following extract from the description of Plotinus' cosmology
in T. Whittaker, The Neo-Platonists (Cambridge, 1918), p. 54: "The accepted
term 'emanation' is derived from one of the metaphors by which Plotinus
illustrates the production of each order of being from the next above. He
compares the cause of all to an overflowing spring which by its excess gives
rise to that which comes after it. This similarly produces the next, and so
forth, till at length in matter pure indetermination is reached. The metaphorical character of this representation, however, is carefully insisted on.
There is no diremption of the higher principle. God and mind do not dis-

misunderstandings between the Dionysii and the per-
plexities of the Cappadocians sprang from the same source,
the impossibility of giving an intelligible account of the
Christian revelation without substituting a trinitarian for
a unitarian conception of unity. For a long time the necessity
for this revision had been concealed by the equivocal status
in theology of the Second Person of the Trinity; the use
of the Logos doctrine hindered as well as helped the recognition in theology of the status which had been His from the
beginning in Christian faith and worship. But in the Arian
controversy that issue had to be faced, and the ratification
of the Nicene decisions by the Council of Constantinople
in 381 showed that the period of equivocation had come to
an end and that in its doctrine of God the Church must
reckon with the full and complete godhead of the Son.
Meanwhile, between the two councils, the Macedonian
controversy had asserted the equal godhead of the Spirit.
What was needed was that into the place hitherto held in
men's thought by the one God of their faith and worship
there should be put *the Trinity as a whole*.

This, whether they knew it or not, was what Dionysius
of Alexandria and the Cappadocians had been trying to
say. This too is what the finally accepted formula, three
Persons in one Substance, implies. But the combined
influence of the fear of tritheism and the mathematical
conception of unity has long prevented this implication

---

perse themselves in individual souls and in natural things, though these
are nowhere cut off from their causes. There is a continual process from
first to last of which the law is the same throughout. Each producing cause
remains wholly in its proper seat, while that which is produced takes an
inferior station. The one produces universal Mind, or Intellect, that is one
with the Intelligible. Intellect produces the Soul of the Whole. This produces
all other existences, but without itself lapsing. Nothing within the series
of the three intelligible principles can be said to lapse in production; the
term being applicable only to the descent of the individual soul. The order
throughout, both for the intelligible causes and for the producing causes
and their effects in every grade always existed and always will exist." Origen
and Plotinus were fellow pupils of Ammonius Saccas; apparently they both
learned to think of multiplicity as derivable non-temporally from unity
without otherwise revising the notion of unity itself.

from being fully grasped and accepted. The notion that in the Trinity one Person may be the fount or source of being or godhead for another lingered on to be a cause of friction and controversy between the East and the West,[1] and still persists into much Christian theology of to-day. The main thesis of these lectures, I have said, is that the act of faith required for acceptance of the doctrine of the Trinity is faith that the Divine unity is a dynamic unity actively unifying in the one Divine life the lives of the three Divine persons. I now wish to add that in this unity there is no room for any trace of subordinationism, and that the thought of the Father as the Source or Fount of Godhead is a relic of pre-Christian theology which has not fully assimilated the Christian revelation.

Of the ancient creeds of Christendom the so-called Athanasian Creed, the *Quicunque Vult*, is the only one which explicitly and unequivocally states the full Christian doctrine of God. In the Nicene Creed the consubstantiality of the Son with the Father, and the association of the Spirit with them in worship and glory, do not necessarily eliminate every trace of subordinationism. When the Son is spoken of as "God of God, Light of Light, very God of very God" and the Spirit is said to "proceed" from the Father (or from the Father and the Son), these phrases might be taken to assert that the Son and the Spirit only share in the Divine substance by derivation from the Father. But the *Quicunque Vult* leaves no room for such misunderstanding. "In this Trinity none is afore, or after other: none is greater, or less than another; but the whole three Persons are co-eternal together; and co-equal." The express rejection in these verses of all subordinationism is good reason for the retention of this document among the official standards of the Church's faith. We may question its suitability for recitation in public worship, but there can be no doubt of its value as controlling the interpretation of the otherwise ambiguous Creed of Nicæa and Constantinople.

The *Quicunque Vult*, moreover, is the standing refutation

[1] *I.e.* on the question of the single or double procession of the Spirit.

of the theory that the doctrine of the Trinity represents the perversion of a simple primitive Christian faith by the intrusion of Greek metaphysics. It shows the truth to be precisely the opposite. The logical outcome of Greek metaphysics, as I have said, was the neo-Platonic worship of undifferentiated unity. The doctrine of the Trinity represents the intrusion into Greek metaphysics of a religious faith based on empirical evidence of Divine revelation which the metaphysics of the time could not assimilate. Philosophy had reached one of those points where its categories were inadequate to include new evidence of the actual world of man's experience. All that the Church could do was to embody the certainties of its experience in what, from the point of view of the philosophy of the time, were a series of contradictions, and insist that their acceptance was necessary to salvation

(iv)

Christianity began as a trinitarian religion with a unitarian theology. The question at issue in the age of the Fathers was whether the religion should transform the theology or the theology stifle the religion. The history of Christian thought in those four centuries is thus one instance of a process often repeated in the history of human discoveries. Whenever empirical evidence conflicts with our presuppositions there has to be a period of suspended judgment before it becomes clear whether the presuppositions must be revised or the evidence discredited. The alleged discovery of black swans in the seventeenth century and of white Indians in the twentieth provoked similar questions: either the notions of swans and Indians must be expanded to include the new instances, or the birds were not really swans or the men really white or really Indian. Such cases, provided that facilities can be provided for further observation of the alleged evidence, are fairly simple. Notions which are themselves generalisations of empirical evidence are easily revised when fresh evidence makes this necessary; in the natural sciences such revision is the normal method of advancing human knowledge. But when the empirical evidence appears to be in conflict with a notion which is accepted as an *a priori* rational concept, there is more difficulty, and the revision of the idea of unity required by the Christian revelation of God was of this kind.

Consider a recent discussion which has points of similarity. It has been urged in some quarters, in connection with the researches of Albert Einstein and the doctrine of relativity, that "space is curved," that therefore we must revise our notion that the shortest distance between two points is the straight line joining them, and even that we must revise our idea of straightness. To this it is replied, to my mind rightly, that the idea of straightness invoked in that axiom is not a generalisation from empirical evidence, it is an *a priori* standard without which we should not know what we mean by curved or by degrees of curvature: that the axiom does not concern the shortest route by which it is possible to travel. What the new empirical evidence proves is that it is impossible as a matter of fact to travel by what would be the shortest route. The evidence does not necessitate a revision of the idea of straightness. It is, indeed, inconceivable that any evidence should do so, for the two things, the idea of straightness and measurements of physical space, are not *in pari materia*. The view that the evidence requires the revision springs from a failure to grasp this fact, from an over-hasty assumption that the idea of straightness is itself a generalisation from empirical evidence and subject to revision in the light of further observations in that field.

Why should not this argument be equally destructive of the position which I have been maintaining in this lecture? Why should the idea of unity be subject to revision in the light of the empirical evidence of the Christian revelation and not be as irreformable by such means as the idea of straightness by the discovery of the curvature of space?

The difference between the two cases is this. I have not

been maintaining that the mathematical idea of unity, *as
a mathematical idea*, either can be or should be revised.
As a mathematical idea it is still as necessary as ever in
theology and in all our thinking. When we say that God
is one, the first thing we mean is that there is none other;
we exclude multiplicity in the mathematical sense. The
revision that was required by the revelation was a realisation
that the internal unity of the Godhead need not be, and
indeed is not, definable by absence of multiplicity in the
same way as the unity whereby He is said to be the one
and only God asserts the absence of any other Gods.

To put the same thing in another way: if the discovery
of the curvature of space has done anything, it has shown
that no actually existent lines in this space-time universe
conform to the mathematical idea of straightness. What
the researches of physicists into the nature of hydrogen
atoms, and of philosophers such as Professor Laird into the
human self, have done is to show that no actually existent
unities conform to the mathematical idea of unity. What
the revelation of God in Christ has done is to show that
neither does the internal unity of the Godhead conform
to that mathematical idea. To the internal unity of God
the unities of the self and the atom are more truly analogous
than that of mathematics. But does this mean that they are
imperfectly one in the same sense that the curved line which
is most nearly straight is still not really straight?

Harnack's treatment of the patristic controversies assumed
this to be so. Of Athanasius and the Council of Nicaea he
wrote:

"Now the question was which of the two was to be adopted, the
Logos κτίσμα or the Logos ὁμοούσιος formula. The former freed
from the latter was indeed deprived of all soteriological content,
but was capable of intelligent and philosophical treatment, namely
rational-logical treatment; the latter, taken exclusively, even supposing that the distinction between the Son and the Father and the
superiority of the Father were maintained in connection with it,
simply led to an absurdity. Athanasius put up with this absurdity:
without knowing it he made a still greater sacrifice to his faith, the

historical Christ. It was at such a price that he saved the religious conviction that Christianity is the religion of perfect fellowship with God from being displaced by a doctrine which possessed many lofty qualities, but which had no inner understanding of the inner essence of religion, which sought in religion nothing but instruction, and finally found satisfaction in an empty dialectic."[1]

In the opinion of Harnack this "absurdity" was sanctioned at Nicaea, with the result that dogmatics were separated from clear thinking, and the anti-rational came to be accepted as characteristic of the sacred. Of the position from A.D. 362 onwards he wrote:

"If up till now orthodox faith had meant the recognition of a mysterious plurality in the substantial unity of the Godhead, it was now made permissible to turn the unity into the mystery, *i.e.* to reduce it to equality, and to make the threefoldness the starting-point; but this simply means that Homoiousianism was recognised which resolved to accept the word ὁμοούσιος. And to this theology, which changed the substantial *unity* of substance expressed in the ὁμοούσιος into a mere *likeness* or *equality* of substance, so that it was no longer a threefold unity, but a trinity, the future belonged, in the East though not to the same extent in the West."[2]

Bethune-Baker has shown convincingly that if Harnack meant that this substitution of substantial likeness or equality for substantial unity was consciously intended or accepted by the Fathers, his exegesis was at fault.[3] But did they, then, without realising it, profess an absurdity? What we have to ask is whether the Church has been mistaken in thinking that it could maintain the "soteriological content" of its faith and its "religion of perfect fellowship with God" without committing itself either to a denial of the true unity of God or to the identification of its dogma with anti-rational absurdity.

Harnack apparently thought that there was no way in which the Church could evade this dilemma. Nor would

[1] A. Harnack, *History of Dogma*, vol. iv. (E.Tr., London, 1898), p. 49.
[2] *Op cit.*, p. 84.
[3] J. F. Bethune-Baker: *The Meaning of Homoousios in the 'Constantino-politan' Creed* (Texts and Studies, vol. vii. No. 1, Cambridge, 1901).

here be if the conception of a unity actively unifying three
Persons in one life is an absurdity. But why should we
dismiss it as an absurdity? There is at least this difference
between the idea of straightness and the idea of unity. The
idea of straightness is only applicable to a spatially extended
universe; although it may be used metaphorically of such
things as thought or conduct, its only literal sense is the
geometrical, and in this sense it cannot be predicated even
analogically of God. But the idea of unity does not necessarily imply either space or time, and it can be used in two
senses neither of which is metaphorical. It can be used
both in the mathematical sense where the criterion is simple
absence of multiplicity, and in the internally constitutive
sense, where the degree of unity is to be measured by
intensity of unifying power. I have argued that it can be
predicated of God in both senses, and that when we pass
from contrasting monotheism with polytheism to speaking
of the internally constitutive unity of God, we pass from
using it in the one sense to using it in the other. The
opinion that the Fathers committed the Church to an
absurdity springs from a confusion of thought whereby
the criterion of the one is applied to the other, where it
is out of place.

Is the idea of internally constitutive unity, then, to be
classed among those which are generalisations of empirical
evidence and not (like that of mathematical unity) among
those which are *a priori* rational concepts? The question
implies that the two are mutually exclusive, whereas the
truth surely is that all generalisations of empirical evidence
are made by ordering the evidence in accordance with
a priori rational concepts of which the idea of internally
constitutive unity is one frequently employed. We could
not raise the questions about black swans or white Indians
were we not concerned with determining what content can
be included in the internally constitutive unity of swanhood
or Indianity. The difference between the two ideas of unity
is this. The mathematical is so simple that one instance is
enough to establish the fact that it cannot exist in mutually

differing varieties of itself, as triangularity can exist in three and only three. In contrast with both these mathematical ideas, the idea of internally constitutive unity is so complex that we have to be continually revising our opinion of what content it will admit of in different instances of itself. Only by studying the empirical evidence in various instances can we determine the possible range of contents of an atom, a crystal, an animal, a man, a nation or a work of art.

At an earlier stage of my argument the idea of organic unity was a useful introduction to our thought about the unity of the Godhead; but it is itself but one instance of the class of internally constitutive unities, and from now onwards it will be best to use the wider term. When we do this we remember that here in this world of space and time we only know the ultimate unities of this type in particular instances of them. We recognise that good men and good deeds have that in common which makes each and all good, but the unifying goodness which constitutes their unity remains in many ways mysterious. So too with the unifying beauty of all beautiful objects and the unifying truth of all true thoughts and words. This world is the world wherein the ultimate unities of reality are made known to us not in their unity but in their multiplicity. Why, then, should we be surprised that in His revelation of Himself to man on earth God makes Himself known in His multiplicity, that He should be revealed to us as Father, as Son, and as Spirit, but that clear understanding of His unity should be beyond our ken? If the neo-platonists had grasped the significance of the earlier parts of their master's *Republic*, if Harnack had reflected upon the nature of human experience in general, they might have seen that "to make the threefoldness the starting-point" and "to turn the unity into the mystery" was neither to reduce unity to likeness nor to embrace an absurdity, but to acknowledge that God's activity in His special revelation of Himself in Christ was of a kind with His activity in that general revelation whereby in every department of human inquiry He enlightens the minds of men.

(v)

In my first lecture I referred to the view of St. Thomas Aquinas that the doctrine of the Trinity expresses a truth known to us only by Divine revelation. I said then that I agreed with St. Thomas on that point, but disagreed with his view of the mode whereby the Divine revelation was communicated to man, and I proceeded to develop an alternative idea of revelation. I have now, I hope, made clear the sense in which I believe that the doctrine is to be accepted as belonging to the special self-revelation of God. To repeat what I then said, "it could not have been discovered by reason apart from that revelation. This is because it could not have been discovered without the occurrence of those events which drove human reason to see that they required a trinitarian God for their cause."[1]

This is, perhaps, the only answer which it is possible to give to those who are dissatisfied with such an exposition of the doctrine as I have tried to present. It is admittedly unsatisfactory, if what is required is such an understanding of the unity as will remove all mystery. Christianity is distinguished by the historical and empirical character of its revelation from all religions which claim to provide such an understanding. It does not profess to proclaim standing truths about God derived either from the *a priori* deliverances of human reason, or from revelation received in the form of ready-made propositions. What it has to proclaim is the gospel, the good news of what God has done and is doing in the history of this world, and its theology, its exposition of standing truths about God, is derived from reflection upon those Divine acts. But this reflection is an activity of the reason, and whilst the first duty in accurate thinking is to accept the given material without denying it, distorting it, or explaining it away, and whilst it may be necessary to acknowledge an element of mystery beyond our understanding, the mystery must not be one which is essentially irrational. What I have been trying

----

[1] Above, p. 25.

to do in these last three lectures is to show that the Divin
self-revelation in action requires the acknowledgemen
of a unity which is mysterious indeed, but not irrationa
Further discussion of its philosophical implications mus
be left for the next lecture, but there are two points whic
I may mention before bringing this one to a close.

It is sometimes asked why the number of Persons i
the Christian doctrine of the Trinity should be neithe
less nor more than three, and some theologians have trie
to find arguments which will demonstrate that this numbe
is a necessity either of thought or of being. Many of thes
arguments seem to me to aim at proving too much, or t
be drawn on wrong lines. Those which argue from analogie
such as the constituent elements in the human self or th
human family assume an unprovable correspondence be
tween things earthly and Divine; those which claim to b
deductions from logical necessities of thought ignore the em
pirical character of God's self-revelation to man. Of cours
if the doctrine of the Trinity does express the final trut
about God, then the triunity of God is a necessity of th
Divine being and so ultimately a necessity for true though
But our belief in it is not due to any power of our own t
decide what is and what is not such a necessity; it is du
to the fact that God has revealed Himself in the way i
which He has revealed Himself in the events of Christia
history as recorded in the Bible and the life of the Church
If we believe that the revelation is complete, and that ther
are no further Persons in the Godhead to be made know
to us, this is because we believe that in Jesus Christ Go
has given us the full and complete revelation of Himself.

The other point to be mentioned here concerns th
personality of the Holy Spirit. It is no use denying tha
this element in the doctrine provides great difficulty fo
our thought. A well known formulation of the doctrin
proceeds on sound lines in so far as it projects into eternit
the life of personal communion between the Father an
the Son which is revealed to us in the Gospels. It the
thinks of the Spirit as the Love which is the *vinculum*

binding Father and Son together in the unity of the Godhead. For this too there is evidence in the Gospels. As we
have seen, it was through the Spirit that the incarnate Son
thought of Himself as guided and empowered on earth
to find and do the Father's will. But in the Gospels the
Spirit is a third He, a Person who can be the object of
blasphemy, the Paraclete who can come to the disciples
as the *alter ego* of the Son. If in thinking of the Spirit as
the principle of unity in the Godhead one is unable to
think of a dynamic unity unifying Persons without being
itself an additional entity, the result is to deprive Him of
this "he-ness." [1] For a long time I was content to accept
this formulation, to argue that the Greek word ὑπόστασις
did not involve the "heness" implied by our modern use
of the word Person,[2] to suppose that the ascription of
"he-ness" to the Spirit was due to a modern misunderstanding of the orthodox patristic formula which did not
require it.[3] But I now see that to do this ascribes too high
a degree of authority to orthodox patristic formulæ as a
source of doctrine. The source must be the revelation of
God as recorded in the Bible, and the formulæ are only
orthodox and authoritative in so far as they truly represent
that revelation. If the "heness" is found in that revelation,
it cannot be dismissed as a modern misinterpretation
of a formula which the language of the time compelled
to represent it ambiguously. It would seem that this formula,
which is too often mistakenly regarded as expressing St.
Augustine's trinitarian theology, was one more attempt
to rationalise the doctrine without the thoroughgoing
revision of the idea of unity which was required. It was
not subordinationist, but it made use of another expedient

---

[1] The impossibility of retaining the "he-ness" of the Spirit in this formulation is well brought out by the Bishop of Oxford (Dr. Kirk) on pp. 224–6
of Rawlinson : *Essays on the Trinity and the Incarnation* (London, 1928).

[2] On this, see the quotation from T. A. Lacey on p. 392 of the same
volume.

[3] This suggestion seems to be implied in Dr. C. C. J. Webb's treatment
of the subject in *Problems in the Relation of God and Man* (London, 1911),
pp. 235, 236.

which was like subordinationism in that it obscured an element in the biblical revelation. However difficult it may be to accept the full personality of the Spirit as in every way equal to that of the Father and the Son, to refuse to do so is to evade the issues presented by God's revelation in history of the mystery of His unity. It does, I think, ease the difficulty somewhat when we remember that the task for our thought is not to start from a patristic formula and ask how we can think of a relation as being a person,[1] but to start from the records of the earthly life of our Lord, or from our experience of possession,[2] and to ask whether we can think of the Mediator of the Father's mind and will as being, in the full sense of the word, a Person.

[1] As was done, for example, by Dr. J. R. Illingworth in *Personality Human and Divine* (The Bampton Lectures for 1894), Lecture III.

[2] As was done by Dr. Kirk, *op. cit.*, pp. 228–237. And see above, Lecture II, pp. 38 ff.

LECTURE V

THE DOCTRINE AND PHILOSOPHY

(i)

TO some of my audience it may seem a strange thing that I should have come so far in these lectures on the Trinity with only one passing reference to the Logos doctrine.[1] Both in the patristic age and in the modern world the Logos doctrine and the doctrine of the Trinity have been so closely associated in human thought that they may well appear to be inseparable. But the association, though useful in its time, has now, I believe, outlived its usefulness, and some discussion of this point will be a fitting introduction to the present lecture which is to deal with the place of the doctrine of the Trinity in the world of philosophical thought. The Logos doctrine arose in the world of philosophical thought, and to that world it belongs. The doctrine of the Trinity, on the other hand, arose in the world of religious devotion; it did not express an *a priori* deliverance of the reason but formulated the results of empirical observation of divine activity in history. Is the philosophical importance of this observation to be found in the fact that it confirmed the understanding of the universe which speculative thought had formulated in the shape of the Logos doctrine?

For this inquiry the first thing to consider is the meaning of the Logos doctrine in itself. We need not concern ourselves for the moment with the disputes about the history of the doctrine and the Greek or Hebrew affiliation of this or that element in it.[2] All we need to notice is that

[1] Above, Lecture IV, p. 101.
[2] See Appendix V, p. 217.

H

whatever its precise origin and history, its philosophical importance is that it has to do with the problem of creation.[1]

The problem of creation, as a philosophical problem, arises in this way. Philosophy, as we saw in the first lecture, begins as an attempt to understand the actual facts of our experience. Its immediate subject matter is provided by the events in this space-time universe, events which we observe by means of our senses, the actual nature of which we seek to determine more precisely by scientific and historical study. These events, as given to us, occur in a process, and the fundamental question of philosophy is whether this process has any intelligible meaning or whether we men and women are just the casual offshoots of a blindly surging stream of mindless energy. If this process be the whole of reality, then it is impossible to find any meaning in it. Without some unchanging point of reference, some standard of perfection, we cannot say whether this event is better than that; we have a series of events which we can only distinguish as relatively earlier or later, not as better or worse. But human thinkers have been unable to rest content with the conclusion that our æsthetic and moral judgments can never express anything more than our fortuitous individual tastes, that the possibility of objective knowledge must be limited to questions of empirical fact. Indeed, they have seen that to do so undermines the validity of those empirical judgments themselves. This has led them to postulate the existence of an eternally perfect reality, by reference to which we can discover some meaning in the space-time process and judge the relative values of different events within it. But the question then arises, what is the point of this space-time process? Can it contribute anything to the perfection of the eternal reality? If it can, then that reality is not eternally perfect; it is no more intelligible than the space-time process; it

[1] The next few paragraphs summarise what I have said more fully in *The Grace of God in Faith and Philosophy* (London, 1936), pp. 48 ff., 105 ff., 154 ff., 161 ff.

cannot fulfil the function for which it is postulated. If it cannot, then why should it exist at all?

Whether we assert the existence of an eternally perfect reality, or whether we deny it, we are alike in being still faced by our original question, how can we find any meaning in the universe and justify our confidence in the objective validity of our judgments?

It is clear that our attempts to answer this question will move along different lines in accordance with these different standpoints. If, discouraged by the apparently negative result of postulating the eternal reality, we reconcile ourselves to having to make do with the space-time process, we shall also seek to reconcile ourselves to contentment with an insuperable relativity in all possible judgments. Such "existential" utterances of subjective impressions, we shall have to hold, are "all we know on earth, and all we need to know." Hence come pluralism, pragmatism, instrumentalism and other kindred philosophies of our day. Of these we shall have to think later. Our present concern is with the other type of thought, for it was as a consequence of belief in the eternal reality that the Logos doctrine arose.

For thought of this kind an ultimate dualism or pluralism is impossible. In the eternally perfect reality must be found not only the criterion of the value of the events of time and space, but also the source and ground of their existence. In what way are we to think of this space-time process as being related to the eternal reality? We are in search of a relation which shall (i) maintain the perfection of the eternal, (ii) account for the events of our space-time universe being what we actually experience them to be, and (iii) allow us to believe that there is some point in its having come into existence and being what it is.

Various metaphors and analogies have been used in attempts to think about this relation. The idea of emanation, which in the patristic age became characteristic of neo-Platonism,[1] is taken from the relation of a stream or a ray

___

[1] See above, p. 100, footnote (IV.).

of light to their respective sources. In certain forms of modern idealism the relation of appearance to reality has been used for the same purpose. These and all similar expedients are alike in that they try to relate the temporal and the eternal in a metaphysical unity, that is to say, a unity in which each is related to the other by the necessity of its being. The eternal is such that it could not be what it is did it not overflow into the temporal, or appear as the universe of our experience.

The idea of creation is different from all these theories, and in radical contrast to them. The analogy is that of the relation between a conscious, intelligent, purposive being and the product of his conscious, intelligent, purposive activity. This is not a relation in which the existence of each term is necessary to that of the other; maker and made are not related as elements in a systematic whole which necessarily expresses itself in them both. The ground of the product's existence is to be found in the purpose which its creator intended to fulfil in it.

To think after this manner of the relation between the space-time process and the eternal reality involves thinking of the eternal reality as a conscious, intelligent, purposive Being, that is to say, as a spiritual Being who thinks and acts in the way that we commonly describe as personal. This way of thinking removes certain difficulties, but others remain. It removes the difficulties connected with the existence of contingency and freedom in the world of our experience. So long as we think of the time-space universe as one mode of the self-expression of the eternal reality, we cannot avoid explaining these away; but when we think of this universe as having that reality which its Creator gives it in order to fulfil some purpose of His own, it is conceivable that this purpose may involve the creation of a world in which there can and shall be genuine contingency and freedom.[1] But the problem of evil becomes,

---

[1] For a fuller discussion of this subject I must refer to my earlier books: *Essays in Christian Philosophy*, *The Grace of God in Faith and Philosophy*, *Towards a Christian Philosophy* and *The Christian Idea of Liberty*.

if anything, more acute. It is conceivable that what appear to us to be good and evil might turn out, *sub specie aeternitatis*, to be different modes of the self-expression of a single impersonal reality. It is more difficult to believe in the goodness, and thus in the intelligibility[1] of a conscious, intelligent purposive God who wills into existence a world containing cancer, the white slave traffic, anti-semitism and the horrors of war.

There are two ways in which in our thought we can try to maintain the goodness of God in spite of the evil in the world of His creation. The one attempts, so to speak, to disconnect God from responsibility for the existence of the evil at the outset. The other boldly asserts that God accepts responsibility for its existence and has Himself provided such a remedy for it that in the end it shall be found that its existence in the time-process has contributed to the fulfilment of the purpose for which that process was created. One may doubt whether man would ever have dared to suggest this latter view, even as a hypothesis, if it had not been proclaimed as divine revelation in the Christian gospel. The Logos doctrine was one variant of the former view, and moreover, was the offspring of an illicit union between the idea of personal creation and impersonal world-production. It came into being as a premature attempt to wed Greek with Hebrew theology, premature because this union needed for its basis the revelation of God in Jesus Christ.

The God of Hebrew theology was always personal in the sense of being a conscious intelligent God who directly controlled the events of this world in which He was working out His purposes. In so far as the self-contemplation which occupied His life was a consciously intelligent, and thus personal, activity, the God of Greek philosophical theology was also personal. But He was not personally in touch with the events of time and space. The unchanging perfection of His eternal being would be destroyed by any

[1] See *The Grace of God, etc.*, pp. 48–51 = *Towards a Christian Philosophy*, pp. 38–40.

concern with this world of change and decay. Yet this world owed its existence to God. However much the evil in it might be due to its being formed out of pre-existent matter for whose being God was not responsible, it only had any genuine reality in so far as it was moved by desire for the divine eternal perfection and successful in imitating it.

We may ignore for our present purpose the dualism involved in the notion of pre-existent matter. The difficulty of relating the Greek God to the world is the same whether we are thinking of its origination or of its control. In either case the difficulty is that any concern with the changing events of time would disturb the unruffled changelessness of His eternal perfection. There is, however, in the world an element which is akin to the divine Being. Man's rational spirit persists and endures through changing circumstances; it can grasp eternal realities and order the chaotic things of earth in accordance with them. By his capacity for rational thought (λογιστικόν) each man can lay hold on the universal reasonableness (Λόγος), which is an "emanation" of the divine in creation. It is but a short step to the thought that each man's λογιστικόν is a personification in him of the universal Λόγος.

We do not know when first this Logos itself was thought of as personal, or as an actively reasoning principle. The point is that, whether personal or not, it was an "emanation" of the divine, informing this world and providing it with whatever it had of genuine reality. As an "emanation" from God it could be thought of as a kind of "overflow" of the divine being, whose emission did not disturb its perfect calm.[1] But in the Alexandrian Logos doctrine, of which Philo is the best known exponent, the personification is clear, and the Logos is identified with the "Word of God" of the Jewish tradition.

We have already had occasion to note that in Hebrew and Jewish thought God was always an active Being, consciously and intelligently purposive, and in that sense

---

[1] See again the quotation from T. Whittaker on p. 100 above.

personal.[1] In this tradition the demand for beings intermediary between God and the world did not come from
philosophical considerations, from any difficulty concerned
with the relation of temporal events to the unruffled unity
of eternal changelessness. Hebrew thought moved in the
language of dramatic, personal relations. I have often
wondered whether the *political* experience of the Jews in
exile did not influence their theological development more
than is commonly recognised. They were living as subjects
of a great empire, where the great King himself was seldom
if ever seen, where he lived in inaccessible splendour and
majesty, where the duty of good citizens was to keep his
law, where from time to time they might catch glimpses
of his representatives as they visited different parts of his
domains, representatives who sometimes bore such official
titles as "the King's Eye."[2] The parallel between this idea
of the earthly monarch and the idea of Jehovah in later
Jewish theology is remarkably close, but I am not sufficiently at home in the history of that thought to be able to
do more than make the suggestion that the resemblance
may point to an influencing of theology by political experience. The equivocal status of the intermediary beings in
Jewish theology, which we had occasion to notice in a
previous lecture,[3] might be due to the fact that in the
Jewish mind a reverence for God's majesty led to their
conception while a reverence for His unity forbade their
birth.

However that may be, the point is that the Jewish ideas
of intermediary beings arose in a "universe of discourse"
which was occupied with the "dramatic" relations of
personal beings, divine, superhuman and human. We must
also remember that both Greek and Hebrew thought were
influenced from other sources; there were Oriental myths
which in their personification were more akin to the Hebrew
than to the Greek mode of thought, in so far as by "Greek"

---

[1] Above, Lecture III, pp. 78.
[2] See *e.g.* Herodotus, I. 114, Aristophanes, *Acharnians*, 92.
[3] Lecture III, p. 80.

we mean "philosophical." In Greek thought, taken as a whole, we have to distinguish between philosophical and other elements, remembering, as Professor Laird has said, that "the distinguishing mark of philosophy and of science is to look for the reasons of things, and to set these down faithfully in order to show their explanatory value."[1] The statement, sometimes made, that the personification of intermediary beings in later Jewish theology is due to the influence of Greek philosophy on Hebrew religious thinking can only proceed from those who have never understood what philosophy is.

In the part of my third lecture to which I have just now referred we distinguished between two senses of the word "personal": (a) consciously and intelligently purposive, and (b) independently hypostatised. Might it not be true to say that in the personification of the Alexandrian Logos the idea of his intelligent and purposive consciousness was drawn from the Jewish tradition, while that of independent hypostatisation, suggested to the Jews by their political experience but inhibited by their monotheism, took heart of grace from association with the Greek philosophical idea of an "emanated," though not necessarily independently conscious, Logos?

The reason why I called the union of the Greek and the Jewish elements in the Logos doctrine "illicit" should now be clear. As a contribution to philosophy its place is in philosophical systems which do not think of God as personal in the sense in which He is personal for Jewish religion and Jewish thought. The reverence which led the Jew to feel that he was unworthy of being directly noticed by the Lord Himself was not due to any idea of God being incapable of doing so without contradicting His own nature. Far from it. God could certainly confront man if He willed to do so. This God has no need of a Logos in order to remain Himself while creating, maintaining, controlling or redeeming His universe. He is Himself the fullness of being, the sole-existent eternal reality, conscious, intelligent

[1] *Theism and Cosmology* (London, 1940), p. 30.

mind, ever active, ever loving. If, for some purpose of His own, He wills to call into existence, "out of nothing" a time-space universe, He can do so. Our task is to study whatever revelation of Himself He has given in this universe, to seek to discover from this His purpose in creation, and to fall in with it. The notion of the Logos as a necessity in order to account for the existence of the world, and for its being what it is, belongs to a system of thought in which the consciously intelligent, active and willing God has to be linked with the time-space universe by some *tertium quid*, something which will account for the world being what it is and yet allow God to remain in that aloofness which is essential to His perfection.

All such systems of thought, as I shall shortly attempt to show, imply an ultimate reality which is impersonal. But let me first finish what I have to say about the part played by the Logos doctrine in the formulation of the doctrine of the Trinity.

We have seen that the doctrine of the Trinity is the projection into eternity of that relationship between Christ and the Father which was revealed in the incarnation, and that this involved the worship as very God of the Lord who had made Himself known in history as Jesus of Nazareth. We have seen how it took time for the implications of this revelation in history to be grasped, and how various expedients, such as modalism and subordinationism, were tried in order to reconcile the worship of Christ with the unity of God. When Christians first began to wrestle with this problem, they did so in a world in which the idea of the Logos was part of the common stock of religio-philosophical speculation and belief. To a Jewish audience, the proclamation that the Messiah had come in the person of Jesus was the obvious way of presenting the Christian message. To the gentile world this would have meant nothing, but to substitute "Logos" for "Messiah" would open their ears. Both in preaching and thinking the identification of the Christ with the Logos was an obvious expedient to be tried.

The use of this expedient by the author of the Fourth Gospel[1] ensured to the term *Logos* and the Latin equivalent *Verbum*, a permanent place in the language of Christian theology. But it no more commits the Church to the philosophy of the Alexandrian Logos doctrine than acceptance of ὁμοούσιος at Nicaea and Constantinople commits the Church to a fourth century metaphysic of substance. Harnack was surely right in holding that the triumph of Athanasius at Nicaea marked the final failure of the attempt to expound the relation of the Second to the First Person in the godhead by means of the idea of the Logos-Creator.[2] The assertion of the full godhead of the Son, "of one substance with the Father," whether or no He might continue to be called Logos or Verbum, meant that He no longer occupied an intermediary position between Creator and created. The Jewish belief in direct creation by the will of a personal God broke free from its uneasy entanglement with an alien and inconsistent metaphysic. Once again the tables were turned, and just as the attempt to interpret the revealed nature of God by the existing idea of unity led to the revision of the idea of unity by the revelation, so the attempt to interpret the function of the Son by the existing idea of the Logos led to the revision of the idea of the Logos by the revelation of the Son in Jesus Christ the Saviour.[3]

(ii)

We have seen that the dilemma presented by the problem of creation forms the great divide between opposing schools of metaphysical philosophy. Many of us here are old enough to have lived through one of those swings of the pendulum from side to side which mark the history of human thought

[1] See my *And Was Made Man* (London, 1928), p. 187.

[2] *History of Dogma* (Eng. trans., London, 1894), vol. iv. pp. 28–29.

[3] For the bearing of this conclusion on Christology, see my contribution to Rawlinson: *Essays on the Trinity and the Incarnation* (London, 1928), pp. 363 ff.

own the ages.[1] In our youth the dominant philosophy was an idealism derived from Kant through Hegel. We have witnessed, and perhaps taken part in, the revolt against that dominance and now live in an age in which the prevailing fashion in philosophy may perhaps best be described as empiricism. I am now going to try to consider the doctrine of the Trinity in relation to these two philosophical outlooks. But first I must be allowed to preface what I have to say with some general remarks about the philosophical world in which both have arisen.

When the Renaissance and the Reformation broke up the unity of mediæval Europe, one result was the emancipation of secular studies from the tutelage of theology. This brought both gain and loss. It brought gain because, as I showed in my first lecture, the existing theology was based on an idea of revelation which was bound to cramp the progress of scientific and philosophical inquiry. It brought loss, because it deprived philosophy of the guidance which God willed it to receive through His revelation of Himself in Christ. A theology resting upon a better understanding of God's way of revealing Himself will some day be able to heal the breach and restore the guidance. But the philosophical world to which belong the present objects of our thought was and is a world in which theological presuppositions had and have no proper part.

That break up of the mediæval unity produced a curious state of affairs, the oddness of which we are only now beginning to appreciate. While philosophers, from Descartes to Hume, were engaged in casting doubts upon the existence of the material world, natural scientists were steadily extending our knowledge of its behaviour and our power of controlling it. So far as I am aware, the scientists were neither grateful to the philosophers who defended the

[1] " Whereas for the people of former generations it was almost self-evident that ultimate reality is eternal and unchanging, for our contemporaries the passing event is alone indubitably real, while the very existence of any eternal object is matter for debate." W. Temple: *Nature, Man and God* (London, 1934), p. 429.

existence of their subject-matter, nor disturbed by those who attacked it. Their own work gave them plenty to do without bothering their heads about epistemology or metaphysics. As for religion, the belief that the world had been created by the God who had revealed His character in Christ their Saviour made no difference to their studies. Whatever might have happened in the past, they were not required to reckon with the occurrence of miracles in the present. So they could continue their worship and their inquiries side by side. The philosophers, likewise, saw no reason to question the accepted faith. There are wide differences between the systems of Descartes, Malebranche, Spinoza. Leibniz, Locke and Berkeley, but all of them take God for granted and present Him in various ways as the ultimate source of all that is. Meanwhile the theologians did little more than to continue to expound the being of God and the scheme of salvation on the old basis of a revelation given in propositions. For a hundred years or more we have the curious spectacle of science, philosophy and theology proceeding independently along separate tracks but all living harmoniously together and unaware that each in its separatedness was steadily undermining the ground of their harmony.

In the eighteenth century the conflict emerged. Scientists began to doubt the need of the hypothesis of God. Deists attempted to secure His existence by removing Him from contact with the world of scientific study. Theologians like Butler and Paley grasped the issue and attempted to grapple with it. But palæontology and Darwinian zoology came to the succour of the secularists, and looking back on the Oxford of 1862 the late Bishop Talbot wrote in 1924 as follows:

"As I came out of my shell in undergraduate days, and got to know more people in and out of college, and to mix at the Union with more of the abler men, I was conscious, of course, that the intellectual 'swim' was against the things which I had been taught to value. . . . This had one definite cause (with others) in the current philosophy of the day. As I knew the intellectual life of Oxford, the

nfluence of John Stuart Mill swept all before it. . . . His influence
vas almost one with that of the science of the day, which was then
haping men's thoughts on almost purely 'naturalist' lines . . . and
vas fighting for its splendid biological and other discoveries uphill
gainst much frightened resistance and some bigotry. . . .

So it was that for a time many of us who felt our religion and
acraments true and holy, could only hold on to what has been called
he 'two pockets' system, keeping our philosophy in one and our
eligion in the other. . . . I speak of what was my experience. I am
ure it was the prevailing one. But of course it was not universal.
dward Caird was coaching in Merton. Gladstone went to him; but,
omehow, nothing got through to me. Mansel, with his cold para-
oxes, counted for little with us. . . . We struggled to get something
orrective of Mill out of Sir William Hamilton's book; but, compared
vith Mill, it taxed us too high. Green was only just showing over
he horizon."[1]

I have quoted this passage because it helps to show why
he absolute idealism which was introduced into these
slands by the Cairds and Green, and was afterwards
leveloped by Bradley, Bosanquet and Pringle-Pattison,
eceived the welcome it did from Christian theologians
nd for half a century dominated British philosophical
heology. There is, I suggest, a parallel between this episode
n the history of British theology, and the Logos-doctrine
period of the patristic age. The early Church, with its
message concerning a Second Person in the Godhead, allied
itself with that strain in secular thought which seemed
to hold a kindred doctrine. The alliance served to bring
the gospel home to the gentile world, and by the time that
the incompatibility of the two doctrines became clear, it
was firmly enough established to be the one to survive.
The Church of the nineteenth century, with its faith in God
as personal, entered into alliance with that philosophy
which gave to mind the supreme directive place in the
universe. In this way it secured the allegiance of thinking
men, and is now in a position to survive the passing of that
philosophy.

[1] Quoted from *The Guardian* of 30th May 1924, p. 505.

It must be remembered that the Church was not ready
with a theology of its own that was adequate to meet the
situation. It was still encumbered with the traditional
theory of revelation as given and received in the form of
propositions. For this to be revised there was needed that
half century or so of intensive devotion to the historical
criticism of the Bible which still lay in the future when
Edward Caird was coaching in Merton and Green was
showing over the horizon. The theologians of to-day, who
criticise the alliance of the Church with Hegelian idealism
on the ground that it ignores the nature of the Christian
faith as revelation, should remember that among their
immediate predecessors they owe to the idealists the fact
that they have the faith at all, and to the historical critics
their ability to hold it as revelation.

The task of philosophy, we saw in my first lecture, is
to seek to understand and make sense of the given material
of our experience. From this point of view the task of
revealed religion is to provide philosophy with material.
Philosophy has then to try to weave into a coherent system
the material which comes from the special revelation with
that which comes from God by other ways. The mediæval
system represented such an interweaving of the material
then available. The period of disunity which has followed
its collapse may be regarded as an age of accumulating
fresh material to be woven into a new and richer unity when
the time is ripe. In this accumulation of material the natural
sciences have made progress more rapidly than theology,
and philosophy has been hampered by the fact that it has
had to try to systematise on the basis of inadequate material.

According to the Christian faith the time-space universe
expresses the will of its consciously intelligent Creator who
gives to it that mode of reality and that degree of independence and freedom which are required by His purpose in
creation. This Creator is the triune God, Father, Son and
Spirit. Whilst the universe and its inhabitants may be
inspired by the Spirit, who thus works "immanently" in
creation, and the Son may enter the history of this world

as God incarnate, in both cases we have activities of God which are, so to speak, not internal to the life of the God-head, but are a going forth of Himself into His creation. This is the truth which has been obscured in the idealistic period of Christian theology, and has revived that misconception of the doctrine of the Trinity which derived from the Logos-theory of the origin of the world.

One may summarise the development of thought as follows. At first, as we have seen, the researches of the scientists involved no breach with the doctrine of creation. But as time went by the orderly functioning of the physical world began to exercise a numinous fascination over the minds of its students, and the discrepancies between their discoveries and what they thought the biblical revelation required them to believe, produced a materialism in which mind was an epiphenomenon, freedom an illusion, immortality a negligible dream, and God an unnecessary hypothesis. The pendulum swung to the side which emphasises the reality of the actual and temporal to the exclusion of the unchanging eternal. The idealistic movement was a reaction to this materialism. It arose at a time when, as a source of philosophic material, the Bible was discredited. It took the universe of the materialist and claimed to show that when subjected to more searching scrutiny it revealed more things in heaven and earth than were dreamed of in that philosophy. Its method was the application of the logical principle of non-contradiction, its conclusion that the space-time universe and finite minds could only be regarded as real if regarded as modes of self-expression of the unchanging Absolute.

The situation was indeed curiously like that in the second and third centuries of our era, the heyday of the Logos-doctrine in Christian theology. There was the same mutual approach to one another of philosophy and theology, each, so to speak, trying to see what use it could make of the other. The earlier period produced various Gnostic systems, the characteristic of which was that current philosophical interpretations of the universe assimilated the Gospel story as a myth expressive of their preconceived metaphysic. Just so did idealist philosophers of our day attempt to find the importance of the doctrines of the incarnation and the atonement in their embodiment of the idea that the Absolute goes forth into the finite and the finite can only establish itself by losing itself in the Absolute.

We are not concerned, however, with the philosophers' use of Christianity. Our subject is the theologians' use of philosophy, and that in connection with the doctrine of the Trinity. I have already mentioned the point that the idealists asserted the directive supremacy of mind in the universe. An added attraction was presented by the researches of these philosophers into the idea of personality. This was forced upon them by the nature of their system of thought. They had to consider the relation of the Absolute mind to finite human minds, whether either or both could be regarded as personal, and if so, in what sense. It was conceived as possible, nay more, as required by the nature of the universe, that personalities should be able to overlap, and that finite personalities might exist in their relative independence while still included in the unifying personality of the Absolute. Moreover, the idea of personality was that of the modern sense of the word, of an intelligent purposive centre of consciousness.

It is true that not all the philosophers would admit this conclusion. McTaggart and H. F. Bradley, for example, concluded to an impersonal Absolute,[1] and in this were followed by Rashdall and others among the theologians. But Lotze, the Cairds, Green, Royce and Bosanquet all argued in favour of the so-called "inclusiveness of personality." Can we wonder that orthodox Christian theologians welcomed their thought as an aid to Christian faith? In the seventeenth, eighteenth and nineteenth centuries the defence of the doctrine of the Trinity had been a long and

---

[1] It is true that Bradley regarded Ultimate Reality as some form of sentient experience, and McTaggart and Rashdall as a Society of Persons. But for reasons given in what follows, and in Lecture VI, p. 164, I do not think that this can properly be regarded as personal.

arduous struggle.[1] Among the opponents of scientific materialism the Unitarians had claimed to take their stand on reason, and had often made the upholders of orthodoxy look and feel like the champions of an obscurantist traditionalism. Now at last they were vindicated. Leading philosophers of the day, men who had started with no theological presuppositions, who had set out to follow whither the argument might lead guided strictly by that most rational of principles, the principle of non-contradiction, these men had decided not only against the materialists, but also against the Unitarians. So far from its being irrational to hold that a single personality may include and unify other personalities, reason now shows that this relationship lies at the heart of all existence!

Here there is an element of permanent gain, for which we too must be grateful to the idealists, which we must be careful not to throw away with the discarding of the idealist metaphysic in general. In their pardonable excitement and enthusiasm the idealist theologians doubtless thought they knew and understood more than they did. They were not sufficiently sensitive to the outstanding difficulties in the conception they so eagerly embraced. What was actually gained may perhaps better be stated negatively than positively. I was arguing in my last lecture that we must be content to find the nature of the divine unity a mystery, but that our experience of the universe is such that to believe in the kind of internally constitutive unity which Christian theology ascribes to God is to accept a rational mystery. The contribution of the idealist philosophers is an assurance that we need not forgo this conclusion on the ground that the constituent elements in the Godhead are each fully personal in the modern sense of being intelligent, purposive centres of consciousness. They have not explained the relationships involved in such a unity in such a way as to deprive it of its mysteriousness, but they have forbidden us to dismiss the belief in its existence as irrational.

[1] See Appendix VI, p. 219.

I

So far, so good. For this the Christian theologian must
be grateful. But he must beware of going further and imagining that the idealist metaphysic is an exposition of the
doctrine of the Trinity itself, that the self-expression of
the Absolute in this world of appearances is a philosophical
statement of the theological doctrine that the Father
expresses Himself through the Son who is the Logos and
principle of creation.

There is a radical divergence between the idealist metaphysic and the metaphysic implied by the Christian revelation. The idealist metaphysic starts from three assumptions:
(i) that reality is a systematic whole which is rational and
intelligible, (ii) that this space-time universe of our experience has its existence within that whole, (iii) that the task
of philosophy is to find the point of view from which it
can be seen how each detail of the universe fits rationally
and intelligibly into that whole. But the metaphysic implied
by the Christian revelation expressly denies that this world
of ours can be made to fit into any rational or intelligible
system of reality by any illumination of our knowledge of
it or any shifting of our point of view. For the world is a
sinful world, and its sinfulness is not a matter of appearance
which can be *thought* away; it is a grim reality which must
be changed in *fact* before the world can become intelligible
for thought. The space-time universe is not the medium
through which God finds expression in order to be Himself.
It is His *creation*, which He has brought into existence
for the fulfilment of a certain purpose, for which purpose
He has given it a relative independence over and against
Himself, and a mode of reality which admits of the existence
of contingency, freedom and sin. This space-time universe
is not internal to the eternal being of God; its relationship
to Him is not the truth unconsciously enshrined in the
Church's doctrine of the Trinity. That doctrine concerns
the eternal being of God as by His Spirit He has opened
our eyes to recognise His activity in ruling this world from
above and in entering into its history in the person of Jesus
Christ in order to reconcile it to Himself.

Among the philosophers this antithesis between the idealist metaphysic and the Christian creed was clearly recognised by the late Professor Pringle-Pattison in his Gifford Lectures for 1913 on "The Idea of God in Recent Philosophy." Among the theologians it was recognised by Mr. F. H. Brabant in his contribution to *Essays on the Trinity and the Incarnation*, published in 1928. "If we are to reach any credible theory of the relations of God and man," wrote Professor Pringle-Pattison, "the traditional idea of God must be profoundly transformed. . . . The accidents of language have combined with the ingrained materialism of our ordinary thinking to make the doctrine of the Trinity a supra-rational mystery concerning the inner constitution of a transcendent Godhead, instead of the profoundest, and therefore the most intelligible, attempt to express the indwelling of God in man."[1]

To this Mr. Brabant replies, "The Father 'eternally begets and loves the Son through the Spirit.' But this activity of God is not the same as the Time process. The eternal begetting of the Son is not the same as the creation of the world. It is here that Professor Pringle-Pattison comes into conflict with Christian tradition. He regards the begetting of the Son as the creation of the world."[2]

In his Gifford Lectures on *Nature, Man and God*[3] the Archbishop of Canterbury has made a gallant and brilliant attempt to reconcile these points of view. He was moved to make the attempt by the consideration that the kind of position which I have been maintaining in these lectures is a "naïve religious view," "rather mythological than philosophic," that it fails to give "a sufficient reason why the Eternal should have launched into being the historical process," and that it "puts together the best points of other views at the cost of compromising all."[4]

This raises the question of the nature and function of philosophy, about which I have tried to say something in my first lecture. I said there that essentially philosophy

---

[1] *Op. cit.*, pp. 407–10.   [2] *Op. cit.*, p. 349.
[3] London, 1934.   [4] Pp. 438–41.

is a quest, the quest for an understanding of the universe as a whole, and that different philosophies arise as different elements in it are taken as the "key-features" for its interpretation. Now it seems to me that in these statements the Archbishop takes as his key-feature those three assumptions of the idealist metaphysic which I have just mentioned. He assumes that any view which does not exhibit the relationship of the space-time universe to God within a rationally intelligible system is naïve and not philosophic.

But why does he call this naïve religious view "mythological rather than philosophic?" Consider again for a moment what the view is. It is based upon the observation that this universe contains many contradictions and irrationalities which cannot be explained away but have to be accepted as realities in the history of this world. It finds a meaning in them through regarding this world as the medium whereby a conscious, intelligent, purposive Creator is bringing into existence a community of free individual finite persons. The ultimate reality is the conscious, intelligent, personal life of God, revealed to us as the life in mutual love of Father, Son and Spirit, and the reason for the creation of this universe is to be found in the counsels and purposes of the Godhead. Our inability to explain these counsels and purposes further is due to the fact that we are men and not God.[1] It does not help to postulate this creative activity as a necessity of the divine nature.

A few minutes ago I was suggesting that we should be grateful to the idealists for having encouraged us to believe in the reasonableness of the idea of a personal life which

---

[1] Cp. the following statement in which Dr. W. R. Inge's Christianity triumphs over his idealism: "We cannot penetrate the mind of the Absolute; and I think we must frankly confess that while the return journey to God, the path of salvation, is known to us, the downward journey, the path of creation, is unknown to us. This has often been made a reproach against the school of philosophy to which I belong. We fail, we are told, to account for the world. Well, the world is a solid fact which we have to accept, not to account for; I see no reason why we should be admitted behind the scenes while our business is on the stage." *Science and Ultimate Truth* (New York, 1926), p. 28.

in its experience unifies the experiences of its internally
constitutive persons. But I pointed out that this conclusion
was not accepted by all the idealists. It seems to me that
those who maintain it do so because they take as their
key-feature the experience of personal life as it is known
to or conceived by us at its highest and fullest and best.
Underestimating the reality of contingency, chance, freedom
and evil, they regard the history of this world as a process
in which there is being actualised a relationship which the
conditions of this world do not allow. What they have
proved is that our experience of life is enough to suggest
to us that such a personal unity of personalities might be
possible if all the persons unified were perfect. Their
opponents remind us that when we are dealing with this
world of ours and with the kind of persons who actually
exist at present in it, the case is different.

It is in the inner being of the Godhead that the Christian
revelation teaches us to find a unity of this kind. The
attempt of so many idealists to extend it to cover the relationship of God to His creation has been, I believe, a failure.
If this be so, then our final judgment on the idealist metaphysic must be the paradox that it is curiously akin to the
materialism against which it revolted. For it implies that
the ultimate reality is not the consciously intelligent Creator
from whose will the space-time universe takes its origin,
but an impersonal necessity expressing itself through the
lives of persons. The use of the words "mythological"
and "naïve" to describe the position which regards the
relationship of personal intercourse as the most real reality
we can conceive, and requires no further explanation of
it in terms of some underlying substratum, betrays the
error common to idealist and materialist alike. This metaphysical subordination of conscious intelligent personal
life must not be allowed to arrogate to itself the exclusive
right to the philosopher's cloak. Nor is it unphilosophical
to admit our ignorance and maintain an attitude of suspended
judgment where the necessary evidence is lacking. The
philosophical conviction that the ultimate reality consists

in personal intercourse is not to be dismissed as mythological, nor is an honest acknowledgment of invincible
ignorance to be put down as naïve.

The Archbishop has been led by these false assumptions
into a brilliant but hopeless attempt to reconcile the irre-
concilable. The result is a formula which barely conceals
its inner contradictions, and surrenders the witness of the
Christian revelation (the key-feature of Christian philosophy)
to the demands of the idealist metaphysic. "In the sense
in which God is necessary to the world," he writes, "the
world simply is not necessary to God. Apart from Him
it has no being; apart from it, He is Himself in plenitude
of being." How is this reconcilable with "Even to the
eternal life of God His created universe is sacramental of
Himself. If He had no creatures to redeem, or if He had
not redeemed them, He would not be what He is?"[1] In the
end the latter of these statements engulfs the former; it is
said that in Christian theology the Hebrew doctrine of
creation by the Living God is incorporated in the doctrine
of the Trinity,[2] and that creation is to God "the means
whereby He is eternally that which eternally He is."[3] There
could be no clearer instance of what Mr. Brabant has called
confusion between the creation of the world and the
begetting of the Son.

(iii)

In the English-speaking world the names of William
James, John Dewey, F. C. S. Schiller and Bertrand Russell
are probably best known as leaders in the revolt against
the idealist metaphysic. But its criticism was not confined
to these popularisers of rival philosophies. At Cambridge
the lectures of Professor G. E. Moore did much to under-
mine its influence and at Oxford my own much revered
teacher, John Cook Wilson, though he described the thought
of Bertrand Russell as "the philosophy of a lunatic asylum,"
was no less critical of the Hegelianism in which he had

[1] Pp. 435 and 494.   [2] P. 489.   [3] P. 495.

been brought up. As I have already said, many of us who are alive to-day have witnessed one of those swings of the pendulum which mark the history of human thought about the problem of creation. We have seen an age which was dominated by its conviction of the reality and importance of the unchanging eternal succeeded by an age in which attention is directed to the changing actualities of space and time. For our seniors the concepts of reason were the most certain of realities, the objects of sense-perception had a very questionable status. For our juniors, verification by the senses is the only guarantee of reality deserving of the name. When we were young, the villain of the piece was David Hume. His greatness was indeed fully recognised; but this meant a recognition that only the most acute and strenuous thought could detect the errors into which he had fallen and counteract the mischief he had wrought. It has been said of the present age in philosophy that one of its outstanding characteristics is the rediscovery of Hume, and of the value of his contribution to thought.

In some quarters this reaction has issued in a complete scepticism with regard to any knowledge of ultimate reality whatsoever. In its extreme form it has produced the logical positivists, with their denial of the possibility of metaphysics, and has led some thinkers to devote the whole of their attention to details of perceptual or linguistic analysis on the ground that any attempt to solve the central mysteries of being would be a vain task, foolishly attempted. This is a kind of philosophical tithing of mint, anise and cummin of which it may be said that it ignores that which ought to be done in its attention to what ought not to be left undone.

Among theologians, the revival of neo-Thomism and neo-Calvinism may or may not reflect a similar scepticism. It does so whenever it despairs of the power of the human mind to distinguish truth from error and falls back on faith in a revelation given in the form of propositions. Of that I have said what I have to say in my first lecture. What I want now to maintain is the value of this anti-

idealist reaction in the attention it calls to the importance
of the empirical and historical. I have said that it is the task
of the human mind to try to order its empirical evidence
in accordance with its *a priori* rational concepts.[1] Where
the empirical evidence refuses so to be ordered, and yet
cannot be denied or shown to be other than it appears,
then the genuinely philosophical thing to do is to accept
the empirical, believe as an act of faith in the ultimate
rational synthesis, suspend judgment as to the method
by which it is attained, and hold provisionally by whatever
theory seems to throw most light upon the problem. The
present *impasse* in both theology and philosophy is due
to the failure of both theologians and philosophers to grasp
the implications of this. Philosophy needs empirical material
on which to exercise its wits. It needs both the material
provided by the universe in general, and the material provided by that divine activity within it which is revelation
proprio dictu. It has been grinding the former by itself in
its mills until it can do so no longer. Without the contribution that only the latter can make its machinery will either
race in idealism, or chop and re-chop the chaff that is all
that remains to it of its given material. What is needed
for the beginning of a new constructive age in both theology
and philosophy is that theology should present God's
revelation in a form in which it invites the attention of
philosophy and that philosophy should develop an interest
in the material thus presented.

It will now be seen how the presentation of the doctrine
of the Trinity which I am attempting to give in these
lectures is meant to appear in the world of philosophy.
It is essentially realist and empiricist, in that it rests on the
view that the task of philosophy, and of philosophical
theology, is to interpret what is given in experience, not
to prescribe what may be given. To quote Mr. D. M.
MacKinnon on the subject of revelation:

"Hume's simple recognition that no individual proposition about
a contingent matter of fact could be established *a priori* holds good

---

[1] Lecture IV, p. 107.

here as elsewhere. It is not for philosophy, whatever philosophy may be, to tell us whether or not God has intervened in the way in which He must have intervened for that intervention to merit the name of revelation. That he has or has not is a matter of fact. We can only look and see. We can only scrutinise evidences; we can only bring ourselves, or allow ourselves to be brought, face to face with Him, to whom both scriptures and prophets testify."[1]

But the empiricism implied in these lectures does not deny the capacity of human reason to distinguish truth from error, or its right to exercise this capacity on whatever is offered to it as revelation. Indeed, it thinks this exercise of it to be not so much a right as a duty. It does not, therefore, demand, after the fashion of some neo-Thomists and neo-Calvinists, that the revelation be given in a form which lifts it above such criticism. "We scrutinise evidences," and if any revelation is to be given which can reach the mind of man, it must be given in such a way as to provide evidences to be scrutinised.

Moreover, it is implied that in this scrutiny the *a priori* canons of logical consistency are valid, and are the instrument with which we have to work. The idealists are to be honoured for their witness to the truth that these canons reflect the nature of the eternal and ultimate reality, and that our experiences in this world are to be scrutinised in the light of its demands. But they go wrong when they conclude that whatever in our experience will not conform to this demand must therefore be in reality something different from what it appears to be. It is equally reasonable to conclude that the relation between the eternal and the temporal may be such as to allow of a different mode of reality in the latter. The Christian doctrine of creation, which finds the reason for our experiences being what they are in the belief that this universe expresses the creative purpose of a conscious, intelligent, good God, is more reasonable than the idealist metaphysic just because it does not have to explain away the empirical objects which are the primary material for our scrutiny.

[1] *God the Living and the True* (London, 1940), p. 33.

We who philosophise can only do so from our place as creatures within this creation. We share in its failure to conform to the canons of logical consistency. We are not only finite but sinful, and this affects our thinking as well as our acting. Because of our finiteness we can each of us only see along the perspectives that radiate from our own point of view. Because of our sinfulness we cannot always be sure of seeing straight along our own perspectives. If we only suffered from finiteness we might, perhaps, by mutual comparison of our various impressions, be able to correct our deficiencies and reach a common knowledge of the common truth. But the distortion caused by our sinfulness is beyond our cure. It is not through trust in reason that we go wrong, but because through our sinfulness our reason is so imperfectly rational. The remedy is not the substitution of some other mode of acquiring knowledge for rational apprehension; it is the education of our reason to enable it to be its true self. This education may have to be a re-education. It may require that a man both be turned about so as to see along fresh perspectives, and also be broken away from definitely false habits of vision.

The Christian doctrine of redemption implies in the intellectual sphere that God the Creator has been and is active in both these ways, as well as in another not yet mentioned, that is, the provision of fresh material to be scrutinised. As we saw in my first lecture, He provides this material both in the evolution of the physical world and the general course of history and also in His special activity in the redemption of the world through Jesus Christ. What we call "conversion" is a turning round to see along new perspectives; in the language of my first lecture it is to see the universe in the light of the gospel story as its key-feature. And it is the work of the Holy Spirit to enable the converted man, as he looks along his new perspectives, to see straight. We must not forget, however, that the God who makes Himself known to us in our Christian faith is the same God who is at work throughout His universe. So far from leading us to deny the value of non-Christian thought, our faith should enable us to recognise the activity of God in confronting, correcting and straightening the vision of men, even when they themselves are unaware of the source of their enlightenment.

If we are genuine empiricists we shall be chary of basing our thought on *a priori obiter dicta* such as "Like can only be known by like."[1] When we free ourselves from these, we see that the recognition of this divine activity does not require us to infer a metaphysic in which each man has in him by nature, in virtue of his creation, a spark of the divine reason or a share in the universal Logos. We can equally well think of God calling this space-time universe into being, giving it its derived and relative yet real independence, and on this planet developing finite centres of consciousness which share the reality and the independence of the world to which they belong. In all this the whole Trinity, Father, Son and Spirit, is unitedly active as Creator. We can then think of the Spirit going forth to illuminate the minds of men and render them *capaces revelationis*, and of its being the function of the Son to present them with those objects of scrutiny in which the knowledge of God is to be found. I submit that a careful scrutiny of the evidence favours this way of thinking rather than that which makes the life of creatures in any sense internal to the life of God.

For the doctrine of the Trinity the empirical evidence consists of the earthly life of Jesus Christ, and all that has sprung from it in the new life of communion with God into which Christians have been taken. The scrutiny of this evidence requires two lines of inquiry; there must be the historical investigation of the records and the philosophico-theological attempt to grasp what must be the nature of the God who makes Himself known in this way.

---

[1] Knowledge, like unity, is indeed an *a priori* conception. We saw in my last lecture that we cannot deduce from the *a priori* conception of unity the nature of its internal constitution. That has to be learned by observation of what actually happens. So, too, we may know what knowledge is *a priori*. But what is knowable, and how knowledge of it may be achieved, must be learned by experience.

The evidence will obviously look different according as it is viewed from within or without the fellowship of those who have entered upon the new life of divine sonship. We who look out from within believe ourselves to have been given by God a new set of perspectives along which more accurate insight may be gained, and that the members of His Church may look for a special guidance of the Holy Spirit to enable them to see straight along them. But this does not mean that we can safely ignore or despise the testimony of those outside to what they see. In the field of historical investigation much work has to be done to which this particular difference of perspective is irrelevant. And in both fields, as we saw in the first lecture,[1] progress comes through the interplay of thought between those within and those without—an interplay whose not least value to the Christian believer is its perpetual reminder that, whatever one's perspective, scientific, historical and philosophical studies must be carried on strictly in accordance with the appropriate canons in each field.

The doctrine of the Trinity is thus an inference to the nature of God drawn from what we believe to be the empirical evidence given by God in His revelation of Himself in the history of this world. I have argued that this evidence, as viewed from within the fellowship of the Christian Church, requires us to believe in a God whose unity unifies three activities each of which is made known to us as a distinct Person in the full sense of that word. Each is a He, none is an it. Now it is part and parcel of the empiricism that characterises these lectures to insist that where we cannot reconcile the deliverances of empirical evidence with the demands of logical consistency, it is better to maintain an attitude of suspended judgment as to the mode of reconciliation than to distort or explain away the evidence in order to procure an immediate result. I therefore make no apology for the fact that in this would-be philosophical lecture I can say no more about the nature of the divine unity beyond what I have already said. I have attempted

[1] Above, p. 34.

to show that the idea of what I have called an internally constitutive unity is not repugnant to reason; I have called attention to certain idealist arguments which encourage us to believe that in God both the Unity and its Constituents may be personal; and I have pointed out that it is generally characteristic of our earthly experience to know the ultimate unities not in their unity but in their multiplicity. There I must let the matter rest. What I am now concerned to assert is that, in the absence of further evidence which it is unlikely that we shall receive on this side of the grave, it is more philosophical there to let it rest than to theorise on lines which involve the denial of the revelation that we have received.

THREE CLASSICAL EXPOSITIONS: AUGUSTINE, AQUINAS, CALVIN

(i)

WE believe God to be the Trinity because we have been adopted to share in the relation of the Son to the Father in the Spirit. This adoption is ours through our incorporation into the life of the Church, and the Church is the body of Christ because Christ is reproducing in it that way of life which was His on earth. We reflect on the historical records of that way of life, and we arrive at a doctrine of God in which the Son is eternally giving Himself to the Father through the Spirit, and each Person, Father, Son and Spirit, is a He. None is an it. Reason and revelation unite to insist that God is One: revelation insists that His unity must be such as to unify the threefold life revealed in Christ and known to us in our adoption. As creatures of time and space we can only know God through the Persons severally; we cannot know His unity directly. But we can believe in that unity by an act of faith which is thoroughly rational: we can argue that its being the unity of three Persons involves not a lesser but a higher, a more intense, degree of unity than any unity known to us on earth; and we may possibly find encouragement in the arguments of some idealists who claim to have proved that the life in which the lives of persons are unified may itself be personal. We have no evidence on which to say anything further with confidence about the inner life of the eternal Godhead. Devotion may be aided by the work of the imagination, and so long as its products are not inconsistent with the evidence that God has given us, it may do more good than harm. But they must be distinguished from the doctrines of theology proper.

That is a very brief statement of what I have so far been trying to say in these lectures. My purpose to-day is to compare this position at which I have arrived with the teaching of three classical Christian theologians, St. Augustine, St. Thomas Aquinas and John Calvin. From this comparison I shall hope to be able to show that my statement of the doctrine of the Trinity agrees with theirs in bearing witness to the central faith of the Christian Church, and that where we differ the differences can be accounted for in such a way as not to impair the strength of our common testimony.

It would seem at first sight as though there might be wide divergences between their teaching and mine in two directions. First, in their discussions of the filiation of the Son and the procession of the Spirit they include in their doctrinal statements a great deal that I exclude as belonging to the realm of imagination. Secondly, their teaching has been held if not to require at any rate to be consistent with a Trinity in which the several Persons are not thought to be fully personal in the modern sense of the word. This is a common opinion in the case of St. Augustine's doctrine of the Spirit, and the late Dean Rashdall maintained that it was the view of St. Thomas Aquinas in regard to all three Persons. I am now going to maintain that the first of these apparent divergences arises from our different ways of using the Bible as the medium of divine revelation, and that the second is due to a misunderstanding of what those classical theologians were intending to teach.

My first lecture will have made clear the difference in our ways of using the Bible. In recalling that to your minds, however, I must point out that underlying this difference here is an essential similarity of great importance. For all of us the Bible provides what I have called the empirical element in our thought. It provides the given material which it is the task of our theology and philosophy to explore and interpret. We are all of us in the opposite camp to those who would use the Scriptures as illustrations of pre-supposed philosophical systems. But St. Augustine was followed by St. Thomas and Calvin in taking over from the Greek tradition that idea of revelation which regarded it as providing statements about things divine ready made in the form of propositions. While we agree in holding that a thinker's first duty lies in fidelity to the empirical evidence, they think that the evidence available gives information of a kind which I cannot accept as being what they think it. Hence the omission from these lectures of much that has occupied a large space in classical discussions of the doctrine of the Trinity must not be regarded as a denial either of the truth of what is there taught or of its value as an aid to Christian devotion. For all I know, it is as likely to be true as not. But as I have not the least idea of what is meant by either filiation or procession in respect of the divine Being, I have not thought it profitable to spend time in discussing the distinction between them in these lectures.

This first divergence, then, is not a serious matter. But the question of the personality of the divine Persons is of cardinal importance, and to deal with it I must attend in some detail to the teaching of the three theologians. I now propose, therefore, to consider in order the treatise *De Trinitate* of St. Augustine, the *Tractatus de Trinitate* in Questions 27-43 of Part I of the *Summa Theologica*, and Chapter xiii of Book I of Calvin's *Institutes*.

(ii)

It is a common impression that by analysing the belief that God is Love St. Augustine arrived at the conclusion that the Holy Spirit is the Love which unites the Father and the Son, and that this is his doctrine of the Trinity. Whilst the Father and the Son may thus be thought of as Persons in the modern sense of the word, the Spirit is the relation between the other two. This impression has caused

great difficulty to those who wish to agree with St. Augustine
and also to think of the Spirit as a He and not an it.
Dr. Illingworth, for example, in his Bampton Lectures on
Personality, Human and Divine,[1] put the case mildly when
he wrote, "the conception of the Word is completed sooner
than that of the Spirit, since a personal object is easier to
imagine than a personal relation." It is not surprising that
other theologians should cut the knot by denying that for
the Fathers in general and for St. Augustine in particular
the word "Person," as used of the Spirit, implied personality
in the modern sense of the word, what I have sometimes
called "he-ness."[2]

What I now wish to maintain is that a careful examination
of St. Augustine's treatise shows that this account of his
teaching misunderstands his use of the word "relation"
and misrepresents his thought—indeed, that what he has
said in the *De Trinitate* is much more like what I have been
saying in these lectures than would commonly be supposed.

Let me begin by noting two obvious points of similarity.
One I have already mentioned, the empirical method of
approach. Bearing in mind that from the philosophical
point of view reliance on Scripture is empiricism, the
empiricism of St. Augustine is obvious throughout his
work. His aim, as he states it in I. 4, is to expound the
doctrine of the Trinity, first setting out the biblical faith,
and then showing that the obscurities are not inherent
in the divine reality but in our capacity for grasping it.
In II. 1 he promises, God helping him, to be diligent
"ad inquirendam substantiam Dei, sive per Scripturam
eius, sive per creaturam."[3] In accordance with this plan
Books I–VIII attempt to set out the Scriptural revelation,
Books IX–XIV to discover the "invisibilia Dei" by analogy
"per ea quae facta sunt."[4] In the search for analogies the

[1] London, 1894, p. 73.

[2] *E.g.* Dr. Wheeler Robinson. See Appendix VII, p. 226.

[3] In seeking to learn about the substance of God, both from His Scripture
and from His creation.

[4] To discover the invisible things of God by analogy from the things that
are made.

inquiring mind is controlled by Scripture:[1] in XI. 3 Romans
i. 20 and Wisdom XIII. 1–5 are quoted as justifying the
use of such analogies at all; in XII. 6 the analogy of the
family is rejected on the ground that in Scripture it is the
individual man who is said to be made in the image of God.
In XIII. 24, after explaining that the things concerning
the incarnate life of Christ are the object of scientia, those
concerning His eternal being the object of sapientia,[2] he
continues: "Ipse nobis fidem de rebus temporalibus inserit,
ipse de sempiternis exhibet veritatem. Per ipsum pergimus
ad ipsum, tendimus per scientiam ad sapientiam."[3] When
this is taken in conjunction with the statement in IV. 4
that Christ the Word, by His incarnation and atonement,
shares with us His life and consequent illumination, it
anticipates very closely the line of approach which I have
taken, though St. Augustine does not follow up the implications of it as I have done.[4] So, too, does his final reflection
on the method he has followed, when in XV. 9 he describes
it as inquiring "si aliquo modo per intelligentiam possumus[5]
videre quod credimus."[6] We believe the empirical evidence;
our task is to scrutinise and try to understand it.

The second point of obvious similarity is the rejection
of all subordinationist theories, and of that confusion
between the begetting of the Son and the creation of the
world which was characteristic of the idealist metaphysic.
Book I. contains a preliminary statement of the doctrine
which emphatically rejects subordinationism—to such an
extent, indeed, that in expounding 1 Cor. xv. 28 St. Augustine

[1] Cp. III. 22. Exstat enim auctoritas divinarum Scripturarum, unde mens
nostra deviare non debet.

[2] There are no English words which of themselves convey to the modern
reader St. Augustine's distinction between scientia and sapientia. The context makes his meaning clear, and it is best to leave them in Latin.

[3] He Himself implants in us faith in the temporal things (i.e. the Gospel
story), He Himself reveals to us the truth of the things eternal. Through
Him we come to Him, through scientia we come to sapientia.

[4] Cp. also I. 22 and XV. 46. Dominus ipse Jesus Spiritum sanctum non
solum dedit ut Deus sed etiam accepit ut homo.

[5] Oratio recta in the original.

[6] If somehow by our reason we can see what we believe.

says that in "qui illi subjecit omnia" the subject is the
Trinity as a whole, and that interpretation is to be given
to "Deo et Patri" in verse 24 (I. 15–17).[1] The Trinity as
a whole indwells in the Christian (I. 19), and "our Heavenly
Father" is the Trinity as a whole (V. 12). When the Son
was sent forth on His incarnate mission to be visible in
forma hominis, He was sent by the whole Trinity, including
His invisible self: "Sic ergo intelligat, illam incarnationem
et ex virgine nativitatem, in qua Filius intelligitur missus,
una eademque operatione Patris et Filii inseparabiliter esse
factam, non utique inde separato Spiritu sancto" (II. 9).[2]
So, too, of the Spirit: "Apud se autem Deus est, etsi nemini
deatur, quia Deus erat Patri et Filio coaeternus antequam
cuiquam daretur. Nec quia illi dant, ipse datur, ideo minor
est illis. Ita enim datur sicut Donum Dei, ut etiam se ipsum
det sicut Deus" (XV. 36).[3]

In IV. 28, 29 and V. 15 the eternal godhead of both Son
and Spirit is clearly distinguished from their temporal
missions. The incarnation and concomitant gift of the
Spirit are not to be confused either with the eternal generation and procession or with the creation of the world.
Moreover, with regard to creation, it must be understood
that when man is said to be made "in the image of God,"
this does not mean in the image of the Son, but of the
Trinity (XIII. 7). Not the Father alone, but the Trinity
is the Creator (I. 2, V. 14).

St. Augustine's thought thus starts from the acceptance
of certain beliefs. These beliefs are accepted on the evidence
of the Bible. He holds them in common with those for whom
he is writing; his aim is to arrive at a deeper intellectual
understanding of the accepted facts; his method is that

---

[1] Who subjected all things to him . . . to God and Father.
[2] Therefore we must understand that the incarnation and the birth from
the Virgin were brought about by one identical operation of the Father and
the Son, working inseparably and not without the Holy Spirit.
[3] He is God in Himself, even though He be given to no one, for before He
was given to anyone He was God coeternal with the Father and the Son.
Nor because They give and He is given is He less than They. For as God's
Gift He is given in such a way that He Himself is God the Giver.

of reflecting upon what for him is the empirical evidence
in accordance with the canons of rational thought. His
empirical data are the unity of God; His self-manifestation
as Father, Son and Spirit; the equal deity of all three Persons
and their status as Creator over against whatever is created.
His problem is to ask how we can intelligibly think of the
God who has thus revealed Himself to man. His canons
of rational thought include certain *a priori* doctrines about
the nature of deity which for him are axiomatic.[1]

The result of all this is a treatise that is far more complicated than would be gathered from that rough and ready
summary of the Augustinian doctrine of the Trinity from
which we started. In its form, it falls into three parts.
Books I–VIII reflect directly upon the biblical evidence
of God's self-revelation. Books IX–XIV follow a separate
line of thought, asking what can be learned about God by
analogy from the image of God in creation, that is, in man.
Book XV summarises what has gone before, and attempts
to draw conclusions. The celebrated trinity of lover, loved
and love is not the analogy which St. Augustine finds in
Books IX–XIV, it is only mentioned incidentally in
Books I–VIII, and its adequacy as an account of the divine
Trinity is inconsistent with Book XV, wherein St. Augustine
expressly denies that depersonalising of the Spirit which
is held by some modern theologians to be its great merit.
Moreover, whatever St. Augustine may have meant by
calling a relation a person, it was not what that theory
requires.

We may as well begin by trying to understand what St.
Augustine means by his language about relations. It occurs
first in V. 6. He is seeking to interpret the scriptural evidence
by the canons of rational thought. The first four chapters
have been devoted to expounding the substantial unity

---

[1] St. Augustine himself incidentally refers to and distinguishes two
sources of information in XIV. 9: "... litterae, quae de his rebus conscriptae
sunt, quas res duce ratione invenit lector: non quas veras esse credit ei qui
scripsit, sicut legitur historia." Writings concerning the things which the
reader discovers by the guidance of reason, not those which, as in the case
of history, he takes on trust from the writer.

and equality of the Persons in the Trinity. Now he comes
to ask in what sense they can be thought of as distinct from
one another, and as his aim is to expound what the Bible
says about them in propositional form, he naturally turns,
for his canons of rational thought, to the traditional logical
doctrine of predicables.

According to this doctrine predicates may be either
substantial, accidental or relative. A substantial predicate
indicates something without which the subject would not
be what it is: man, for example, is by definition a rational
being, and "rational" is therefore a substantial predicate.
But men may be white or black, tall or short, sick or well:
these, therefore, are accidental predicates. And men may
also be in certain relations to one another and to other
created things, as are fathers and sons or teachers and
pupils, not to mention relations in time and space; these
are indicated by relative predicates.

In speaking of God, says St. Augustine, nothing can
be predicated accidentally. As He is eternally perfect and
therefore unchanging there is nothing in Him which might
be other than it is; all His attributes must be predicated
of Him substantially (V. 3). What is predicated of God
substantially is predicated equally and univocally of all
three Persons: the Trinity as a whole, for example, and
each of the divine Persons, is equally omnipotent and
omniscient. But this is not the kind of predication involved
when the Bible speaks of God as being Father, Son or
Spirit.[1] Therefore we must take these words as relative
predicates, that is to say, as indicating relations within the
godhead: "Trinitatem relatarum ad invicem personarum"
(IX. 1).[2]

What, in the first instance, are the predicates that are
predicated relatively of the three Persons severally? Paternitas and filiatio, fatherhood and sonship, are obviously

---

[1] Cp. VIII. 3 where it is stated that the Son is called "wisdom" substantially and "word" relatively. What corresponds to "verbum" is "nata
substantia."

[2] A Trinity of Persons mutually interrelated.

two. But what is the third? St. Augustine says "Munus," gift, and this is important because it bears witness to the fundamental empiricism of his thought. In the course of this world's history God has made Himself known to us men in Christ as Son, through Christ as Father, in the gift of the Spirit as Spirit. Just as the incarnate life of the Son has given us the evidence for the eternal sonship, so the gift of the Spirit to the Church has given the evidence for His eternal existence in the Godhead. Pentecost was a new mode of giving the same Spirit who had spoken by the prophets (IV. 29). The Spirit did not come into existence when there were creatures to whom He could be given. He proceeds eternally from the Father and the Son as *donabile* and therefore *donum*, for *donum* must be distinguished from *donatum*. His becoming *donatum* did not involve any change in His substance any more than the creation of the world involved a change in the substance of the Son as He became its Lord. Creatures have changeable accidents, and thus there are changes in them when they become servants of the Lord or receivers of the Spirit. There is no change in the substance of eternal God (V. 16, 17).

God is Spirit, and each Person is Spirit. God is holy, and each Person is holy. But the third Person is called "the Holy Spirit" in a special sense, and this name, as a proper name, is predicated relatively not in virtue of His being Spirit, but of being God's gift. Giver and gift are relative terms, corresponding to Father and Son (V. 12). But the biblical evidence shows the Spirit to be the gift of both Father and Son (IV. 29). He is not eternally begotten as a Son, but eternally proceeds as a gift.

So far nothing has been said which implies that the Spirit Himself *is* a relation. All that has been said is that there are three Persons in the Trinity, that there exist between them two types of relation, filiation and procession, and that the names Father, Son and Spirit may be used of the Persons who are substantially one, but distinguished through being related to one another in this way. The word "relation" has not been used of the love which unites Father and Son; it has been used of filiation and procession, or of fatherhood, sonship and "givenness."

Here there is another point to be noted. Besides the logical doctrine of predicables St. Augustine includes in his canons of rational thought the axiom that God *is* His attributes. He is not great, for example, by participating in a greatness which is other than Himself, as is the case with a great house or a great mountain or a great mind, which are only great by participation in His greatness. "Ipse sua est magnitudo. Hoc et de bonitate, et de aeternitate, et de omnipotentia Dei dictum sit, omnibusque omnino praedicamentis quae de Deo possunt pronuntiari" (V. 11).[1] For this reason, God the Father is His fatherhood, God the Son is His sonship, God the Holy Spirit is His givenness. In other words, in whatever sense St. Augustine calls the Holy Spirit a relation, in that same sense the Father and the Son are also relations. The Holy Spirit is His givenness in the same sense that the Father is His fatherhood, the Son is His sonship, and God, the Trinity in unity, is His omnipotence and omniscience.

But now we must consider the passages in which the Spirit is identified with that "ineffabilis quaedam Patris Filiique communio (V. 12); consubstantialis et coaeterna: quae si amicitia convenienter dici potest, dicatur; sed aptius dicitur charitas"—the identification which leads to the famous saying: "et ideo non amplius quam tria sunt;

---

[1] He Himself is His own greatness. And the same thing must be said of His goodness, His eternity, His omnipotence, indeed of all the predicates that can be predicated of God. Cp. also VI. 8, VII. 1, VIII. 2. Much that St. Augustine says on account of this axiom, for example the repeated assertion that in God each attribute *is* all the others, I find quite unintelligible. It seems to me to derive from that neo-Platonic idea of unity which I have shown in Lecture IV to be inadequate for our thought about the unity of God. I believe that he was right in holding that in God, and in God alone, *esse* and *existentia* coincide, but that his exposition of this truth was hampered by this inadequate idea of unity. That, however, is a different point from the one involved in my present argument, and does not affect it.

unus diligens eum qui de illo est, et unus diligens eum de quo est, et ipsa dilectio" (VI. 7).[1]

St. Augustine did not make this statement as a result of asking what must be the inner constitution of the Godhead if the Godhead as a whole be love. He was led to it by the simple method of fitting Scripture passages together, and his treatment of the Spirit as *caritas* is precisely parallel to his treatment of the Son as *sapientia*. The Spirit is known to us as the gift whereby the love of God hath been shed abroad in our hearts (Rom. v. 5), and the context in 1 John iv. shows that "God is Love" refers to the Spirit (XV. 31). Similarly, in 1 Cor. i. 24 Christ is called the "power and wisdom of God" (VI. 1). Are we then to hold that the Father and the Spirit are not *sapientia*, and that the Father and the Son are not *caritas*? No, the Father and the Spirit are also *sapientia*, but the Son is called "sapientia" *proprie*. "Si ergo proprie aliquid horum trium charitas nuncupanda est, quid aptius quam ut hoc sit Spiritus sanctus? Ut scilicet in illa simplici summaque natura, non sit aliud substantia et aliud charitas; sed substantia ipsa sit charitas et charitas ipsa sit substantia, sive in Patre, sive in Filio, sive in Spiritu sancto, et tamen proprie Spiritus sanctus charitas nuncupetur" (XV. 29).[2]

Having thus arrived at the thought that the Spirit is *caritas* in the same way that the Son is *sapientia*, St. Augustine does remark in VI. 7 that this way of thinking gives us a trinity, the trinity of lover, loved and love. But he merely touches the idea and leaves it at once. He only recurs to it once again in quite a different connection: in VIII. 14 he is speaking of the love wherewith we are to love God

---

[1] A certain ineffable communion of Father and Son, which may quite well be called "affection," but is more fittingly called "love." . . . And therefore there are not more than three, One who loves Him who is from Him, One who loves Him from whom He is, and the Love itself.

[2] If therefore any one of these three is especially to be called Love, what is more fitting than that this should be the Holy Spirit? In the simplicity of the divine nature the Substance is not one thing and the Love another, but the Substance is itself the Love and the Love is itself the Substance, in the Father and in the Son and in the Holy Spirit—and yet the Holy Spirit is called Love especially.

and our neighbour, and he remarks again that all love
involves the trinity of lover, loved and love. He makes no
attempt to treat this as an analogy of the divine Trinity.
In his conclusions in Book XV he does not revive this
line of thought. As I have suggested, it is easy to see why
he does not. He is concerned to emphasise that full personality of the Spirit which this way of thinking tends to
obscure.

The passage in VIII. 14 marks the transition to the second
part of the whole treatise. The statement in Gen. i. 26, 27
that man is made in the image of God suggests to St.
Augustine that light may be sought by looking in the image
for a trinity analogous to that in the original.[1] We need not
stop over Books IX–XIII, in which he gives his reasons
for rejecting various trinities as not providing any true
analogy. Finally, in Book XIV, he finds what he is looking
for. An image of the divine Trinity is to be found in the
human soul when that soul is engaged in the purely intellectual activity of self-knowledge. For that activity
involves the knowledge which begets what is known of
it and the activity of the will which unites begetter and
begotten. This is the trinity of memoria, intelligentia, and
amor, for amor is "valentior voluntas"[2] (XIV. 8, XV. 38,
41). "Ecce ergo mens meminit sui, intelligit se, diligit se:
hoc si cernimus, cernimus trinitatem; nondum quidem
Deum, sed iam imaginem Dei" (XIV. 11).[3] The analogy
gives no ground for treating the personality of the Spirit
differently from that of the Father and the Son; in this
connection memoria and intelligentia are on precisely the
same footing as voluntas or amor.

So we come to Book XV, in which St. Augustine sums
up his work and states his conclusions. More than once
he has said that the meaning of the word "persona," as

---

[1] This line of thought has been anticipated by a passing reference in
IV. 30.

[2] More powerful will.

[3] So, you see, the mind remembers itself, knows itself, loves itself. If we
see this, we see a trinity. We do not indeed as yet see God, but we now see
the image of God.

used of the Trinity, is obscure. It is a technical term which
is used for want of a better, because some word is needed
to express the scriptural teaching.[1] But there is nothing
to suggest that the word is to mean anything different as
applied to the Father and the Son, and to the Spirit. The
doctrine, therefore, is not to be expounded by studying
the etymology of technical terms. The study of technical
terms, and the study of the image of God, must both be
subordinated to the biblical revelation.

This being so, the main part of Book XV is devoted
to pointing out the inadequacy of the analogy from the
image of God. Whereas each man is one person, and the
trinity which is the image is in his mind, the divine Trinity
is God, and is not one but three Persons (11). Moreover, we
men only remember with the memory, know with the
intellect, and love with the will; but in the divine Trinity
each Person does all three. The Son is begotten and the
Spirit proceeds, but as begotten and proceeding each is
complete, is memory, intellect and love (12). In particular,
the Spirit is spoken of as personal in the sense of being
consciously and intelligently purposive: "In tantum ergo
Donum Dei est, in quantum datur eis quibus datur. Apud
se autem Deus est, etsi nemini detur, quia Deus erat Patri
et Filio coaeternus antequam cuiquam daretur. Nec quia illi
dant, ipse datur, ideo minor est illis. Ita enim datur sicut
Donum Dei, ut etiam se ipsum det sicut Deus. Non enim
dici potest non esse suae potestatis, de quo dictum est
'Spiritus ubi vult spirat,' et apud Apostolum. . . . 'Omnia
haec operatur unus atque idem Spiritus, dividens propria
unicuique prout vult.' Non est illic conditio dati et dominatio
dantium, sed concordia dati et dantium" (36).[2] Finally,

---

[1] V. 10, VII. 7, 8.

[2] Therefore He is only the gift of God in so far as He is given to those
to whom He is given. In Himself He is God, even though He be given to
no one, for before He was given to anyone He was God coeternal with the
Father and the Son. Nor because they give and He is given is He less than
they. For as God's gift He is given in such a way that He Himself is God
the giver. For one cannot say that the giving is not of His own power, seeing
that of Him it is said "the Spirit bloweth where He wills," and (by the

n paragraphs 42 and 43 St. Augustine repeats the point
hat whereas in each of us the analogous trinity exists in
one person, the divine Trinity is a unity in which each
member is a complete Person. Whatever may be
he etymological history of the words ὑπόστασις and
persona, it is impossible to avoid the conclusion
that St. Augustine regarded each Person in the
Godhead as being personal in whatever sense the word
s used of conscious, intelligent and purposive human
beings.

There is thus essential agreement between these lectures
and the *De Trinitate*. In both it is the duty of Christian
doctrine to bear witness to the biblical revelation, and the
duty of theology to try to understand that revelation
without distorting it. In both, despite the different conceptions of the mode in which it is given, the revelation requires
us to believe in God as the divine Trinity wherein each
person is fully personal in the modern sense of the word.
In both the nature of the divine Unity is a mystery which
we are forbidden by the evidence to deny. I have suggested
that we may perhaps find some light on this mystery by
measuring degrees of unity by intensity rather than by
simplicity. Such a way of thinking never occurred to St.
Augustine. Nevertheless it is what his thought would seem
to anticipate and look forward to when he writes: "Nec
rursus quemadmodum ista imago quod est homo habens
illa tria una persona est, ita est illa Trinitas: sed tres personae
sunt, Pater Filii, et Filius Patris, et Spiritus Patris et Filii.
. . . Non tamen, sicut in ista imagine Trinitatis non haec
tria unus homo, sed unius hominis sunt, ita in ipsa summa
Trinitate cuius haec imago est unius Dei sunt illa tria, sed
unus Deus est, et tres sunt illae, non una persona. Quod
sane mirabiliter ineffabile est, vel ineffabiliter mirabile,
cum sit una Persona haec imago Trinitatis, ipsa vero summa

apostle) "All these things worketh the one selfsame Spirit, divid-
ing to each severally as He wills." In these sayings there is no con-
ditioning of the given by controlling givers, but a concord of given and
givers.

Trinitas tres personae sint, inseparabilior est illa Trinitas personarum trium quam haec unius" (XV. 43).[1]

There remains one obvious point of difference. I have argued that we should think of the unity of God as a unity wherein no one of the Persons has any metaphysical priority over another, that the strain in traditional theology according to which the Father is the *principium* of the Godhead is a relic of subordinationism due to an inadequate grasp of the nature of unity as disclosed by the Christian revelation. In St. Augustine the metaphysical priority of the Father is unquestioned. I have described the process by which theology arrives at the doctrine of the Trinity as one of "thinking away" those elements in the incarnate life of Christ and the temporal mission of the Spirit which are incidental to the historical revelation in time and space. St. Augustine adopts this method in I. 22–27 where he explains various statements in the gospels as being made about Jesus "secundum formam servi." The difference between us is that I go further in this direction than he does, and do not regard the passages which speak of filiation or procession as revealing the existence of anything that may be called derivation "secundum formam Dei."

The belief that the eternal character of these relationships is a guaranteed truth of revelation leads St. Augustine to devote a great deal of time to expounding the different modes of "procession" of Son and Spirit. In this he is followed by St. Thomas and by Calvin. But the real ground of the speculation is metaphysical. It is by locating the *principium* of the Godhead in the Father that St. Augustine,

---

[1] Nor again is the Trinity a trinity after the same manner as is that image of it, since the image, man, has the three in one person, while the Father of the Son and the Son of the Father and the Spirit of the Father and the Son are three Persons. . . . Again, in that image of the Trinity the Three are not the man but are of the man, whereas in the divine Trinity itself (of which that is an image) the Three are not of one God, but are the one God, and themselves are three Persons, not one Person. And—what is marvellously ineffable or ineffably marvellous!—although this image of the Trinity is one person and that divine Trinity is three Persons, yet that Trinity of three Persons is more unified than this of one.

who is working with what I have called the "mathematical" conception of unity, believes himself able to maintain unity.[1] This is why he regards the modes of derivation implied by the words filiation and procession as valid "secundum formam Dei." The reason for my holding this to be unnecessary, and indeed mistaken, is, of course, equally metaphysical. The difference between us lies in a realm in which no man can know the truth for certain until we know "even as we are known." Meanwhile both views are compatible with the practice of trinitarian religion. I have explained the grounds on which I hold the one I believe to be true, and I am of opinion that if St. Augustine, St. Thomas and Calvin were alive to-day they would be glad in this respect to revise what they have written.

(iii)

This somewhat detailed discussion of St. Augustine will enable us to deal more briefly with St. Thomas Aquinas, for, apart from differences in style and arrangement, the *Tractatus* is a repetition of the theology of the *De Trinitate*. The first thing we notice is the difference of arrangement. St. Augustine, as we have seen, sets out to ask how we may understand what we believe. He starts from the empirical evidence, he inquires what must be the nature of the God revealed in the temporal "sending" of Son and Spirit. St. Thomas begins from the other end. He has the completed Augustinian doctrine of the Trinity all ready for exposition

[1] Cp. XV. 47. "Cum Spiritum sanctum genitum non dicamus, dicere tamen non audemus ingenitum, ne in hoc vocabulo vel duos patres in illa Trinitate, vel duos qui non sunt de alio quisquam suspicetur. Pater enim solus non est de alio, ideo solus appellatur ingenitus, non quidem in Scripturis, sed in consuetudine disputantium et de re tanta sermonem qualem valuerint proferentium." Although we do not call the Holy Spirit begotten, yet we dare not call Him unbegotten, lest this word should be thought to mean that in that Trinity there are two Fathers, or two who are not from any other. For the Father alone is not from another, therefore He alone is called unbegotten—not indeed in Scripture, but according to the custom of theologians, who for so high a matter have to make use of the best word they can find.

and sets out to expound it in logical order. There is, he says, "procession" within the Godhead. This is of two kinds and involves four "relations," and five "notions." Only at the end, after this detailed discussion of the internal constitution of the Godhead, does St. Thomas pass in Qu. 43 to speak of the temporal mission. Nevertheless there is an underlying kinship of treatment between the two writers. Though St. Thomas is expounding the accepted orthodox doctrine, his foundation is the empirical evidence of Scripture. Thus he opens his exposition with the assertion that "divina Scriptura in rebus divinis nominibus ad processionem pertinentibus utitur" (27, i).[1] And his method of exposition by way of asking and answering difficult questions betrays the same desire as that of his predecessor to try to see how what is believed may be understood. St Thomas, too, is seeking to order the material of faith in accordance with the canons of rational thought.

Again, St. Thomas takes for granted the rejection of subordinationism and of any confusion between the generation of the Son and the creation of the world. The sense in which the Father is called the Father of the Son must be carefully distinguished from that in which God is called the Father of creatures (33, iii); the sense in which the Son is called the Image of the Father must be carefully distinguished from that in which man is said to be made in the image of God (35, ii).

St. Thomas also assumes that the Father is the *principium* of Godhead. In 33, i, ii he states categorically that this is so, and that this is why the Father is called Father. But there follow some interesting signs of coming cracks in the structure of this relic of subordinationism. As in St Augustine, the ground of the belief is an alleged metaphysical necessity: "sicut in quolibet genere oportet ponere unum primum, ita in divina natura oportet ponere unum principium, quod non sit ab alio, quod ingenitum dicimus. Ponere igitur duos innascibiles est ponere duos Deos e[

[1] Concerning things divine Holy Scripture uses words that belong to [the idea of] procession.

luas naturas divinas" (33, iv ad 4).[1] In 39, viii, although
ﬡe states that the existence of the Father alone is an actual
ﬦpossibility,[2] he suggests that the doctrine of His *prin-
ipium* implies the logical possibility of unipersonal exist-
ﬤnce: "Unitas dicitur absolute, non praesupponens aliquid
ﬗliud; et ideo appropriatur Patri, qui non praesupponit
ﬗliquam personam."[3] Now in 29, i–iii he has approved of
שׂoethius' definition of persona as "naturae rationalis in-
ﬦividua substantia,"[4] and of the emendation whereby
ﬧichard of St. Victor had sought to make it more directly
ﬧpplicable to the divine Persons: "divinae naturae incom-
ﬦunicabilis existentia."[5] Divina natura is stated to be
ﬗtionalis in the sense of communiter intelligibilis. It would
ﬤem, then, that in approving the Boethian definition St.
ﬨhomas implies that a person is essentially one among
ﬢthers.[6] There is thus a latent contradiction between the
ﬥgical implications of the definition of persona and the
ﬦoctrine of the *principium*. There is not much of that
ﬦoctrine left when, in 41, iii, he explains that in the Godhead
"generation" has none of the meaning of "derivation"
﬩taching to it in earthly sonship, and in 41, iv he almost
ﬨuggests, but not quite, that the Father's power to generate
ﬧ the mode in which the generative power of the Godhead
ﬧ a whole operates through Him.

In accepting this definition from Boethius St. Thomas
ﬦent a step further than St. Augustine, for whom the word
ﬢersona was a technical term taking whatever theological
ﬦeaning it was to have from the relations which it was
ﬦtended to describe. But this does not make much differ-

---

[1] As in every genus we must posit a primary unity, so in the divine nature
ﬦe must posit a single principle which is not from another, which we call
ﬦbegotten. Therefore to posit two unbegottenables is to posit two Gods
ﬦd two divine natures.

[2] Unitas autem statim invenitur in persona Patris, etiam, per impossibile,
ﬤmotis aliis personis.

[3] Unity is spoken of absolutely, as not presupposing anything else.
ﬨherefore it is used of the Father, who does not presuppose any person.

[4] The individual substance of a rational nature.

[5] The incommunicable existence of the divine nature.

[6] On this see C. C. J. Webb: *God and Personality*.

ence to St. Thomas' general treatment. For the most part
he follows St. Augustine in saying that the Persons describe
relations, that there are the four relations (paternitas, filiatio
spiratio, processio, 28, iv),[1] and consequently the five
"notions," or properties whereby the Persons are known
(these are the same as the relations with the addition of
innascibilitas,[2] 32, iii). In 39, viii he quotes with approval
what St. Augustine had said about the Spirit being the
Love which unites Father and Son, but in 37, i he has
already followed St. Augustine in saying that the Spirit
personifies the Father's Amor in the same way that the
Word personifies the Father's Intelligentia. For both
theologians the background of this thought is the axiom
that both the Trinity as a whole and each Person does not
have but is His attributes.[3] As I have already argued, the
application of this axiom to the Son as *proprie* sapientia
prevents the identification of the Spirit with amor from
implying in His case a different kind of personality. In
43, viii the Son and the Spirit are on a level in their
ability to send themselves and each other on temporal
missions.

There is no need to labour this point further, especially
as it is St. Augustine and not St. Thomas who is usually
alleged to have made the distinction. But I must
attend to the interpretation of St. Thomas which was
given by the late Dean Rashdall. If he was right, these
lectures are in flat contradiction to the teaching of the
Summa.

Dean Rashdall maintained that God is an unipersonal
Being who is at once "Power or Cause (Father), Wisdom
(Son), Will (Holy Ghost); or, since the Will of God is

---

[1] Fatherhood, sonship, inspiring, procession.

[2] Inability to be born.

[3] *E.g.* Relatio autem in divinis non est, sicut accidens inhaerens subiecto,
sed est ipsa divina essentia . . . Sicut ergo deitas est Deus, ita paternitas divina
est Deus Pater, qui est persona divina (29, iv.). But in the Godhead a relation
is not as an accident inhering in its subject, but is the divine essence itself.
So as the deity is God, so the divine fatherhood is God the Father, who is
a divine Person.

lways a loving Will, Love (Amor) is sometimes substituted
or Will (Voluntas) in explanation of the Holy Spirit."
This, he said, was "St. Thomas' explanation of the Trinity,"
nd he added, "How little St. Thomas thought of the
Persons' as separate consciousnesses is best seen from his
doctrine (taken from Augustine) that the love of the Father
or the Son *is* the Holy Spirit. The love of one Being for
Himself or for another is not a Person in the natural,
ormal modern sense of the word: and it would be quite
northodox to attribute Personality to the Son in any other
ense than that in which it is attributed to the Holy Ghost."
n support of his contention Dr. Rashdall quotes as follows:
In . . . 37, i the 'conclusio' is 'Amor, personaliter acceptus,
roprium nomen est Spiritus sancti,'[1] which is explained
o mean that there are in the Godhead 'duae processiones:
na per modum intellectus, quae est processio Verbi; alia
er modum voluntatis, quae est processio amoris.'[2] So
gain (45, vii): 'In creaturis igitur rationalibus, in quibus
st intellectus et voluntas, invenitur repraesentatio Trini-
atis per modum imaginis, inquantum invenitur in eis
Verbum conceptum et amor procedens.' "[3]

Taken apart from their context, these passages, together
vith some others which Dr. Rashdall does not quote[4] might
ossibly bear the interpretation that he puts upon them.
But the context includes not merely the *Tractatus de
Trinitate*, and not merely the rest of the *Summa* and of the
orks of St. Thomas. It includes the whole theological
radition in which he stands. To the passage in 27, iii where
e uses the kind of language on which Dr. Rashdall relies,
is Turin editor adds the note: "Ita ratiocinantur Tatianus,
Athenagoras, S. Irenaeus, S. Cyrillus, Tertullianus, S.

---

[1] Love, taken personally, is the proper name of the Holy Spirit.
[2] Two processions, one in the mode of intellect, which is the procession
f the Word; the other by the mode of will, which is the procession of Love.
[3] Therefore in rational creatures, in which are intellect and will, there
found a representation of the Trinity in the way of an image, in so far
there is found in them the word conceived and love proceeding. See
ashdall: *Philosophy and Religion* (London, 1909), p. 183.
[4] *E.g.* 27, iii; 39, viii.

Basilius, S. Athanasius, praecipue S. Augustinus, et fere omnes theologi."[1] Writing a few centuries after St. Thomas, Calvin said of Sabellius: "Si in certamen ventum est, fatebatur se credere patrem Deum, filium Deum, spiritum Deum: sed postea elabi promptum erat, nihil se aliud dixisse quam si Deum fortem et iustum et sapientem vocasset."[2] It was to refute such doctrines as this, says Calvin, that the word "persona" was introduced. It makes no difference in principle whether one regards the doctrine of the Trinity as the assertion that God is power, wisdom and love or that He is strength, justice and wisdom. If Calvin is right, the Turin editor shows St. Thomas to have been following a tradition which expressly repudiated the type of theology advocated by Dr. Rashdall. If Dr. Rashdall is right, either Calvin was mistaken about the intentions of "fere omnes theologi," or St. Thomas was standing out as an exception to the tradition.

That Dr. Rashdall is wrong seems to me clear from the following consideration. He himself held a purely exemplarist doctrine of the atonement which did not require a christology involving the exercise of personal relations between the Father and the Son.[3] That the man Jesus should have been the medium through which the unipersonal God revealed His character of love was all that he required. But this was not the doctrine of St. Augustine of "fere omnes theologi," or of St. Thomas himself. For them the sacrificial self-offering of the incarnate Son, His triumphant resurrection, His ascension and heavenly session and the certainty of His judgment were no mere myths illustrative of the divine benevolence. They were the ultimate realities of time and of eternity. Is it conceivable that the author of the Eucharistic hymn Adoro te devote should ever have thought the words "the eternal Son"

---

[1] So argue Tatian, Athenagoras . . . and almost all theologians.

[2] Institutes (1559), I, xiii, 4. When he was pressed, he confessed that he believed the Father to be God, the Son to be God, and the Spirit to be God but afterwards was quick to fall back and say that he had said no more than if he had called God strong and righteous and wise.

[3] See The Idea of Atonement in Christian Theology (London, 1919).

to mean no more than that God is wise as well as being
powerful and loving?

> "In cruce latebat sola deitas,
> At hic latet simul et humanitas:
> Ambo tamen credens atque confitens
> Peto quod petivit latro poenitens.

> "Plagas sicut Thomas non intueor
> Deum tamen meum te confiteor:
> Fac me tibi semper magis credere,
> In te spem habere, et diligere.

> "Jesu, quem velatum nunc adspicio,
> Oro, fiat illud quod tam sitio,
> Ut te revelata cernens facie
> Visu sim beatus tuae gloriae."[1]

Set in this context the interpretation of the two passages
quoted by Dr. Rashdall is surely clear. They are both
reminiscent of passages in St. Augustine, and were meant
in the same sense. The second of them (in 45, vii) referred
to the analogous trinity in the human mind—the analogy
which St. Augustine refused to press because to do so
would have landed him in the position of Dr. Rashdall.
The title of the Article (37, i) from which the first quotation
was taken is to be noted: "Utrum Amor sit proprium nomen
Spiritus Sancti."[2] In *De Trin.* XV. 39, 30 St. Augustine
had given the fact that words are often used in wider and
narrower senses as justifying such twofold use of sapientia
and amor in theology: although, for example, the Father
and the Spirit are also sapientia, the Son is called sapientia
proprie. St. Augustine had been trying to expound the
language of Scripture taken as giving revelation in the form
of propositions. St Thomas is following in his footsteps.
St. Thomas, like St. Augustine, distinguishes between the
ascription of amor to the Godhead as a whole and to the
Spirit: in the one case it is predicated *essentialiter*, in the
other *personaliter*.

---

[1] See also the questions dealing with the Atonement and the heavenly
session and perpetual priesthood of Christ in *S.T.* III. 46–9, 58, xxii.

[2] Whether Love be the name proper to the Holy Spirit.

The religion of St. Thomas is a full-blooded trinitarianism. In his theology he is wrestling to express this in terms
of a philosophical notion of unity which cannot contain
it. The result is that the abstract terms in which he attempts
in the *Tractatus* to describe the relations of the divine
persons appear somewhat like the "bloodless categories"
of Bradley's famous phrase. But St. Thomas surely never
meant his theology to be used for the purpose of desiccating
the revelation which God had given through the activity
of Son and Spirit in the incarnation, the atonement and
the continued life of the Church. Through that revelation
he worshipped three Persons in one God. He sought, by
logical analysis of the nature of being, to show how this
could be, and how predicates could rightly be used of the
Persons severally and of the Trinity as a whole. But the
Persons themselves, though they might be thought and
spoken of as existing in the five notions and the four relations, or as power, wisdom and love, were always more than
this. The living content of each was given by that which
He made known of Himself to faithful worshippers.

In my last lecture I was arguing against the view that
it is "philosophical" to postulate some impersonal reality
underlying personal life, and that to regard the impersonal
as grounded in the personal is "naïve and mythological."
Both St. Augustine and St. Thomas assert the priority
of the personal. It is involved in the axiom that God *is*
His attributes and His relations, for the import of that axiom
is that there is no more ultimate impersonal reality, beyond
the personal being of God. This is very clearly stated by
St. Thomas in 40, i and iv. "In divinis idem est abstractum
et concretum, et deitas et Deus. . . . Proprietates personales
sunt idem cum personis, ea ratione qua abstractum est
idem cum concreto . . . oportet quod praeintelligatur relatio
actui notionali, sicut persona agens praeintelligitur actioni."[1]

---

[1] In divinity abstract and concrete, godhead and God, are one. . . . Personal properties are the same as the persons in the same way as abstract and
concrete. . . . It is necessary for a relation to be *prior* in thought to a notional
act, as a person acting is prior in thought to an action.

The same truth is otherwise expressed in the statement
that in God nothing is done by nature which is not also
done by will: The Son, for example, is begotten of the
Father both by nature and by will.[1] I cannot help thinking
that the difficulties in both Augustinian and Thomist
trinitarian theology are due to the fact that under the
influence of contemporary philosophical tradition they
forget to be true to this principle. The Trinity of God's
self-revelation is no impersonal system of relations between
hypostases in an essence; it is the living, loving communion
of Father, Son and Spirit into which we are adopted in
Christ. Neither in St. Augustine nor in St. Thomas can
their logical apparatus conceal the fact that this is the living
reality in which they believe, about which they are trying
to think and write.

(iv)

Calvin ends his chapter on the Trinity by commending
the writings of St. Augustine on the subject, and by saying
that he himself has only aimed at refuting live errors, not
at discussing every conceivable question that might be
raised in connection with the doctrine. "Certe nihil astute
praeterii quod mihi adversum esse putarem: sed dum
ecclesiae aedificationi studeo, multa non attingere con-
sultius visum est, quae et parum prodessent, et lectores
gravarent supervacua molestia" (29).[2] His approach is
empirical in the same sense as had been that of St. Augustine
and St. Thomas. He will only philosophise within the
limits set by the biblical evidence: "Equidem hic, si quando
alias in reconditis Scripturae mysteriis, sobrie multaque
cum moderatione philosophandum: adhibita etiam multa
cautione, ne aut cogitatio aut lingua ultra procedat, quam

---

[1] St. Augustine, *De. Trin.* IV. 12, XV. 38; *S.T.* I. 41 ii. ad 1.

[2] Be assured that I have not cunningly omitted what I thought opposed
to me. But as my care is for the edification of the Church, it has seemed to
me wiser not to touch on many things which would not contribute much
and would burden readers with tiresome trivialities. The references are all
to Book I, Chap XIII. of the *Institutio Christianae Religionis* (1559), Ed.
Baum, Cunitz & Reuss, Brunswick 1864.

verbi Dei fines se protendunt" (21).[1] Like St. Augustine
and St. Thomas he clearly distinguishes between the
generation of the Son and the creation of the world. Sections
7–13 are a catena of biblical proofs of the godhead of the
Son, and in more than one passage Calvin rejects in anticipa-
tion the use of the doctrine of the Trinity made by idealists
such as Professor Pringle-Pattison: "Ego vero longe secus
concludo: quum in ipso momento quo dixit Deus: fiat
lux, sermonis virtus emerserit et exstiterit, ipsum multo
ante fuisse. Quam dudum autem, si quis inquiret, nullum
exordium reperiet. Neque enim certum temporis spatium
terminat quum dicit ipse (John xvii. 5): pater illustra
filium gloria quam apud te initio possedi, antequam
iacerentur mundi fundamenta. Neque hoc praeteriit
Ioannes: quia antequam ad mundi creationem descendat,
principio sermonem apud Deum fuisse dicit. Constituimus
ergo rursum, sermonem extra temporis initium a Deo
conceptum apud ipsum perpetuo resedisse: unde et aeter-
nitas et vera essentia et divinitas eius comprobatur" (8).[2]

[1] For me here, as elsewhere in the deep mysteries of Scripture, one
should philosophise soberly and with great moderation, taking great care
lest either thought or speech should go beyond the limit of God's word.

[2] Cp. 22. Prodigiosum vero hoc commentum, personam nihil aliud esse
quam visibilem gloriae Dei speciem, non longa refutatione indiget. Nam
quum Ioannes nondum creato mundo λόγον fuisse Deum pronuntiet, longe
ab idea discernit. Si vero tunc quoque et ab ultima aeternitate λόγος ille,
qui Deus erat, fuit apud Patrem, et propria sua gloria apud Patrem insignis
fuit, non potuit certe externus esse aut figurativus splendor: sed necessario
sequitur fuisse hypostasin, quae in Deo ipso intus resideret.

My conclusion is far different. When in the very moment in which the
Father said "Let there be light," the power of the Word came forth and
stood out, the Word Himself had existed long before. If anyone asks "How
long?" he will find no beginning. For He gives no definite period of time
when He Himself says, " Father, glorify thy Son with the glory which I
had with Thee in the beginning, before the foundations of the world were
laid." Nor did John overlook this point, for before coming down to the
creation of the earth he speaks of the Word having been with God in the
beginning. Therefore once again we affirm that the Word took His beginning
from God outside time, that His seat has been with God perpetually, whence
are proved His equal eternity and true essence and divinity.

Cp. Surely the prodigious error, that a Person is nothing more than the
visible appearance of God's glory, needs no long refutation. For when John
says that the Word was God while yet the world was not created, he dis-

The Bible also requires us to distinguish the Holy Spirit from creation in the same way: "Aeternum igitur spiritum semper in Deo fuisse tunc apparuit, dum fovendo sustinuit confusam coeli et terrae materiam, donec accederet pulchritudo et series" (22).[1]

Calvin starts with the passage I referred to in my first lecture: In His self-revelation, he says, God "ita se praedicat unicum esse, ut distincte in tribus personis considerandum proponat" (2). He then justifies the use of the word "persona" by reference to *Hebrews*, i. 3: "Certe ex apostoli verbis colligimus propriam esse in patre hypostasin quae in filio refulgeat. Unde etiam rursus facile elicitur filii hypostasis, quae eum a patre distinguat" (2).[2] This leads on to a discussion of the use of technical terms. Persona, subsistentia, πρόσωπον and sometimes substantia, he says, have all been used as synonyms to describe the distinct Persons in the Trinity. He is not concerned to fight about words, and non-scriptural words may rightly be used where they are necessary to expound and safeguard the true meaning of Scripture (3). Historically, ὁμοούσιος was introduced to refute Arius, persona to refute Sabellius (4). "Dic *in una Dei essentia personarum Trinitatem*: dixeris uno verbo quod Scripturae loquuntur" (5).[3]

Calvin thus accepts the traditional orthodox formula as expressing the biblical revelation. And when he goes on to treat of the distinctions in the Godhead, he follows

tinguishes Him widely from an idea. If then and from ultimate eternity the Word, who was God, was with the Father and was glorious with the Father with His own glory, He could not have been any merely external or apparent splendour. It necessarily follows that He must have been a hypostasis which had its being within the Godhead itself.

[1] Therefore it was clear that the eternal Spirit had always existed in God while by His care He maintained in being the confused material of heaven and earth until there should be given to it beauty and order. See also the biblical proofs of the godhead of the Spirit in 14, 15.

[2] We may certainly learn from the words of the Apostle that there is in the Father a special hypostasis which is reflected in the Son. Whence also one may easily deduce the hypostasis of the Son which distinguishes him from the Father.

[3] Say "A trinity of persons in the one essence of God": you will have said what the Scriptures say in one phrase.

tradition in calling them distinctions of relation: "Personam igitur voco subsistentiam in Dei essentia, quae ad alios relata, proprietate incommunicabili distinguitur. . . . Iam ex tribus subsistentiis unamquamque dico ad alias relatam proprietate distingui" (6).[1] But Calvin takes a definite step forward when he tries to expound the content of the distinctions. He is not content simply to refer to the relations of filiation and procession. Although the divine existence in three Persons is not to be confused with God's creative activity, yet it is through His self-manifestation in and to His creation that we find the evidence for our belief in His eternal threefoldness. Calvin, in fact, anticipates the argument of these lectures that we arrive at the doctrine of the Trinity by asking what must be the eternal nature of the God of this particular temporal self-manifestation. "Proprietatem filio a patre esse distinctam ostendunt loci, quos iam citavimus: quia sermo non fuisset apud Deum, nisi alius esset a patre: neque gloriam suam habuisset apud patrem nisi ab eo distinctus. Similiter patrem a se distinguit, quum alium esse dicit qui testimonium sibi perhibet (John v. 32, viii. 16). Atque huc tendit quod alibi dicitur, patrem per verbum omnia creasse: quod non poterat nisi ab ipso quodammodo distinctus. Praeterea non descendit pater in terram, sed is qui a patre exiit: non mortuus est, nec resurrexit, sed qui ab eo missus fuerat. Neque ab assumpta carne exordium habuit haec distinctio, sed antea quoque unigenitum in sinu patris fuisse manifestum est (John i. 18). Quis enim asserere sustineat, tum demum sinum patris ingressum filium, quum e coelo descendit ad suscipiendam humanitatem? Erat ergo ante in sinu patris et suam apud patrem gloriam obtinebat. Spiritus sancti a patre distinctionem Christus innuit, quum dicit eum a patre procedere: a se ipso autem, quoties alium vocat; ut quum alium consolatorem ab se mittendum

---

[1] Therefore by "person" I mean a subsistence in the essence of God, which by being related to the others is distinguished by an incommunicable property. . . . I say that of the three subsistences each being related to the others is distinguished by its own special property.

denuntiat, et alibi saepius—John xiv. 6, xv. 26, xiv. 16"
(17).[1]

It is indeed characteristic of Calvin that he confines
himself to stating the scriptural evidence and arguing that
the traditional formula expresses the teaching of the Bible
and nothing else. In spite of his commendation of St.
Augustine, he differs from him markedly in one respect.
St. Augustine had searched widely for analogies which
should help towards intelligent faith in the Trinity. Calvin
looks for no help in that direction: "Enimvero ad vim
distinctionis exprimendam, similitudines a rebus humanis
nescio an expediat" (8).[2] Hence there is nothing in his
treatment which suggests the minimising of the idea of
personality as attributed to any one of the three Persons.
In this respect the Spirit is treated as parallel to the Son:
"Denique in ipsum omnia, ut in filium, conferuntur quae
maxime propria sunt divinitatis officia" (14).[3] Commenting
on 1 Cor. xii. 11 ff. Calvin writes: "Omnia distribuit unus
et idem spiritus prout vult. Nisi enim esset aliquid in

[1] That there is a special property for the Son distinct from the Father is
shown by the passages we have already quoted. The Word could not have
been "with God" if He had not been other than the Father. He could not
have had His own glory with the Father if He had not been distinct from
Him. Similarly He distinguishes the Father from Himself when He says
that there is Another who bears witness to Him. This is confirmed by that
other saying that the Father created all things through the Word; He could
not have done this if He had not been in some way distinct. Moreover, the
Father did not come down on earth, but He who came forth from the Father:
the Father neither died nor rose again, but He who had been sent by Him.
Nor did this distinction have its beginning at the incarnation, but it is clear
that before that also the only-begotten had been in the bosom of the Father.
For who could maintain that then and then only did the Son enter the
Father's bosom when He came down from Heaven to put on humanity?
Therefore He existed beforehand in the bosom of the Father, and was
receiving His own glory with the Father. And Christ indicates the distinction
of the Holy Spirit from the Father when He speaks of Him as proceeding
from the Father: He indicates His distinction from Himself as often as He
speaks of Him as another, *e.g.* when He promises to send another comforter,
and often elsewhere.

[2] Indeed I doubt if similitudes from things human are of any real use for
giving the force of the distinction.

[3] In a word, all the things that are the proper functions of divinity are
conferred on Him as on the Son.

Deo subsistens, minime ei daretur arbitrium et voluntas. Clarissime ergo Paulus spiritum insignit divina potentia, et in Deo hypostatice residere demonstrat" (14).[1] Again, St. Peter, in rebuking Ananias, "quod spiritui sancto mentitus esset, non hominibus mentitum esse dicebat, sed Deo" (15).[2] The doctrine of the double procession is accepted because it is taught in the Bible "multis id quidem locis, sed nusquam clarius quam cap. 8 ad Romanos, ubi scilicet idem Spiritus, nunc Christi, nunc eius qui suscitavit Christum a mortuis, promiscue vocatur" (18).[3] When Christ said "God is Spirit" He was uttering the truth that the Divine essence is wholly spiritual, not using the word Spirit, as it is used in other passages, to mean the third Person hypostatically. κύριος, the New Testament word for Jehovah, is similarly used sometimes for Christ and sometimes for the Godhead as a whole (20).

Two passages (Eph. iv. 5 and Matt. xxviii. 19) taken together are enough to prove for Calvin the truth of the doctrine of the Trinity in Unity. "Nam Paulus haec tria sic connectit, Deum, fidem et baptismum, ut ab uno ad aliud ratiocinetur: nempe, quia una est fides, ut inde unum esse Deum demonstret: quia unus est baptismus, inde quoque unam esse fidem ostendat. Ergo, si in unius Dei fidem ac religionem initiamur per baptismum, nobis necesse est verum censere Deum in cuius nomen baptizamur. Nec vero dubium est quin hac solenni nuncupatione perfectam fidei lucem iam esse exhibitam testari voluerit Christus, quum diceret: baptizate eos in nomine patris et filii et spiritus sancti. Siquidem hoc perinde valet atque baptizari in unius Dei nomen, qui solida claritate apparuit in patre, filio et spiritu: unde plane constat in Dei essentia

---

[1] All these things distributes one and the same Spirit as He will. Unless He were something subsisting in God, He could not be given choice and will. Therefore most clearly does Paul endow the Spirit with divine power and show that He exists in God hypostatically.

[2] Acts v. 4.

[3] In many places indeed, but nowhere more clearly than in Romans viii where the same Spirit is described indifferently as the Spirit of Christ and the Spirit of Him who raised Christ from the dead.

residere tres personas in quibus Deus unus cognoscitur"
(16).[1] If only everyone would accept the substance of the
Bible doctrine, how happy he would be to be done with
argumentation! "Utinam quidem sepulta essent nomina,
constaret modo haec inter omnes fides: patrem et filium
et spiritum esse unum Deum: nec tamen aut filium esse
patrem, aut spiritum filium, sed proprietate quadam esse
distinctos" (5).[2]

Nevertheless in one particular a metaphysical assumption
controls his thought. That relic of subordinationism, the
doctrine of the *principium* of the Father, remains. Its first
introduction is quite innocuous. Referring to the empirical
evidence of the threefold activity of God in His historical
self-manifestation, Calvin writes, and writes truly: "Ea
distinctio autem est quod Patri principium agendi, rerumque
omnium fons et scaturigo attribuitur: Filio sapientia,
consilium, ipsaque in rebus agendis dispensatio: at Spiritui
virtus et efficacia assignatur actionis" (18).[3] But the attempt
to regard this *principium* of the Father as an element in
the eternal being of God produces great difficulty. He is
puzzled by the contradictory language used by orthodox
theologians: "Nunc enim Patrem Filii principium esse

---

[1] For Paul joins together these three, God, faith and baptism, in such
a way that one can argue from one to another. He says there is one faith
that therefrom he may show that there is one God; one baptism to show
one faith. Therefore, if by baptism we are initiated into the faith and religion
of the one God, it is necessary for us to think of the true God in whose name
we are baptized. Nor is it doubtful that Christ willed to show forth the
perfect light of the faith in His solemn proclamation, when He said, "Baptize
them in the name of the Father and of the Son and of the Holy Spirit."
This must mean the same as being baptized in the name of the one God, who
has appeared with unmistakable clarity as Father, Son and Spirit. From
this it is certain that there exist in the essence of God three Persons in whom
the one God is known.

[2] Would that the words could be buried, if only this faith could be established among all: that the Father, the Son and the Spirit are one God, and
yet the Son is not the Father or the Spirit the Son, but each is distinguished
by a certain special property.

[3] There is this distinction, that to the Father is attributed the origination
of the action: He is the fount and source of all things. To the Son are assigned
wisdom, counsel and the actual carrying out of the action, to the Spirit its
power and efficacy.

tradunt: nunc Filium a se ipso et divinitatem et essentiam
habere asseverant, adeoque unum esse cum Patre principium" (20).[1] He sees clearly that the *principium* cannot
involve an ontological priority. Indeed, in spite of his
commendation of St. Augustine's treatment of the subject,
he seems to me to see more clearly than either St. Augustine
or St. Thomas had done that the unity of the divine essence
involves the Son being "essentiator sui." "Nam quisquis
essentiatum a patre filium esse dicit, a se ipso negat esse.
Reclamat autem spiritus sanctus, illum Iehovah nominans"
(23).[2] His solution is to ascribe to the Father a primacy
of "ordo" and "gradus" which, nevertheless, does not
imply any priority in "gradus divinitatis." "Nam etsi
fatemur ratione ordinis et gradus principium divinitatis
esse in patre, detestabile tamen esse dicimus commentum
illud, solius patris essentiam esse propriam, quasi filii
deificator esset" (24).[3] "Atqui ex scripturis docemur unum
essentialiter Deum esse, ideoque essentiam tam filii quam
spiritus esse ingenitam: sed quatenus pater ordine primus
est, atque ex se genuit suam sapientiam, merito, ut nuper
dictum est, censetur principium et fons totius divinitatis.
Ita Deus indefinite est ingenitus: et pater etiam personae
respectu ingenitus" (25).[4] ". . . nomen Dei non sumi
indefinite, sed restringi ad patrem quatenus deitatis est
principium, non essentiando, ut fanatici nugantur, sed

[1] For sometimes they say that the Father is the *principium* of the Son,
and sometimes assert that the Son has His divinity and essence from Himself,
and so is one *principium* with the Father.

[2] For whoever says that the Son derives His essence from the Father
denies that He is from Himself. But the Holy Spirit refutes this by calling
Him Jehovah.

[3] For although we confess that in respect of order and rank the *principium*
of divinity is in the Father, yet we express abhorrence of the error which
says that the essence belongs to the Father alone, as though He were the
deifier of the Son.

[4] We are taught by Scripture that God is essentially one, and that therefore the essence both of the Son and of the Spirit is unbegotten. But in so
far as the Father is first in order, and has begotten His Wisdom from Himself,
He is rightly thought (as has just been said) to be the *principium* and source
of the whole Godhead. So God as a whole is unbegotten, and the Father is also
unbegotten in respect of His person.

ratione ordinis" (26).[1] "Nam et hac de causa Filium verum esse Deum asserit Ioannes, ne quis secundo deitatis gradu subsidere putet infra Patrem" (26).[2]

Why does Calvin, in spite of his expressed distaste for verbal sophistries and argumentation, twist and turn about in so lengthy an attempt to state the doctrine of the principium of the Father? It is because he, like his predecessors, believed that doctrine to be necessary to the maintenance of the unity of God. Two passages make this clear. "Atqui non observant, quamvis Dei nomen filio quoque sit commune, tamen κατ᾿ἐ ξοχὴν patri interdum adscribi, quia fons est ac principium deitatis: idque ut notetur simplex essentiae unitas" (23).[3] "Atqui alibi ab hac calumnia se purgat, ubi patrem vocat principium totius deitatis, quia a nullo est: prudenter scilicet expendens specialiter patri ascribi Dei nomen, quod nisi ab ipso fiat initium, concipi nequeat simplex Dei unitas" (29).[4] *Simplex unitas.* The simplicity of unity! It is just this notion that unity is a simple thing that is exploded by the empirical evidence which is the basis of the doctrine of the Trinity. If we grasp the implications of this evidence, and think of the unity as unifying the Three Persons of whom none is afore or after another, we have no further need of the doctrine of the *principium* of the Father. The twists and turns and contradictions of Calvin and his predecessors are due to the fidelity with which they bear witness to the evidence while hampered by an unrevised and inconsistent notion of unity.

[1] . . . the name of God is not used indefinitely, but is used of the Father only in so far as He is the *principium* of Godhead, not by being the source of the essence, as the fanatics pretend, but in respect of order.

[2] For this reason John asserts that the Son is true God, and that He does not sit below the Father in a second rank of Godhead.

[3] They fail to notice that although the name of God is common to the Son also, yet it is sometimes applied *par excellence* to the Father, because He is the fount and *principium* of Godhead. This is in order to make plain the simple unity of the essence.

[4] Elsewhere he clears himself of this accusation by calling the Father the *principium* of the whole Godhead, because He is from none. Wisely to be sure does he use the name of God especially of the Father, because if all did not begin from Him it would be impossible to conceive the simple unity of God.

(v)

As we now look back over the whole development of the doctrine of the Trinity, there emerges a story of a definite and consistent pattern. It does not begin with any intellectual formulation of doctrine, but with the self-revelation of God given in the form of mighty acts to which the Bible bears witness. Adopted to share in the sonship of Christ, Christian theologians seek by rational reflection to grasp and expound the doctrine of God entailed by the empirical facts of His self-revelation. This means philosophical thinking, and philosophical thinking is the attempt to order empirical evidence in accordance with the canons of rational thought. But we human thinkers are not by nature endowed with infallible knowledge of what is and what is not rational. We may presuppose with the absolute idealists that "the rational is the real," but we may have to correct our idea of what is rational in the light of what is empirically given as real.

The empirical evidence of God's self-revelation in Christ required a revision of the accepted idea of unity. That the ultimate unity of God must be a "simple" unity, of what I have called the mathematical type, was a quasi-axiomatic presupposition of philosophical thought. There was thus created a situation analogous to that produced in the scientific world by the alleged discovery of black swans. One of three things had to happen: (a) The evidence of the alleged revelation might be called in question. (b) An attempt might be made to reconcile the evidence with the existing idea of unity. (c) The idea of unity might be revised in the light of the evidence.

It is my contention in these lectures that the third of these ways is the one that reason must take. But this has required so radical a revolution in ways of thinking that it is not surprising that it should have taken nearly two thousand years for the astounding evidence to have taught its lesson to the human mind. It is not surprising, therefore, that the classical theologians should have found it necessary to follow the second of these three ways.

Of the three whom I have tried to discuss to-day, Calvin has suffered least from the inevitable contradiction between the evidence and the idea of unity. This is because he was more content than the others to confine himself to setting forth the evidence, leaving aside the philosophical problems involved. By the use of various analogies St. Augustine made strenuous efforts to reconcile the evidence with the idea of unity, but in the end he had to confess himself beaten. St. Thomas achieved an apparent reconciliation in a form of words which referred to abstractions rather than to the living realities with which he had to deal. It is not by their success in reconciliation, but by their failure, that they bear witness to the truth.

For the truth surely is that true unity exists only in God. We must not use our own notions to prescribe to Him what the nature of His unity must be; we must be content to learn its nature by scrutinising the evidences that He gives us, and in the light of them must criticise, not only our own imperfect actual unities, but our idea of unity itself. By the honest intellectual labours of St. Augustine, St. Thomas and Calvin, by their refusal to deny the evidence in order to secure their end, God was revealing the necessity of the change and preparing the way for it. By the labours of post-renaissance scientists He has familiarised our minds with the idea of internally constitutive unities, and thus opened them to receive a fuller grasp of His revelation of Himself. If we are to be true successors of the classical theologians, we must try to think as honestly in the terms of the thought of to-day as they did in those of their time.

TRINITARIAN RELIGION

I HAVE now to the best of my ability set forth what the doctrine of the Trinity is, have given an account of its origin and development, and have indicated its relation to that inquiry into the nature of the universe which is the task of philosophy. In this last lecture I am going first to speak of its place in the practice of the Christian religion and then to say something about its implications for our thought about certain matters of practical as well as theoretical importance.

(i)

We saw in my second lecture that the doctrine of the Trinity is the statement of the doctrine of God implied by the Christian life, and that the Christian life was a new thing brought into the history of this world by Jesus Christ as He took His followers to share in His divine sonship and reproduced in them that way of life which had been His upon earth. Trinitarian theology is thus the interpretation of trinitarian religion. Religion and theology act and react upon each other. We do not really believe the creed, we only pay it lip-service, so long as it makes no difference to the way we worship and live. Conversely, the theology has no meaning for us unless it interprets our living religion.

If I am not mistaken, the doctrine of the Trinity suffers more than other central doctrines of the Christian creed from not being thus closely related to the practice of the Christian religion. This need not be so. Dr. Albert Mansbridge, for example, in his autobiography *The Trodden Road*, has written:

"This is the Christian faith revealed to me by those who have borne witness to it, and responded to by me in the power of my own spirit. It is mysterious, but the doctrine of the Trinity in Unity of God meets the needs of human nature—God above, God incarnate, God inspiring. The whole being vibrates to its truth. Those who accept, or who are proceeding to the acceptance of its truth, are in the blessed company of all faithful people, and are immunised from capture by the spirits of evil—Satan and his angels—although they may be sore let and hindered, even injured, in their bodies and minds."[1]

That is well said. But how many Christians to-day, when trying to speak of the faith by which they live, would select the doctrine of the Trinity as that to whose truth their whole being vibrates? How many laymen would not rather regard it as an unintelligible metaphysical doctrine which orthodoxy requires them to profess, but which has no direct relevance to their life or their prayers? How many clergy, as Trinity Sunday draws near, groan within themselves at the thought that it will be their duty to try to expound this dry and abstract doctrine to congregations for whom they anticipate that it will have but little interest? It will indeed be of little interest so long as for the preacher it is a dry and abstract doctrine, so long as for the congregation the sermon is not an interpretation of the religion which its members are practising.

Our efforts to teach the doctrine will always, I am convinced, be futile so long as we try to teach it as an intellectual truth without having prepared the ground by teaching our hearers to live a trinitarian religion. Only when we are speaking to men and women who are living trinitarian lives shall we be able, by "speaking to their condition," to kindle their interest in our exposition of the doctrine. Our first task, therefore, must be to consider how to teach trinitarian religion, how to initiate our congregations into the trinitarian way of life.

What is needed in the first instance is not so much a matter of the intellect as of the imagination, practice in the maintaining of a certain attitude towards life. In my second lecture I referred to the experience of many a

[1] P. 224.

M

parish priest who has known members of his flock fall away
to find their spiritual home in some sect which teaches
them to live as those who are seeking to express the divine
spark within them. Often, in such cases, they greet one
with a new light in their eyes, as men and women who have
found the religion that really grips and helps them. I then
suggested that the reason of their falling away may be that
they go to seek the help they need in the home of false
theology because it has not been offered to them in the
home of true.[1]

This suggests the starting-point. We may begin by
practising ourselves, and teaching and encouraging others
to practise themselves, in living as men and women who have
been adopted to share in Jesus Christ's relationship to
the Father in Heaven and to the Father's world, in the
Spirit. The formula for the Christian life is seeking, finding
and doing the Father's will in the Father's world with the
companionship of the Son by the guidance and strength
of the Spirit. That is the meaning of our membership of
the Church. This adoption was not of our own doing. It
was the act of God, who reached out through His Church
and baptized us into the fellowship. Just as in virtue of
our physical birth many things are true of us of which
we are quite unaware, and we grow in grasping what is
already true of us by growing in the life which that birth
has given us, so it is with our re-birth through water and
the Spirit. The Church in its teaching can tell me about
this act of God, about "my Baptism; wherein I was made
a member of Christ, the child of God, and an inheritor
of the kingdom of heaven." I have to make that truth my
own by practising myself in living by it, until the lesson
which was taught to my intellect takes possession of my
whole being and becomes, as we might say, my second
nature. I must cure myself of any tendency I may have
to live as though I were myself the self-contained centre
of my world, seeking to reconcile my earthly interests with
my duty to the God who is a mysterious threeness in oneness

[1] Above, p. 56.

above the skies. I must practise myself in substituting
for this the attitude of one who is trying by the guidance
of the Spirit to see the world as Christ sees it, that is, to
see it as our heavenly Father's world, in which our Father's
work is waiting to be found and done by those whose eyes
are opened to find it.

The best place to begin to practise this is in our prayers.
As we kneel to pray, we pause to recollect who we are and
what we are doing. Moved by the Holy Spirit we are coming
into the presence of our heavenly Father, brought in by
the Lord Jesus whom we adore and worship as He takes
us by the hand and presents us to our Father. We have
turned aside out of the world. But as "we offer ourselves, our
souls and bodies," we bring with us all our worldly interests,
for they are His interests—or should be. We offer our sins
that they may be forgiven; we offer the interests He cannot
share that He may wean us from them; we offer our thanks
for the victories and joys that He has given us, our petitions
and intercessions for all those people, causes and things
with which He wills us to be concerned. And as we rise
to return to our life and work in the world, we look out in
our mind's eye beyond the wall of the room or church
where we may be, we look out into all the world around
as those who are being sent forth, united with Christ and
enlightened by the Spirit, in order that we may share God's
joy in all that is good and true and beautiful, His grief
at all that is ugly and base and sinful, His labour in over-
coming the evil and building up the good.

There is nothing that sounds new in all this—and yet
to many of us it may be something quite new if we are
clearly and consciously realising our distinct relationship
to each Person of the Blessed Trinity. We may sometimes
address ourselves to the Spirit or to the Son as well as to
the Father, for each is a He, none is an it.[1] But we shall
not be confusedly addressing ourselves sometimes to One
and sometimes to Another without knowing when or
why. We shall speak to the Spirit as to the Lord who moves

[1] See Appendix VIII, p. 232.

and inspires us and unites us to the Son; we shall speak
to the Son as to our Redeemer who has taken us to share
in His sonship, in union with whom we are united to His
Father and may address Him as our Father. We shall be
entering into the meaning of that old English saying, "God
encompasseth us."

It has been said, I forget (if I ever knew) by whom, that
holding the true Christian doctrine of God is like walking
along a razor's edge, carefully avoiding slipping off into
the error of tritheism on the one side or into that of unitarianism on the other. This is a deplorable metaphor,
suggesting as it does that orthodox Christianity is a matter
of timidity and caution, forgetting that "God hath not
given us the spirit of fear; but of power, and of love, and
of a sound mind."[1] In the fourth lecture we remembered
that in this world of space and time we have direct experience of ultimate unities only in their multiplicity; our
experience of the multiplicity leads us to believe in the
unity by an act of rational faith.[2] It is one of the conditions
of our life here on earth that in our religion God makes
Himself known to us not directly in His unity, but in His
several Persons. It is better that we should enrich our
spiritual life by exploring to the full the possibilities of
our threefold relationship to Him than that for fear of
tritheism we should impoverish it and never enter fully
into the heritage of our Christian revelation. The more
progress we make as men who in their earthly thoughts
and words and deeds acknowledge the Trinity, the more
we shall find ourselves drawn on to worship the Unity.

Among other things, we need to remember a practical
application of the fact that in the case of the Holy Spirit
we speak of "possession" rather than "communion."[3]
We need to remember that there is no inconsistency in
believing both that it is often our duty to throw our whole
self into what we are doing, and also to believe that in our
doing of it we are guided and inspired by the Holy Spirit.
Let me explain this by giving an instance of the kind of

---

[1] 2 Tim. i. 7.   [2] See above, p. 108.   [3] See above, pp. 38 ff.

thing I mean. As I listen to sermons, I am impressed by the fact that over and over again preaching fails in effectiveness not because of defects in the preparation of the subject-matter, but because the preacher is not putting his whole self into the delivery of his message. One recognises that the material is good, well and carefully thought out and put together. But it fails to catch fire and kindle answering sparks in the congregation because its utterance gives the impression of being the performance of a routine duty. It has been a great help to me personally to realise that what I have to pray for to the Holy Spirit, as I kneel before entering the pulpit, is that for the next twenty minutes or so I may be enabled to forget everything except this message and this congregation, and to put my whole self into bringing it home to them. Then, when I am in the pulpit, the time for prayer is past, the time for action has come. So too it is with all our activities. The gift of the Spirit for which we need to pray is the gift of concentration. The fruit of the Spirit is to be found in our power to bring our whole mind to bear upon the matter in hand.

If in the ways I have indicated we exercise ourselves in the practice of trinitarian religion and in living trinitarian lives, and lead our congregations along these paths, then both we and they will be interested in the exploration and exposition of trinitarian theology, for it will be interpreting and illuminating the religion by which we live and the lives we are living. But if we try to think or speak of it except on the basis of such prayer and action, both we and they will find it a jejune weaving of abstractions, for we shall be thinking and speaking of truths which, though they may be true, have no apparent relevance either to religion or to life.

A further point must be mentioned, a point of intellectual as well as practical interest, before we leave this subject. I have spoken of our sonship of the Father and our possession by the Spirit as privileges of the Christian consequent upon his adoption into membership of the body of Christ. How are these related to the universal fatherhood of God, and the activity of the Spirit inspiring the prophets of the Old Testament, the philosophers of Greece, and many another man and woman outside the borders of the Christian Church?

Here, as elsewhere, we have suffered too much from *a priori* methods of argument. If we follow the empirical method to which I have tried to be faithful in these lectures, our scrutiny of the New Testament evidence compels us to recognise that the coming of Jesus Christ did initiate a way of life among men which was the life of a community sharing His sonship and His mode of possession by the spirit. This was a new thing in history. To the evidence for it which was given in the second lecture I need now only add that when the author of the Fourth Gospel wrote "The Holy Ghost was not yet given; because that Jesus was not yet glorified,"[1] he was stating simply and straightforwardly a historical fact. The new life, the life in the Spirit, had not begun for any of the disciples before Pentecost, any more than St. Paul's new life in the Spirit had begun before he was made a new creature by his conversion on the road to Damascus and his baptism by Ananias. It was through the one Lord, the one faith and the one baptism that Christians entered into their sonship of the one God and Father of us all.

But we go beyond the evidence, and are led astray by *a priori* considerations if we conclude from this that God is in no sense Father of all men, or that what look like signs of the working of the Holy Spirit elsewhere are not really what they appear to be. Whilst we can never cease to be grateful for the adoptive act of God whereby He has taken us to share in the sonship of Christ, as we grow in knowledge of Him through entering into the privilege of this special sonship, it should lead us to understand more deeply the fatherly care with which He watches over all His creation. And our inside knowledge, so to speak, of possession by the Spirit should make us increasingly able to recognise His working wherever it is to be seen,

[1] John vii. 39.

even in the lives of those who are quite unaware of or may
deny the source of their inspiration. The way in which
to formulate precisely the distinction between His mode
of exercising His fatherhood and inspiration in the two
cases may be beyond our power to express. As genuine
empiricists we may have to suspend our judgment about
that. We must be content to recognise the two modes,
denying neither the reality of both nor the distinction
between them.

(ii)

I pass now to another subject. Although in this world
we only meet the ultimate unities in their multiplicity,
and God is revealed to us in His Persons severally, yet
the divine unity is implied in this trinitarian revelation,
and in it there is revealed to us the pattern for all true
unity. As I said in my fourth lecture: "The Christian
doctrine of God . . . asserts that all the actual unities of our
earthly experience, from the unity of the hydrogen atom
to the unity of a work of art, of the human self, or of a
human society, are imperfect instances of what unity truly
is. . . . It is through the revelation of God in Christ that
we find the unity of God to be of such a kind as to cast light
upon all our lesser unities."[1] I want now to say something
of the practical implications of this with regard to the
unity of the human self, of political and international
unity, and of the unity of the Church.

For this purpose, the essence of the doctrine of the Trinity
is the doctrine that true unity is what I have called "internally
constitutive unity," that is to say, a unity which by the
intensity of its unifying power unifies distinct elements
in the whole. A unity can be deficient *as unity*, it can fail
to exhibit perfection of unity, in either or both of two ways:
either by failing to maintain its elements in their distinctness, or by failing in its power to unify them, or both.

Most of us know what it is to be torn in different directions by different elements in our personality; we know

[1] See above, p. 96.

what the psalmist meant when he wrote "With the pure thou shalt be pure, and with the froward thou shalt learn frowardness." In the early morning, it may be, we kneel before God's altar, we are caught up to share in the worship of angels and archangels. We see the tawdriness of the world, the hatefulness of our sins. It is inconceivable that we should ever again be interested in anything except the service of our Lord. Later in the morning we are in the company of scholars, or engaged in scholarly work, and feel, in the words of Harnack, that "if piety should suffer in the process well, there was and is a stronger interest than that of piety —namely, that of truth." The afternoon is occupied with administrative business, and as the fascination of it grips us we feel that the only life worth having would be one spent in ordering the affairs of men. A visit to an art gallery may bring out yet another self, and at tea we may meet a girl who makes us feel that all this world and the next would be well lost for love. As we relax among our friends after dinner, and vie with one another in telling tales and making remarks that will provoke laughter and appreciation, how dull and distant seems the heavenly worship of the early morning compared with the immediate reward of witty remarks, tinged though they may be with malice or impropriety. So, when the day is done, and we look back over it, and see this creature dragged hither and thither by this interest and that, we may well ask "Which of these things is the real I? Am I really anyone at all?"

Practising psychologists know well that this problem of unifying the heterogeneous elements in a man's make up is one of the central problems in human life. There are at least four false ways of dealing with it, ways which lead into their consulting rooms. There may be so complete a failure to unify that the result is the pathological state of divided personality. There may be a less complete and obvious failure, issuing in a sense of frustration at the apparent futility of life. There may be unification round a false or inadequate centre which produces in extreme forms monomaniacs, and in lesser degrees fanatics of various kinds. There may also be unification around the true centre achieved by suppressing or repressing elements which take their revenge in neurotic conditions.

But the true pattern of unity for men who are made in the image of God is one in which there is a place for all our different selves, so far as they are good selves, a unity in which each is to remain its own self in order that it may play its part in enriching the whole. The scholarly self with its passion for truth, the self which finds expression in efficient administration, the self which falls in love, the sociable self which enjoys good company, the self which is drawn by music, drama, painting or literature, all these and others, together with the self which aspires after the worship of heaven, have their value and their place.

We are, however, finite. Life is not long enough for each of us to give full expression to all his many selves. The love which is to unify them has therefore to take the form of recognising the value of those which cannot be indulged. They are not to be suppressed or repressed as evil; they are to be offered in willing surrender to God because He wills us to give precedence to some other self as the centre of the particular work that he has for us to do on earth. The man who is called to be a scholar must curb his desire to engage in manifold practical activities. If for a while he has to go and be a soldier, he must put aside his civilian pursuits. If he is called to work in which marriage is impossible, he must be continent with a good grace. But he will only do any of these things with a good grace if he maintains a gracious attitude towards the selves he cannot satisfy, if he avoids the temptation to seal up the doors of his mind against the interests he cannot pursue and lets a love for them fertilise and enrich, without distracting, the self which is to be the centre of his life.

This graciousness cannot be achieved by man except by the grace of God. Our natural pride makes us disinclined to acknowledge that we are finite beings who cannot foster all kinds of good; it inclines us to justify our self-limitation

by holding that we have chosen what is better and renounced what is worse. So long as we are trusting in our
own strength, our natural weakness requires us to buttress
our self-denial by building up a sentiment of reprobation
or scorn towards the interests we have renounced. Thus
the achievement of a false unity in our own lives makes
us incapable of taking a further step in graciousness, and
appreciating the contributions which others can make to
human life, just because they are different from our own.
It may be that they are called to put in the centre selves
which we have to put on one side. It may be that they can
express selves which we do not seem to have in us at all,
which may indeed even be uncongenial to our tastes.

For want of this graciousness we are a divided and dis-
tracted world. The business man despises the artist, and
the artist returns the scorn with interest. The scientist
thinks that the classic wastes his time among dead languages,
the classic thinks that the scientist is blind and deaf to the
higher ranges of human culture. White men, red men,
yellow men and black men dislike one another for not
being like themselves. Mutual appreciation between Jews
and Gentiles, between Nordics and Latins, between
Englishmen, Frenchmen, Germans, Slavs and Greeks,
Turks and Bulgars, is hard to come by. Within Christ's
Church protestants and catholics, Lutherans and Calvinists,
Thomists, Barthians, liberals and modernists have this
in common, that each wants to make the others as like to
himself as possible and finds it difficult to join in worship
otherwise.

It does not seem to be natural to men to appreciate other
kinds of people because they are different, to want them
to remain different while prospering equally. This well-
spring of mutual antagonism in our hearts is the mark
of the defacing of the image of God in us. The doctrine
of the Trinity reminds us that though the capacity to love
may not be in human nature as we have it, it is the essence
of God's nature. What is Christianity, if it be not the
message that God has entered into the history of this world

for the purpose of restoring the image, of re-making our human nature after the pattern of the divine, of changing us beyond our capacity to change ourselves?

Thus the doctrine of the Trinity is directly relevant to all our endeavours to promote the peace and unity of mankind. For the unity of different types of churchmanship within the Church, for the unity of different groups and classes within a nation, for the unity of different nations within the commonwealth of mankind, we need to look to the pattern of unity which has been shown us in the mount. We need to pray that the Church, by contemplating the unity of the divine Trinity, may find its own true unity and thus be able to lead the groups, classes, races and nations of mankind into that peace and unity which is God's will for them.

(iii)

When a Christian declares his belief in the resurrection of the body he is asserting, among other things, that in the life of the world to come each of us shall retain his individual personality, able to recognise and be recognised by his fellows. The connection between this belief and the doctrine of the Trinity was first brought home to me some fifteen years ago in conversation with an Indian philosopher. We were discussing the question of immortality, and he was maintaining the view that our destiny, if and when we shall ever be perfected, will be an absorption into the being of God in which we shall at last be rid of our individual self-consciousness. As the conversation proceeded, it became clear that this belief was implied by and deduced from his conception of the unity of God. Since for him the unity of God was the perfection of what I have earlier called the mathematical type of unity, a unity characterised by the absence of all internal distinctions, he had to believe that the incorporation of a man into that unity would involve the loss of his individual selfhood.

This conversation well illustrates a point that I made in my fourth lecture, that acceptance of the doctrine of the Trinity requires a revision of the idea of unity. The Indian's expectations with regard to the future life were not dictated by his religion but by his philosophy. Since the only reasonable form of theism is monotheism, he argued, and since unity is the complete absence of internal multiplicity, union with God must mean absorption into that undifferentiated unity. Given the premisses, the conclusion must follow. The only way to dispute the conclusion was to attack the premisses.

I have argued in these lectures that scrutiny of the empirical evidence provided by the historical facts of the Christian revelation necessitates a revision of that idea of unity as applied to God. I need not now go over that ground again. My present purpose is to exhibit the logical connection between the Christian doctrines of the Trinity and of immortality.

This connection is implied in the prayer ascribed to our Lord in St. John xvii. 20–24:

"Neither pray I for these alone, but for them also which shall believe on me through their word; that they may all be one; as thou, Father, art in me and I in Thee, that they also may be one in us: that the world may believe that thou has sent me. And the glory which Thou gavest me I have given them; that they may be one, even as we are one: I in them, and Thou in me, that they may be made perfect in one: and that the world may know that Thou hast sent me, and hast loved them as Thou has loved me. Father, I will that they also, whom Thou hast given me, be with me where I am; that they may behold my glory, which Thou has given me: for Thou lovedst me before the foundation of the world."

"That they may be one, even as we are one." These words point to the connection between the two doctrines. It is as members of Christ, sharing in the immortality that is His by nature and ours by adoption and grace, that we look forward to life beyond the grave. Because for us the unity of God, which is the archetype and pattern of all true unity, is a life in which the divine love eternally unites and yet keeps distinct the Persons of the Trinity, therefore we, when we are taken up to share in that life, may hope

:ach to be united with God, and with his fellows in God,
n a life of love which shall preserve eternally our personal
listinctness. Through countless ages, by means of our
)odily life in space and time, God our Creator has been
ashioning us into uniquely individualised personalities.[1]
This creation is no transient illusion, or mere appearance,
is certain monistic and pantheistic theologies would have
is think. God has given to this world such reality that He
ias Himself entered into its history, in order that He may
ulfil His creative purpose by redeeming the souls that He
s creating for union with Himself. And He Himself is such
:hat that creative purpose can be fulfilled, as He takes those
:reated souls to be one while remaining many in the unity
)f the Blessed Trinity.

(iv)

In the year 1928 a mild flutter was caused in religious
:ircles in the United States by a paper which was read before
the American Society for the Advancement of Science
ind reported sensationally in the daily press. Its author
proclaimed that discoveries in astrophysics had made it
impossible for intelligent men who were aware of the
progress of that science to believe any longer in the Christian
conception of God. God, if He exist, must be the God
of the whole universe. The Christian idea of God was
formed in days when men believed this earth to be the
centre of the universe and had, moreover, no realisation
of the vastness of interstellar space as it is now known to
us. Now that our eyes have been opened to see that this
planet is but an insignificant speck in a universe so vast as
to baffle our imagination, it is absurd to think that the
redemption of man from his sins could be the central
interest of its God.

In making this judgment Dr. Elmer Barnes doubtless
fell into the error of confusing physical with spiritual
greatness. But his utterance performed the useful service

[1] For an expansion of this sentence, see my *Grace of God in Faith and
Philosophy*, pp. 127 ff. = *Towards a Christian Philosophy*, pp. 173 ff.

of calling attention to a mistaken notion of what the Christian idea of God is, and the flutter it caused showed that the mistake was not unknown among Christians themselves. The importance of the incident for our purpose is that it is a mistake from which we should be saved by a right apprehension of the doctrine of the Trinity.

In his Gifford Lectures on *God and Personality* Dr. C. C. J. Webb argued, to my mind rightly, that the idea of personality implies a plurality of persons. We cannot think of any life as truly personal unless it be a life of intercourse between persons. If, therefore, we are to think of God as unipersonal, we must think of Him as eternally related to some object of His personal attention. For this reason the idea of creation as the eternal object of God's personal love and care has always been congenial to unitarian theology. But the doctrine of creation, in orthodox Christianity, asserts that the created universe is not necessary to the being of God. It is entirely dependent upon God for its being, but God has no need of it in order to be entirely Himself in all the full richness of His Godhead.

The doctrine of the Trinity implies that in the eternal being of God, quite apart from creation, there exist all the elements necessary for a fully personal life. It enables us to believe that the life of God is essentially and eternally personal without denying the implications of the doctrine of creation. Taken together, the doctrines of the Trinity and of creation expressly forbid us to assert that this whole vast universe, let alone this world and the life of man upon it, are the centre of interest in the life of God. Thus the criticism of Dr. Elmer Barnes was not relevant to the orthodox Christian doctrine of God but to a perversion of it.

But this does not imply any diminution in our estimate of God's love and care for this world and for man. It is here that we must avoid being led astray by any confusion between physical and spiritual greatness. When we are dealing with the latter, inability to be fully cognisant of and concerned with details is a mark, not of greatness, but of the reverse. The fact that the general manager of a large railway company cannot be intimately concerned with the personal life of every least employee is due to his human finiteness and limitation, not to his greatness. God does not need this universe in order to be Himself. But, having created it, He knows its every detail, and gives to each that love and care which it needs in order that His purpose for it may be fulfilled. The gospel of His revelation of Himself in Christ is the proclamation of the depth of His love for us men. "God so loved the world that He gave His only begotten Son." "What is man, that thou art mindful of him? . . . We see Jesus, who was made a little lower than the angels for the suffering of death, crowned with glory and honour; that he by the grace of God should taste death for every man. . . . For verily . . . he took on him the seed of Abraham."[1]

The doctrine of the Trinity thus enables us to keep the right proportion in our faith, to acknowledge with humble gratitude God's infinite love for man and also to adore Him in the glory and perfection of His own being:

"For God has other Words for other worlds,
But for this world, the Word of God is Christ."[2]

(v)

"For this world, the Word of God is Christ." In my first lecture we saw that this was a word spoken in deeds, God's revelation of Himself given in the incarnate life of Christ, the Word made flesh. In the next two lectures we tried to grasp the implications of that historical revelation for our thought about the eternal being of God. This was the life of Him whom we believe to have been God living as man, and the records of His human life show it to have been the life of finding and doing His heavenly Father's will through the Spirit. Those records go on to exhibit His followers as taken up to share with Him in that way of life, and we saw that the Church's doctrine of God

[1] John iii. 16; Heb. ii.
[2] H. E. Hamilton King: "The Sermon in the Hospital."

is formed by looking back on that historic life from within our adoptive sharing in it, trying to think away whatever was conditioned by His incarnate mode of existence in space and time, and asking what must be the nature of the God of this universe if that life of His and our sharing in it are taken as the key-features for its interpretation. We found this to be a doctrine of God according to which there is an eternal life of personal communion, Father and Son eternally giving themselves in responsive love to one another through the Spirit. Moreover, we found that according to the evidence the Spirit is to be thought of as personal in the same sense as the Father and the Son, as a He, not an it. This left us face to face with the question whether the doctrine of God required by God's revelation of Himself could be reconciled with the demand of our reason for a monotheistic faith.

In the fourth lecture I argued that this could be done, but only if we allow the empirical evidence to convince us of the reality of what I called an "internally constitutive unity," a unity which must in many ways remain mysterious to us so long as we are living and thinking in this world of time and space. I tried also to show that in the historical development of the doctrine of the Trinity the empirical evidence was driving the mind of the Church, in the teeth of its philosophical presuppositions, to assert, without realising what it was doing, this revised notion of unity. The fifth lecture was devoted to a discussion of the relation between the doctrine of the Trinity and philosophical inquiry. I maintained that the doctrine is not the offspring of *a priori* philosophical speculation, but claims philosophical attention as a doctrine arrived at by scrutinising the evidence in accordance with the canons of rational thought.

Having shown that the doctrine of a mysterious unity, uniting by the intensity of its unifying power, three Persons, each equally personal in the full sense of the word, was empirically necessary and philosophically respectable, I next asked, in the sixth lecture, whether this was the doctrine professed by the Christian Church down the ges. An examination of the teaching of St. Augustine, St. Thomas Aquinas and John Calvin led to the conclusion that this was the doctrine which basically they believed.

In other words, the first three lectures were designed to show that this doctrine had its origin not in philosophical speculation, but in the fidelity of the Christian community to the revelation it had received. The next two lectures argued that the doctrine thus formulated commends itself to our reason when we philosophise aright. The sixth lecture showed that the chief cause of our philosophising wrongly and going astray is the assumption that we know more than we do. Where St. Augustine, St. Thomas and Calvin were content to bear witness to the Christian revelation, they bore witness to the doctrine as I have tried to present it. Passages which obscured their true faith were due to arguing either on the assumption that they knew *priori* all about the nature of unity, or to the belief that the Bible had given them inside information concerning the interrelations of the Persons in the Godhead.

To-day we have come back from these intellectual pursuits to end this course of lectures where the doctrine took its origin, not in theology or philosophy, but in the practice of the Christian religion. We have seen that the doctrine of the Trinity, as the distinctively Christian doctrine of God, gives its character to the distinctively Christian way of worshipping and serving God; that it guides our paths by giving us the pattern unity for individual and social life; that it illuminates and deepens our hope of immortality; and that it enables us to see God and man in their right proportion as Creator and created.

Founded on fact, illuminating the mind, guiding the life, the doctrine of the Trinity draws forth our grateful adoration of the God who has thus blessed us in revealing Himself to us. How better, then, can I close than in the words of the traditional prayer of the Christian Church? Almighty and everlasting God, who hast given unto us thy servants grace by the confession of a true faith to acknowledge the glory of the eternal Trinity, and in the

power of the Divine Majesty to worship the Unity: We
beseech thee, that thou wouldest keep us steadfast in
this faith, and evermore defend us from all adversities
who livest and reignest, one God, world without end
Amen."

REASON AND REVELATION IN THE *SUMMA THEOLOGICA* AND THE *INSTITUTES*

IN I. 1, i St. Thomas distinguishes revealed theology from philosophy as being "scientia divinitus inspirata" and not the discovery of human reason. In I. 1, vii, 2 and ad 2 the content of revealed theology is apparently identified with the contents of the Bible, but in II². 5, iii and 10, xii this is expanded to include whatever the Church authoritatively teaches.

In I. 12, xiii ad 1, and II². 1, vi the trinitarian nature of God is stated to be a truth of revelation. The reason for this is given in I. 12, xi: so long as our souls are embodied they can only know by natural reason such truths as are mediated through the senses. The doctrine of the Trinity is a truth about God's essence and "per naturas rerum materialium divina essentia cognosci non potest."

From this it is clear that St. Thomas' teaching on revelation is bound up with his views on epistemology, so that to discuss it we must examine what he has to say about *intellectus* in I. 75–89 and about *fides* in II². 1–10.

Since vegetative, nutritive and sensitive life are found in the lower orders of creation, but not intellective, "propria . . . operatio hominis, inquantum est homo, est intelligere" (I. 76, i). St. Thomas accordingly often uses "intellect" or "intellective principle" as apparently equivalent to "soul." (Compare the title of I. 76 with that of its first article.) The difference seems to be that "soul and body" is a comparatively rough and ready phrase while a nicer discrimination distinguishes the specifically human intellective principle from its vegetative, nutritive and sensitive body. In either case St. Thomas is careful to deny that the two elements are to be thought of as having actual existence as separate entities. The intellective soul is the *forma substantialis* of the man; it is only as the bodily element is informed by the soul that there comes into being the actual existent, the man (I. 76, iv and vii ad 3; 77, vi).

There are here two difficulties in St. Thomas' account. (1) The apparent equivalence of soul with intellect requires the nutritive and sensitive elements to belong to the side of the body. But in I. 76, iii they are stated to belong to the side of the soul and in I. 77, v to both sides. (2) In I. 75, ii, iii a human soul is said to differ from that of an animal by the fact that it subsists. This subsistence, which is bound up with the thomist view of the soul's incorruptibility and immortality (I. 75, vi) is inconsistent with the denial of actual existence to the soul apart from the body. An attempt to reconcile these two views is made in I. 89, i.

On the second of these difficulties I should myself maintain that the doctrine of the natural immortality of the soul based on its alleged subsistence is untenable, if what are in question are the individual souls pf particular persons.[1] I should hold that an *individual* human soul only comes into actual existence as its content is provided by its bodily experiences.[2] St. Thomas seems to endorse this view in I. 79, ii ad 2, where what subsists anterior to the bodily experiences is merely potential. I should also hold that the equivocal position of the nutritive and sensitive elements in St. Thomas' thought is due to his attempting to deal with successive stages in a continuous process of growth by a logic which requires them to be placed in mutually exclusive classes. This being an impossible task, his inconsistency is not a fault but a virtue.

We may then ignore those passages which suggest that the human soul has an independent existence apart from and prior to its association with the body. So far as life in this world is concerned, St. Thomas is as clearly convinced as any modern evolutionary thinker that the human intellect needs the experiences provided by its vegetative, nutritive and sensitive life in the body in order to have any content. "Anima autem intellectiva . . . intantum quod non habet naturaliter sibi inditam notitiam veritatis, sicut angeli, sed oportet quod eam colligat ex rebus divisibilibus per viam sensus. . . . Unde oportuit quod anima intellectiva non solum haberet virtutem intelligendi, sed etiam virtutem sentiendi. Actio autem sensus non fit sine corporeo instrumento. Oportuit igitur animam intellectivam tali corpori uniri quod possit esse conveniens organum sensus" (I. 76, v). "Non enim potest dici, quod anima intellectiva corpori uniatur propter corpus; quia nec forma est propter materiam, nec motor propter mobile, sed potius e converso. Maxime autem videtur corpus esse necessarium animae intellectivae ad ejus propriam operationem, quae est intelligere, quia secundum esse suum a

---

[1] See *e.g.* the criticism of this doctrine in John Baillie: *And the Life Everlasting* (O.U.P., 1934).

[2] See my contribution to Rawlinson: *Essays on the Trinity and the Incarnation*, pp. 367 ff., and my *Grace of God in Faith and Philosophy*, pp. 127 ff. = *Towards a Christian Philosophy*, pp. 173 ff.

corpore non dependet. Si autem anima species intelligibiles secundum suam naturam apta nata esset recipere per influentiam aliquorum separatorum principiorum tantum, et non acciperet eas ex sensibus, non indigeret corpore ad intelligendum: unde frustra corpori uniretur" (I. 84, iv; cp. vii, viii). Hence in this life we cannot know immaterial things directly or completely, but only in so far as they can be apprehended in and through what is material (I. 88).

The intellect is both passive and active. By "passive" is meant that until it receives sense impressions it is a *tabula rasa*, devoid of all content. But in its reception of these impressions it is by no means a wholly passive *tabula rasa*; the senses passively receive their physical stimuli, but these are grasped by the intellect as *phantasmata intelligibilia*, and this grasping is an *activity* of the intellect. "Quia phantasmata non sufficiunt immutare intellectum possibilem, sed oportet quod fiant intelligibilia actu per intellectum agentem, non potest dici quod sensibilis cognitio sit totalis et perfecta causa intellectualis cognitionis, sed magis quodammodo est materia causae" (I. 84, vi). I take it that what St. Thomas is here saying is that hunger, for example, as felt by a man who knows he is feeling hungry is something more than hunger as felt by an animal; it is *intelligibly* felt, *i.e.* it is an intelligible phantasm, and owes this to the fact that the intellect is active in the experience of feeling. This intelligible awareness of the feeling as being a feeling of hunger shows that through the phantasm grasped in the particular sense-experience the intellect "abstracts" the species to which the particular experience belongs (I. 85, i). The species, however, is not an actually existent thing, and so is not the object of the knowledge; it is the instrument whereby the intellect recognises the sense-object for what it really is. Only in the secondary stage of reflecting upon its own activity in perception does the intellect perceive the existence in itself of the phantasmata and species whereby it has been able to recognise the sense-objects for what they are. The sense-objects, recognised as instances of species, are the primary objects of the intellect (I. 85, ii).

The fundamental activity of the intellect, therefore, is the recognition of an object as what it is: "Objectum . . . proprium intellectus est quidditas rei" (I. 85, vi). The discursive activity of reason, which moves step by step from one intellectual apprehension to another, is a mode of activity belonging to the same intellectual potency (I. 79, viii; II^2. 8, i ad 2). This process of reasoning works *componendo et dividendo* (I. 85, v), and what this means appears from the statement in I. 85, iv that the intellect cannot grasp more than one thing at a time unless it sees them as parts of a single whole. In a syllogism, for example, the intellect first grasps the major premiss, then grasps the minor premiss, then looks at the two together. If they are capable of being combined, *componendo* it sees in them the conclusion they entail, but if they are not, then *dividendo* it says "non liquet." All three acts of the intellect are acts of immediate apprehension; the process of reasoning is made up of a series of acts of immediate apprehension by the intellect.[1] We can now see why the *phantasmata* have to be introduced, why St. Thomas could not, after the manner of "naïve realism" regard the intellect as apprehending the sense object directly. The reason is that the objective world, which we are seeking to understand, remains unaffected by our inquiry; the process of reasoning is a process whereby we subjectively learn more about the reality which all the time has been what we discover it to be. What in this process we put together and set apart cannot be the objective reality itself. Nevertheless, it is this reality which we are observing. Hence the *phantasmata* are not (like the "impressions" and "ideas" of Locke and his successors) obstacles interposed by nature to our direct apprehension of objects; they presuppose such direct apprehension, for they are literally abstracted by the intellect from the apprehended object to be used as counters in the reasoning process whereby the understanding of the object (of its *quidditas*) may be increased.

How is it that the intellect is able thus to apprehend and understand the external world? The answer is that the prototypes (rationes aeternae) of all created things exist in the mind of God and that our intellects are illuminated by participation in the light of the divine mind and thus have the power to recognise things for what they are when we abstract the intelligible species from the sense data: "Ipsum enim lumen intellectuale, quod est in nobis, nihil est aliud quam quaedam participata similitudo luminis increati, in quo continentur rationes aeternae. . . . Quia tamen praeter lumen intellectuale in nobis exiguntur species intelligibiles a rebus acceptae ad scientiam de rebus materialibus habendam; ideo non per solam participationem rationum aeternarum de rebus materialibus notitiam

---

[1] This account of the syllogism is similar to that in J. Cook Wilson, *Statement and Inference*, vol. ii. p. 440. I do not know how far Professor Cook Wilson was familiar with the thought of St. Thomas; the similarity may be due to the fact that Aristotelian logic was the starting-point for both thinkers.

habemus, sicut platonici posuerunt quod sola idearum participatio
sufficit ad scientiam habendam" (I. 84, v). It is important to keep
in view both sides of this balanced statement: in his earthly life
man cannot know the *aeternae rationes* directly, he can only know
them in the impressions made by their material embodiment on
his senses (I. 84, iv, vii, viii); but when he receives these impressions
he can recognise the objects for what they are through the God-
given illumination of the intellect. The *aeternae rationes* do not,
like Plato's ideas, have any substantial existence of their own; they
are the adjectival qualities of created things.

Although sense objects are the only things we can know, we can
argue from them to the existence of God (I. 2). What we immediately
apprehend in this case is not God but the necessitation of God's
existence. But since the argument implies that He must be a cause
adequate to His effects, it implies certain qualities in Him, such
as simplicity, perfection, infinity. Thus we can be said by the reason
to know some things *about* God. But other things, *e.g.* the Trinity
and the Incarnation, can only be known by revelation (I. 12, xiii;
II^2. 1, v, vi). Still, in every case the knowing is the activity of the
same reason or intellect, which as a potency is capable both of
the "inferior" knowledge of sensible objects and of the "superior"
knowledge of things eternal. "Unde una et eadem potentia rationis
est ratio superior et inferior, sed distinguuntur, secundum Augus-
tinum, per officia actuum, et secundum diversos habitus" (I. 79, ix).

We now turn to the treatment of faith in II^2. 1–10. In II^2. 1, iii
faith is defined as "virtus perficiens intellectum," and in 8, viii ad 2
certitude of faith is the fruit of the gift of intellect: intellect and
faith mutually interact, there cannot be the certitude of faith without
the prior gift of intellect, but the intellect is only perfected through
the virtue of faith. The object of faith is *veritas prima, i.e.* God (1, i).
God, being both Truth and Goodness, is the object of both intellect
and will; hence faith is a virtue of the will as well as of the intellect,
and a distinction is drawn between *fides informis* and *fides formata*.
Faith is "formed" by love, but this only applies to the will side of
the virtue; on the intellectual side there is no difference between
formed and unformed faith (4, iv), and so the distinction is of no
importance for our present purpose.

But on the purely intellectual side there is also involved an element
of will, for in 2, i St. Thomas says that believing is the giving of
assent in a process of deliberation, faith is an act of the intellect
determined by the will. This repeats the statement made in I. 111, i

where he speaks of "a habit of the intellect whereby it is disposed to obey the will which strives towards divine truth" (see also II². 2, ii; 4, ii). This does not mean, however, that we may choose our beliefs without proper intellectual grounds for them: the heretic is condemned because "quae vult tenet et quae non vult non tenet" (II². 5, iii), and in order to have faith a man must have credible things presented to his mind in such a way as to bring conviction (I. 111, i ad 1; II². 2, ix ad 3). The act of will involved would therefore seem to be that whereby the conscientious scholar is resolute to accept the objective facts even if they conflict with his own theories, and this would seem to be the meaning of the statement that a man should accept matters of faith not on grounds of human reason but of divine authority (II². 2, i, x).

Faith is only faith when what is believed is true (II², 1, iii; 4, v), and when a man has such faith he has a knowledge which is absolutely certain (1, iv; 2, iv) although subjectively he may not always feel this certainty (I. 1, v ad 1; II². 4, viii). This faith is necessary to salvation because "ultima beatitudo hominis consistit in quadam supernaturali Dei visione" (II². 2, iii, vii).

Faith would thus seem to be the effect produced in man by the divine illumination of the intellect, as described in I. 1, iv; 84, v; 79, ix. So far there is nothing to prove that St. Thomas is doing more than giving a Christian account of certain empirical facts about the working of the human mind. The fundamental activity of the mind is the recognition of truth presented to it, and all discursive reasoning is a series of such immediate apprehensions. But men differ in their opinions; how then are we to distinguish true apprehensions from false opinions? In the last resort, there is no criterion that can be applied; the insight or intuition which grasps the truth is an ultimate and unique kind of experience, irreducible to and inexplicable in terms of anything other than itself. It comes through a resolute perseverance in determination to seek the truth and to accept nothing less, whatever may be the effect on one's interests, tastes, desires or theories, and when it comes it comes with a certainty which is absolute. These being the observed facts of human experience, St. Thomas gives a Christian interpretation of them. What makes the pursuit of truth worth while is that apprehension of truth is apprehension of God; the apparently incalculable manner in which this man "hits upon" a truth and that man does not show that such insight or intuition is a gift of God's free grace, given as and where He wills (cp. II².

6, 8, 9). In all this the divine assistance is regarded as illuminating the rational intellect and enabling it to apprehend both sensible objects and things eternal. Moreover, in a passage anticipatory of Hume and his successors, the faith which gives certain knowledge is said to be concerned with hypothetical statements about standing relations, not with matters of empirical fact (II². 1, iii ad 4). There is nothing which requires the conception of revelation as the provision of information embodied in propositions. The teaching so far considered is consistent with the view contained in my lecture, both as regards the divine assistance of the one and only mode of working of the human intellect, and of the connection of faith (=true belief) with "saving faith."

But when we turn to consider the nature of the *credibilia* we find that these are identified with the contents of the Bible and the teaching of the Church (II². 2, v; 5, iii), and the act of will involved in faith is readiness to accept whatever is contained in the Bible or taught by the Church, whether one knows what this is or not. Certain cardinal doctrines must be explicitly accepted, but for the rest it is enough to give, as it were, a "blank cheque" to the Bible and the Church.

Why does St. Thomas hold this? Three suggestions "may be made.

(i) "Faith" is admittedly not the same thing as knowledge"; its object cannot be said to be "known" in the same sense in which that word is rightly used of the normal activity of the human mind. We do not say we "believe" that water finds its own level, or that the angles of a triangle are equal to two right angles. "Nec fides nec opinio potest esse de ipsis visis aut secundum sensum aut secundum intellectum"; "Non autem est possibile quod idem ab eodem sit visum et creditum" (II². 1, iv, v; cp. II². 8, ii). But theology is by definition concerned with matters unverifiable either by empirical observation or by logical deduction from first principles, for while we are in the flesh we can only have such knowledge as comes through the senses, and "per naturas rerum materialium divina essentia cognosci non potest" (I. 12, xi). St. Thomas sees clearly that the question is not that of possible "mystical" revelations through dreams and visions (cp. I. 12, xi; 86, iv ad 2). It concerns that knowledge of God and heavenly things which man does receive in his one and only intellect (I. 79, ix). Now for St. Thomas the embodied intellect of man on earth can only know such realities as are apprehended through sense perception, and the subject-matter of revelation belongs *ex hypothesi* to another sphere. His epistemology therefore necessitated the postulation of some other avenue into the intellect for that revealed knowledge of God and heavenly things which man has by faith.

(ii) However much a man might be subjectively uncertain in matters of faith (I. 1, v ad 1; II². 4, viii), there could be no doubt that objectively anything revealed by God to the intellect and properly apprehended must provide the most certain kind of knowledge conceivable (I. 1, v; II². 1, iv; 2, iv). Now according to St. Thomas' epistemology certain knowledge could never be obtained about matters of empirical fact (II². 1, iii ad 4). But among the objects of Christian faith are such empirical facts as historical events in the earthly life of Christ. Hence again there was need to postulate some abnormal avenue into the human mind for the facts of faith.

(iii) If I am right in the lecture (p. 20) in assuming that in early Christian thought the Bible succeeded to the place held by mythology in the Greek philosophical tradition, then St. Thomas' acceptance of the Bible as containing divine revelation expressed in propositions needs no further explanation. It provided what his epistemology required, and gave it in the form in which he would naturally expect it to come. And it was in accordance with his thought to regard the Church corporately as the authorised exponent of the Bible, so that its formulated doctrines were *credenda* equally with the contents of the Bible. It is interesting to notice here that the creeds, unlike the Bible, may be revised to meet the needs of different ages, the Church corporate exercising its authority to do this through the Pope: "Prohibitio et sententia synodi se extendit ad privatas personas, quarum non est determinare de fide; non enim per hujusmodi sententiam synodi generalis ablata est potestas sequenti synodo novam editionem symboli facere, non quidem aliam fidem continentem sed eamdem magis expositam. Sic enim quaelibet synodus observavit, ut sequens synodus aliquid exponeret supra id quod praecedens synodus exposuerat, propter necessitatem alicujus haeresis insurgentis. Unde pertinet ad summum pontificem, cujus auctoritate synodus congregatur, et ejus sententia confirmatur" (II². 1, x ad 2).

For St. Thomas this way of accepting the Bible was not obscurantism. As we have seen, the expectation that religious truths would be communicated to men in the form of ready-made propositions was the common expectation of the world of his day, of the learned world as well as the uneducated. Christianity excelled over other religions in rationality because its "mythology" was history, and since the divine doctrines were *miraculis confirmatae*, "ille qui credit habet sufficiens inductivum ad credendum" (II². 2, ix ad 3). To believe "non propter rationem humanam sed propter auctoritatem divinam" was to conform one's theories to objectively given truth, and not *vice versa*—a sound principle in every inquiry in every age.

Although St. Thomas never freed himself from the notion that divine revelation is to be expected and received in the form of propositions, there is one passage which perhaps looks towards the view maintained in these lectures. In explaining why the propositions of the Old Testament were given to men by angels and those of the New directly by Christ Himself, he says "conveniens fuit ut lex perfecta novi Testamenti daretur immediate per ipsum Deum hominem factum" (II¹. 98, iii). This surely prepares the way for the view that primarily the revelation is given in the *activity* of God, in deeds rather than words, of which the climax was the earthly life of the Word made flesh.

The relevant passage in the *Institutes* (1559) is Book I, Chapters i–x. There is here nothing corresponding to the epistemological analysis in the *Summa*. The statement at the end of v. 9 that our human minds are better able to see the goodness of God in His works than by contemplating Him directly is in keeping with St. Thomas' thought, but Calvin is not interested in tracing this to the connection between the intellect and the senses, nor does he find in it the ground of our need of revelation. For him that need springs from our incapacity to read aright the witness which creation bears to its Creator.

It may be well first to notice some points of agreement between our two authors. For Calvin, as for St. Thomas, "ultimus beatae vitae finis in Dei cognitione positus est" (v. 1). Again, faith gives a knowledge of God which has a certainty otherwise lacking: "Hinc tamen apparet, si naturaliter tantum edocti sunt homines, nihil certum, vel solidum, vel distinctum tenere" (v. 12). This being so, acceptance of the divine revelation is the subordination of one's theories to the objectively given truth: "Pia mens Deum non quemlibet sibi somniat, sed unicum et verum duntaxat intuetur: neque illi quodcunque visum fuerit affingit, sed talem habere contenta est qualem se manifestat ipse, summaque diligentia semper cavet, ne audaci temeritate ultra voluntatem eius egressa perperam vagetur" (ii. 2). And the whole Bible is to be accepted entire (vii. 2).

But Calvin does not, like St. Thomas, equate the contents of the Bible with the teaching of the Church. The Bible, he says, needs no credentials beyond its own inherent self-evidence. One might as well demand some external authority to tell us how to discern between light and dark or black and white or sweet and bitter (vii. 2). To give the Church the right to determine what in the Bible is to be accepted and what not is to submit the eternal truth of God to the judgment of men (vii. 1). At first sight this seems to imply that the individual Christian will be a better judge than the Church corporately, but in vii. 3 he refers to an occasion on which St. Augustine "universale ecclesiae iudicium profert, in quo adversariis erat superior." His meaning becomes clear in vii. 4, 5. The Bible explains itself to those who have faith through the indwelling Spirit, and this gift of the Spirit is not given to the Church corporately but to certain chosen persons: "Singulari privilegio illic Deus solos electos dignatur, quos a toto humano genere discernit." Thus Calvin agrees with St. Thomas that the meaning of Scripture is revealed only to those who have received from God the gift of faith; he differs from him in not regarding the organised visible Church as the Spirit-bearing body authorised officially to promulgate the inspired interpretation of God's word.

But for our purpose the chief difference between the two theologians is on the relation between the gift of faith and human reason. Whereas for St. Thomas reason can discover certain truths, including certain truths about God revealed in nature, for Calvin human reason apart from faith can have no such certain knowledge at all. The Bible is like a pair of spectacles which enables a man to read the revelation in nature (vi. 1). Without it, man's idea of God is not merely imperfect, it is hopelessly wrong (v. 11, 12). He worships the self-spun products of his own corrupt imagination (iv. 1; v. 13). "Neque Paulus (Rom. i. 19), ubi tradit patefieri quod cognoscendum est de Deo ex mundi creatione, talem manifestationem designat quae hominum perspicacia comprehendatur: quin potius eam ostendit non ultra procedere nisi ut reddantur inexcusabiles" (v. 14).

Nevertheless Calvin is unable to avoid the use of language inconsistent with this position. I. i. 1 certainly suggests that we can to some extent realise our imperfections even before their full extent is revealed by being seen in the light of God. In ii. 1 all truth and goodness come from God: "nusquam, vel sapientiae ac lucis, vel justitiae, vel potentiae, vel rectitudinis, vel sincerae veritatis gutta reperietur quae non ab ipso fluat, et cuius ipse non sit causa." That this does not simply apply to the virtues of the faithful seems clear from II. ii. 15: "Si unicum veritatis fontem Dei spiritum esse eputamus, veritatem ipsam neque respuemus, neque contemnemus, ubicunque apparebit, nisi velimus in spiritum Dei contumeliosi esse." Again, Calvin commends his sceptical view of human reason by arguments which depend on the validity of our reasoning process, that process which we have seen to imply our capacity to make a series of apprehensions of truth. The statement at the end of viii. 13: "inepte faciunt qui probari volunt infidelibus, Scripturam esse verbum Dei" seems inconsistent with the passage in viii. 11 where "isti nasuti censores" are to be convinced by being made to listen to the reading of St. John's Gospel. Moreover, the position itself can only be maintained by thoroughly bad arguments. The simile of the eye and the sun in i. 2 could only produce Calvin's conclusion by a *non sequitur*; the treatment of human ideas of truth, goodness and God as self-generated (as in iv. 1 and v. 13) is a *petitio principii*; and if all our judgments and achievements are relative, it is as erroneous to dismiss them as absolutely worthless as to mistake them for things of absolute worth.

Calvin, like St. Thomas, regarded the Bible as containing a revelation given in the form of propositions, to be accepted as such. The eyes of its authors were opened to enable them to understand the witness of nature to its Creator: "Hunc ordinem ab initio ergo ecclesiam suam tenuit, ut praeter communia illa documenta verbum quoque adhiberet. . . . Sive autem per oracula et visiones patribus innotuit Deus, sive hominum opera et ministerio quod deinde per manus posteris traderent, indubium tamen est insculptam fuisse eorum cordibus firmam doctrinae certitudinem, ut persuasi essent atque intelligerent, a Deo profectum esse quod didicerant" (vi. 1, 2). To enable succeeding generations to share in their illumination God willed these "oracula quae deposuerat apud Patres" to be written down. In these days there is no longer such inspiration as was given to those Fathers, and so we must simply accept what they have written. "Sed quoniam non quotidiana e coelis redduntur oracula, et Scripturae solae exstant quibus visum est Domino suam perpetuae memoriae veritatem consecrare: non alio iure plenam apud fideles auctoritatem obtinent, quam ubi statuunt e coelo fluxisse, ac si vivae ipsae Dei voces illic exaudirentur" (vii. 1). Thus the faith, which in v. 14 is said to open man's eyes to recognise God's revelation of Himself, works differently in the authors of the Bible and in their later readers. It enabled the former to recognise the revelation directly; the latter must first accept their writings and only then are enabled to grasp the revelation.

I have argued in my first lecture that what actually happens is that by faith our eyes are opened to see what the biblical writers saw, but that this does not mean that we shall accept as literally true every proposition they penned. Since *omnis determinatio est negatio*, we can agree with Calvin when he speaks of the Bible as a fence to exclude error (vi. 2). We can also agree with him in all that he says positively in vi. 2 and elsewhere about the necessity of the Bible to teach us to know the true God and of our redemption in Christ. But these positive assertions can be, and should be, disentangled both from the notion that the Bible consists of indistinguishably inerrant propositions, and from the exaggerated negative assertion that all other ideas of God have absolutely no truth or value in them at all.

PSYCHOLOGICAL PREDISPOSITIONS TO BELIEF

WE start from the patent fact that the same evidence when considered by different minds often leads to the drawing of different conclusions. If, for example, we compare *Ecclesiastes* with the Sermon on the Mount, we find that the Preacher and our Lord gave to the same facts precisely opposite interpretations. To the Preacher the fact that one event happens alike to all was evidence that all is vanity and a striving after wind; to Jesus Christ it bore witness to the perfection of the love of God.[1]

The extent to which this is characteristic of human experience is a thing which we are often slow to grasp. The keen young Christian and the keen young communist are equally sure that they can present evidence which will demonstrate the truth of their creeds to all but the wilfully blind. The persistence of this illusion into middle age is a form of infantilism. It is a mark of the truly educated man to have formed the habit of assuming that those who disagree with him may be equally honest and intelligent as himself. For many of us this is one of those lessons which only time and experience can make us capable of learning. A certain form of the doctrine of existential judgments, and the popularity in some circles of the view that alleged intellectual difficulties in the way of Christian belief are always "smoke screens" concealing moral obliquity, are in opposite ways evidence that Sir Richard Livingstone is right in stressing our need of extended adult education.[2] The former takes the fact of disagreement to imply that there is no common objective truth open to the discovery of human reason; the latter assumes that personal consciousness of guilt is the only obstacle to all men seeing the truth alike.

Both of these extremes were avoided by the classical theologians when they ascribed the capacity to accept the Christian revelation to a direct gift of God. In itself this doctrine is simply an accurate description of the experience of the believing Christian. He is conscious that his eyes have been opened to see the truth, and that this has not been due to any merits of his own; it has, so to speak, just come to him. If others are to see it too, their eyes must be opened

[1] Eccles. ii. 15–17, vi. 8, 9, ix. 11; Matt. v. 44–8.
[2] See *The Future in Education* (Cambridge, 1941).

likewise. Why are they not? The rejection of the doctrine that this divine favour is distributed in accordance with human deserts is a rejection of the "smoke screen" theory, and the question has to be left open as one of the inscrutable mysteries of Providence.

I have argued in the lecture that this position is essentially sound, but needs revision at two points. The giving and withholding of this gift needs to be divorced from connection with the question of justification, and the apparent directness or immediacy of the gift needs to be considered in the light of the psychological antecedents of the persons concerned. On the former of these enough has been said in the lecture itself. But the latter must have some further attention.

It is surely the presupposition of all sane thought that truth exists to be discovered, that the mind of man is capable of discovering it, and that when discovered it will be found to be one and the same for all men. If this were not so, there would be no point in argument or discussion. Although as finite human beings we each approach the one common truth along the perspective dictated by his own past history, our aim in discussion and argument is so to explain to one another our diverse ways of looking at it that at last we may all come to understand how it is that it has appeared so differently to us from our different approaches. Such perfect understanding alone would provide knowledge according to the Aristotelian canon: ἐπίστασθαι δὲ οἰόμεθ' ἕκαστον ἁπλῶς ... ὅταν τήν τ' αἰτίαν οἰώμεθα γινώσκειν δι', ἣν τὸ πρᾶγμά ἐστιν ὅτι ἐκείνου αἰτία ἐστὶ, καὶ μὴ ἐνδέχεσθαι τοῦτ' ἄλλως ἔχειν.[1]

Objectivity of this kind is, as I have said elsewhere, the thinker's El Dorado.[2] Each seeks with the aid of his fellow thinkers to transcend his own subjective limitations. But it is only in a comparatively narrow range of objects of thought, when these are abstracted from the concrete whole of experienced reality, that we can attain this goal. There are demonstrable truths of mathematics, and in certain of the more exact sciences there are approaches to an equal degree of certainty. But in the studies which seek to deal with more concrete objects of thought, in biology, psychology, history, economics, sociology, theology and philosophy we are hindered by difficulties

---

[1] *Anal. Post.* 71 b.

[2] This is briefly summarising what I have argued at greater length in *Essays in Christian Philosophy*, XII. = *Towards a Christian Philosophy*, Chap. II. See also A. C. Ewing: *Reason and Intuition* (reprinted from Proceedings of the British Academy, Vol. xxvii.), London, 1941.

at both ends. Not only are the subject matters of our studies complicated and obscure, but we also find it more difficult to transcend our own subjective prejudices.

What is needed is to retain our faith in the existence of the common objective truth and the possibility of its discovery, and at the same time to keep our eyes open to our subjective liability to distorted vision. Certain tendencies in twentieth-century thought illustrate this. The war of 1914–1918 disrupted settled and orderly life throughout the civilised world, and especially on the continent of Europe. The disruption in the world of affairs had its counterpart in the world of thought. Philosophy and theology were affected no less than politics and economics. One may sum it up by saying that whereas before 1914 men were certain of the existence of the common objective truth but under-estimated their own liability to distorted vision, since 1919 there has spread over the world from the continent of Europe a tendency so to emphasise the subjective limitations of human thought as to destroy faith in its common object. In the political sphere the League of Nations was probably built on an insecure foundation because based on the assumption that nations could easily transcend their "existential" outlooks in obedience to the vision of a common good. Its breakdown has been hailed in some quarters as evidence that the idea of a common good was the unreal phantasy of a sentimentalised imagination. The assurance of scientists that they were discovering the true nature of the physical world has been disturbed by the question whether they do more than find the answers to sums of their own devising. The Hegelian idealists' confidence in the power of human thought to grasp reality has been succeeded by the assertion that metaphysics is nonsense. The evangelical Christian who was brought up to be at ease in Zion finds himself ill at ease among the worshippers of *Deus absconditus*.

In all this it is possible to see the influence of psychological predispositions on human thought. The beginning of the twentieth century was the ending of an unusually long period of comparative peace in the political sphere. The consequent sense of security both strengthened belief in a common good and a common truth and concealed the extent of existing disagreement concerning them. The widespread and profound sense of insecurity which has followed upon the breaking of that peace is what underlies the prevailing scepticism with regard to the power of human reason to discover any common good or truth. The lesson to be learned from these events is to correct the balance of our earlier outlook without falling over on the other side. This means that we must be more cautious in assuming that our views represent the whole truth, more ready to suspend judgment while, with the aid of our fellows, we try to look along as many perspectives as possible in search of an ultra-stereoscopic apprehension of reality. When, for example, we are told that the sufferings of a persecuted European church have opened its eyes to see the truth of God in ways not opened up to comfortable Anglican theologians, we must be eager to sit at the feet of martyrs and confessors and to learn from them what they have learned. But there are also lessons to be learned through the calmer vision of churches which have been spared the intenser conflict. Each experience both helps and hinders. It opens the eyes to some aspects of the truth and blinds them to others. If either despise the other, neither will be able to distinguish the truth from the error in its own vision. But by comparing their experience on the basis of a common act of faith in a common objective truth each can enter into the apprehension of the other, and by so doing correct its own errors and enrich its own store.

Reflection on the history of human thought in our own lifetime thus brings home to us the necessity of recognising the importance of the influence of psychological predispositions on our interpretation of evidence and our apprehension of truth. It is clear that they must be taken into account as factors predisposing towards or inhibiting from acceptance and understanding of the Christian revelation.

One may reasonably ask, for example, whether the widespread recrudescence of belief in God as a mysterious ("numinous") terrible Judge may not have such an origin. The reports of anthropologists, travellers and missionaries remind us how deep-seated in our psychological inheritance is fear of the terrible unknown background of human life.[1] In the history of mankind the revelation of God's love to the chosen people through the prophets and in Christ is a very recent episode. Moreover, that revelation makes its way into the human mind by way of conscious apprehension and acceptance. Sometimes the mind is so much under the control of inherited fears (of which it may be quite unconscious) that it simply cannot believe the good news to be true; preaching of the gospel addressed to the intellect has to be prepared for by influences

[1] See also E. Bevan: *Hellenism and Christianity* (London, 1921), p. 81, and A. N. Whitehead: *Science and the Modern World* (New York, 1925), p. 18.

affecting underlying levels of the self.[1] When the revelation is accepted, the believer has the task of training his whole self to live in accordance with the truth to which his mind has given its conscious assent, and often this will involve a struggle to avoid relapsing into the attitude of his earlier and lower self.[2] In times of great nervous and emotional strain we are always in danger of losing our most recently and consciously acquired psychological characteristics. If these have not become sufficiently deeply rooted in our innermost selves they may be stripped off, leaving the more primitive elements to come to the surface. Thus we may well ask whether certain "savage and inhuman theologies"[3] in vogue at the present time are not "rationalisations" of a psychological failure to maintain faith in the Christian gospel against the uprush of more primitive emotions.

On the other hand, it is probably true that a good deal of the liberal theology, both catholic and protestant, which was in vogue in the early years of this century was too easily at ease in Zion, that it lacked depth for want of having felt sufficiently deeply the fact of sin.

These various illustrations of the influence of psychological predispositions on human thinking help us to understand how it is that the same facts may be to one man evidence of the activity of the God whom Christians believe in and worship, while to another they bring no such conviction. They help us to understand how it is that the Christian believer must always thank God for the faith by which he has been enabled to receive His revelation, for this opening of his eyes has come to him through elements in his psychological constitution for which he is not responsible, has come as a gift. At the same time they forbid us to regard those who are less fortunate as thereby incurring God's condemnation. "Therefore

---

[1] Cp. Mr. C. S. Lewis on the function of rhetoric and poetry in *A Preface to Paradise Lost* (Oxford, 1942), chaps. viii, ix.

[2] Something of this kind may well have been involved in St. Peter's relapse into a refusal to eat with gentiles at Antioch (see Gal. ii. 11, 12). St. Paul suggests another motive, but in such cases motives are seldom single. And cp. the following passage from the late Bishop Gore's exposition of Romans viii. 1–11: " Unless we are continually practising ourselves in this conception of life, we find ourselves falling back again into the attitude of one standing over against God with God for his taskmaster. And that is the false and always ruinous idea." C. Gore: *St. Paul's Epistle to the Romans*, vol. i. (London, 1899), p. 282.

[3] The phrase is quoted from a leading article in *The Guardian*, No. 5054 (Oct. 16, 1942). See, too, my *The Lord's Prayer* (London, 1934), pp. 58–60.

judge nothing before the time, until the Lord come who both will bring to light the hidden things of darkness, and will make manifest the counsels of the hearts: and then shall every man have praise of God."[1]

Thus we are driven to seek for some other interpretation of God's purpose in allowing such variety of psychological predispositions, as I have tried to do in the lecture.

[1] 1 Cor. iv. 5.

THE DISTINCTION BETWEEN JUSTIFYING AND SAVING FAITH

THE use made of this distinction is not novel, though the terminology may be. In the following seventeenth-century passage, for example, "acceptance" and "perfection" correspond to my "justification" and "salvation." "I do not speak this, as if I would discourage a Heathen from doing the Best that he is able; or condemn those reasons upon which he proceedeth in his Vertuous Deeds; No, nor as if all this were necessary to the Acceptance of an Action. But to show how highly Christianity does ennoble the Soul of Man, how far more sublime its Principles are, and how far more perfect it makes his Actions: When they are what they may be: And withal to provoke Christians to a more Intelligent and lofty Practice of Christian Vertues, lest they differ not in their Morals from the better sort of Heathens. All these things are necessary to the perfection of an Action, though not to its Acceptance."[1]

Recent discussions of the underlying question are to be found in Kirk: *Ignorance, Faith and Conformity* (London, 1925), Chaps. II–V, and Karrer: *Religions of Mankind* (Eng. trans., Watkins, London, 1936), Chaps. XII, XIII.

Both writers are dealing with the question as it has been discussed by St. Thomas Aquinas and subsequent Roman Catholic theologians. The starting-point of the discussion was Heb. xi. 6: "He that cometh to God must believe that he is, and that he is a rewarder of them that seek after him." If this defines the minimum faith required in this life for a man to be on the road to Heaven, can the heathen or the atheist who honestly tries to live up to the best he knows be held to have the necessary qualification? Dr. Kirk regards the consensus of opinion as tending to answer "No." Fr. Karrer affirms that the best opinion undoubtedly answers "Yes," that the condemnation of justification by *fides late dicta* does not affect justification by obedience to conscience.

Dr. Kirk's account of the discussion illustrates admirably the inadequacy of the idea of revelation as given in propositions. Not only was the statement in Heb. xi. 6 taken as the premiss of the whole argument, but it was held to define justifying faith as con-

[1] Thomas Traherne: *Christian Ethics* (London, 1675), p. 112.

sisting in the acceptance of two propositions: that God is, and that He is a rewarder. The question was then put, Could a man be saved by "invincible ignorance" of these propositions? "Is invincible ignorance, that is to say, of the same efficacy as justifying faith? If so, it would appear at least that faith is not unique and absolutely necessary for salvation, and the distinctive character of Christianity is gone. . . . The Church wanted to maintain both—the unique content and the unique attitude—and not even compassion for the heathen would reconcile her to the surrender of either. The most that she would do was to reduce to a minimum—though by no means to a negligible minimum—the content of that faith which was essential to salvation. . . . The faith which was *necessary* for salvation was generally understood, therefore, to mean explicit acceptance of the existence of God and His remunerative character, and no more."[1]

The case is altered if the Christian's acceptance of revelation is regarded as the recognition in Jesus Christ of God in action rescuing His world from the powers of evil. This implies the recognition of sin as the root of evil, and thus affirms the prophetic proclamation of God as the Righteous One who looks primarily for righteousness in His worshippers. But if this be so, then the fundamental act of faith in God is for a man to try to do what he honestly believes to be right and to trust the Power behind the universe to support him in the effort. Thus the heathen or atheist who is trying to do what he honestly believes to be right is therein actually manifesting faith in the God made known to us in the biblical revelation. On this view of revelation there is no need to seek to determine the minimum content of intellectual belief which is required for justification; what is looked for is not some lowest common measure of propositional statement but the moral "set" of a man's life. By this reasoning, based on the thesis of my lecture, we arrive at the same position which Fr. Karrer reaches along different but converging lines, and which he regards as the true position of catholic theology.

On this understanding of revelation the uniqueness of Christianity derives from the once-for-all character of the divine activity. This is incompatible with "subjective" doctrines of the atonement of the Abelard-Rashdall type. But given belief in the atonement as an objective divine accomplishment, in virtue of which forgiveness is ready and waiting for penitent sinners, it is possible to regard its benefits as extending to all who are trying to do their moral best,

[1] Kirk, *op. cit.*, pp. 79, 81, 84.

and to regard them as justified through the death of Christ even though they may never have heard of Him, or may have found themselves unable honestly to accept what they have been told of Him.

This view also has biblical authority in the sense of being in accordance with the mind of Christ as revealed in the Gospels. He endorsed the Baptist's revival of the moral emphasis of the prophetic message. In Matt. v. 8, vi. 22 He commends the pure heart and the single eye. Mark iii. 5, 28–30; Matt. xv. 1–20; Luke xii. 57 show that what He looks for is genuine obedience to an unsophisticated conscience; Matt. xxi. 31–32 contrasts the publicans and harlots with the chief priests and elders as having been more honest in their attitude to the Baptist. The parable of the talents (Matt. xxv. 14 ff.; Luke xix. 12 ff.) commends the moral virtues of faithfulness, the teaching about the widow's mite and the shewbread (Mark xii. 42, ii. 23 ff.) and the prophecy of judgment in Matt. xxv. 31 ff. commends that of charity, and the reply to the rich young man (Matt. xix. 18, 19) omits from the list of necessary precepts the requirement of explicit faith in God.

It may be argued that all this evidence is irrelevant because Jesus was talking to Jews who already accepted the propositions that God is and is a rewarder of them that seek after Him. This argument attaches too much importance to what was an "inseparable accident" of His historical redemptive activity. He came to call the chosen people to a mission of service on behalf of mankind; He died and rose again to open the way to that service for those who responded to the call, whom He constituted the new Israel. He sent them forth to do in the world at large what He had done in the narrower circle of the chosen people: "As my Father hath sent me, even so send I you." "Go ye and make disciples of all nations."[1] What He had looked for among the Jews, they were to look for among the gentiles—the heart that was set upon doing right according to its best light. Any other view implies a repudiation of the prophetic teaching of the righteousness and love of God, the teaching in which the incarnate Lord found His inspiration and His key to the understanding of the Old Testament.

[1] John xx. 21; Matt. xxviii. 19.

FATHER THORNTON ON THE DISTINCTION BETWEEN THE RISEN LORD AND THE HOLY SPIRIT IN THE NEW TESTAMENT

BY a careful analysis of the relevant New Testament passages Fr. Thornton shows that their descriptions imply throughout a clear and consistent distinction between the Risen Lord and the Holy Spirit. The truth about the Christian life—whether it be the life of the individual Christian or of the Church—is that each is in process of growing into his (or its) true self. This true self is being given by God and received by man. It is indeed Christ Himself, in whom each man, and the whole Church, finds his (or its) true self. In this process the Spirit works within the creature disposing it to receive from above its true self which is Christ. To quote Fr. Thornton: "Both Christ and the Spirit dwell in the Christian soul, but not in the same way. Christ is the indwelling content of the Christian life. He is being 'formed' in us. . . . St. Paul nowhere says that the Spirit is formed in us, or that we are to be conformed to the image of the Spirit. . . . The indwelling of the Spirit involves the indwelling of Christ; consequently the indwelling of Christ is inseparable from the quickening. But the Spirit is never regarded as the *content* of the quickened life. He is the agent of revelation who brings the content of truth to the spirit of man; and by consequence we have the mind of Christ. . . . The Spirit is the quickening cause; and the indwelling of Christ is the effect of the quickening. . . . Christ is the objective ground of salvation; the Spirit is the effective cause of the new life in us." The scriptural references will be found on pp. 322 ff. of *The Incarnate Lord* (London. 1928), from which these quotations are taken.

THE MEANING OF *LOGOS* IN GREEK THOUGHT

SOME twenty years ago the late Professor J. A. Smith read a paper on this subject to the Oxford Philological Society. So far as I know, this paper has never been published, and I can only give some of the main points as I remember them.

According to Professor Smith the original meaning of λόγος was just talk, conversation, prose as distinct from poetry. Thus the familiar fragment of Heraclitus, τοῦ λόγου τοῦδ' ἐόντος αἰεί, ἀσύνετοι γίνονται ἄνθρωποι, has nothing to do with the eternity of a supernatural being. It simply states that while the discussion of some unidentified question is endless, men find it difficult to understand what it is about.

From this original meaning the word came to be used for what is said about something, and so for the definition of things, *i.e.* their description in words. An extension of this usage led to its meaning a diagram, for in answer to the question, "What is the *logos* of a triangle?" a man might draw one on a blackboard. In this way the word λόγος became connected with the idea of reason, for only that which is rational is definable. There can be a definition of a triangle, but not of a square circle. Only the rational is λογικόν.

Professor Smith then denied that the word was ever used in the Greek tradition for the active reasoning faculty in man, or for a cognate principle in the universe. The phrase for this faculty, he said, was τὸ λογιστικόν, and there is no instance of λόγος being used for τὸ λογιστικόν. The roots of that later usage, he said, were probably to be found in Hebrew thought. Through such men as Philo the word λόγος came to be used to translate the Hebrew *Memrah*, and theologians in their ignorance had read back the later meaning, with which they were familiar, into earlier writings where it was out of place.

To prove his thesis Professor Smith took *seriatim* a number of passages in which theologians are accustomed to see anticipations of the Hebrew-Christian Logos doctrine, and offered alternative translations based on the distinction between λόγος and τὸ λογιστικόν. Besides the quoation from Heraclitus already mentioned, I only remember his treatment of the λόγοι σπερματικοί of the Stoics. This phrase, he suggested, described a biological theory according to which the fact that the offspring of horses are horses and of goats goats is due to the fact that in each case the male spermata are miniature copies of the full-sized animals.

There were present at the reading of this paper certain classical and philosophical scholars who were at home in the world of pre-Christian Greek thought. I gathered from the ensuing discussion that they regarded the thesis favourably.

I am not myself competent to make a judgment on the question, and have long regretted that the paper has not been published, so as to enable it to be criticised by those who are. On *a priori* grounds, for the reasons given on pp. 113 ff. above, I should be inclined to expect Professor Smith to be right. In any case, having heard his paper, I cannot disregard the fact that the traditional view has been challenged and that the question is an open one.

THE CONTROVERSIES OF THE SEVENTEENTH AND EIGHTEENTH CENTURIES

THE British unitarianism of the seventeenth and eighteenth centuries was born of belief in the competence of reason to criticise traditional doctrines, and it was impatient of any conception of unity other than the "clear and distinct idea of it" given by mathematics.

"You add yet more absurdly, that there are three Persons who are *severally and each of them true God*, and yet there is but one true God: this is *an Error* in counting or numbring; which, when stood in, is of all others the most brutal and inexcusable; and not to discern it is not to be a Man."[1]

"Let it be admitted, that you had proved the supreme divinity of Christ and the Holy Spirit, the natural conclusion would have been three distinct Gods, which is a doctrine expressly condemned by Scripture and reason."[2]

"It must be universally true, that *three things* to which the same definition applies can never make only *one thing* to which the same definition applies. . . . If, therefore, the three persons agree in this circumstance, that they are each of them *perfect God*, though they may differ in other respects, and have peculiar relations to each other and to us, they must still be *three Gods*; and to say that they are only *one God* is as much a contradiction, as to say that three men, though they differ from one another as much as three men can do, are not three men, but only one man."[3]

"If *ideas* are attached to the words employed, Trinitarianism is, in reality, either Tritheism or Sabellianism."[4]

The orthodox doctrine of the Incarnation was found equally open to criticism.

[1] *A Brief History of the Unitarians, called also Socinians*, p. 24. (Published anonymously, but ascribed to John Biddle.) 1687.

[2] *The Trinitarian Controversy Reviewed: or a Defence of the Appeal to the Common Sense of all Christian People*, p. 338. By the Author of the Appeal. London, 1760.

[3] Joseph Priestley, in *Tracts*, vol. i. p. 182. Printed and published by the Unitarian Society. London, 1791.

[4] *An Examination of the Charges made against Unitarians and Unitarianism and the Improved Version by the Right Rev. Dr. Magee, Bishop of Raphoe*, p. xxx. By Lant Carpenter, D.D. Bristol, 1820.

"To suppose the Son of God, when he was upon earth, to be assisted by the Spirit of God; and at the same time to suppose that he was supreme God himself, and equally possessed of divine power with the Father, is such a gross and palpable contradiction, as disinterested Christians could not possibly swallow down, if they exerted those reasonable powers which God hath given them."[1]

This rationalism, however, was not of the type which is inconsistent with belief in divine revelation and supernatural events.

"He is also the Son of God, because he was begotten on blessed *Mary* by the Spirit or Power of God, Luke i. 35."

"John iii. 13. . . . The Socinians do (generally) understand this Text literally, and say, that 'tis here intimated that before our Lord entered upon his Office of Messias, he was taken up to Heaven to be instructed in the Mind and Will of God (as Moses was into the Mount, Exod. xxiv. 1, 2, 12) and from thence descended to execute his Office, and declare the said Will of God."

"He that could multiply the Loaves and Fishes, and the Wine at the Wedding of *Cana*, need not have wanted any of the Comforts of Life."[2]

"He has this title [*i.e.* Son of God] because He was born of the virgin Mary in a miraculous manner, Luke i. 35. 2. He is stiled Son of God upon account of his office, John x. 34. 3. Of his resurrection, Acts xiii. 33, and Rom. i. 4."[3]

"Christ being made by the immediate hand of God, and not born in the usual course of generation, is no reason for his not being considered as a man. For then Adam must not have been a man."[4]

"Dr. Graves dwells greatly on the miraculous powers of our Lord: where is the Unitarian who would say less, except as it respects the source of those powers?"[5]

These passages show that the unitarians as well as their opponents, accepted the Bible as containing revelation given in the form of propositions, after the manner criticised in my first lecture. Two further passages are interesting illustrations of this method of interpretation.

"But when you infer that Christ is upon an equal footing with God, because he is represented as standing at the right hand of God, you may with equal reason infer the same thing with respect to the angels of God; for they are set forth in Scripture *as standing by him on his right hand and on his left*, 1 Kings xxii. 19.[6]

"[On John x. 35.] Now if Christ had been conscious to himself

---

[1] *Defence*, p. 225.
[2] *Brief History*, pp. 4, 91, 124.
[3] *Defence*, p. 68.
[4] Priestley, p. 20.
[5] Carpenter, p. xx.
[6] *Defence*, p. 301.

that he was the *true and very God*, and that it was of the utmost consequence to mankind that they should regard him in that light, this was certainly a proper time for him to have declared himself, and not to have put his hearers off with such an apology as this."[1]

On both sides of the controversy the appeal to reason was to the use of reason for the purpose of finding the right interpretation of the Bible as containing the divine revelation given in the form of propositions. In this, both sides regarded themselves as carrying on the work of the Reformation, furthering the rescue of the Bible from concealment under popish misinterpretation and restoring it to the scrutiny of reason and common sense. The trinitarians, however, regarded the history of Christian thought in the first five centuries as showing the church engaged in drawing out the true meaning of the biblical revelation and expressing it in the Nicene and Athanasian creeds. The unitarians claimed to be more thorough-going in their fidelity to Reformation principles in that they went back behind all human inventions and speculations, those of the fourth and fifth no less than of later centuries, to the Bible itself. They maintained that the Nicene doctrine of Christ's deity, and the trinitarianism of the *Quicunque Vult*, were first steps in that corruption of the primitive Christian faith which ultimately reached its climax in the Roman errors of their own time.

"Their silence upon a point deemed important, undeniably demonstrates that the Apostles never entertained any such notion; neither did they require any such belief of the first Christians; and it lies upon you, as a sincere Christian, to show what right Christians had, who lived several hundred years after their days, to make that necessary to salvation, which Christ and his Apostles never made so."
"As for subtle metaphysical inquiries, whether God eternally willed that all fulness should dwell in Christ, or not, I meddle not with them: it is sufficient for my understanding, that the Scripture hath expressly determined, that Christ was the first being whom God produced."[2]

There are many such passages, in which the theology of the creeds is regarded as metaphysical speculations of human origin and con-trasted with the divinely revealed truth. Particular criticism is levelled against the use of the word "God" for a "tripersonal substance."

"When, therefore, you maintain that God, taken absolutely,

[1] Priestley, p. 18.   [2] *Defence*, pp. 69, 210.

cannot be said to be a Person, you introduce nothing but confusion: For God is always described by the sacred writers, as a Person. . . . When you speak of God being an intelligent Agent, and at the same time deny him to be a Person, you talk in a language not possible to be understood. . . . Again, whether the terms Essence, and Substance, have the same signification, or whether they signify different things, I think of little importance, and not worth a particular discussion. It is high time that all such metaphysical terms should be banished from Christian professions, and Christian debates."[1]

On the other side, the trinitarians tried to show that the Fathers who wrote the creeds rightly and reasonably interpreted the sacred text. Samuel Clarke's *Scripture-Doctrine of the Trinity* (1712), which consisted of a very full catena of texts interpreted in the unitarian direction, called forth in reply Daniel Waterland's *Vindication of Christ's Divinity*.[2] This consisted of a collection of texts arranged in groups; to each group were appended a number of queries and a discussion of each query. A second volume, answering criticisms of the first, and developing its arguments, was published in 1723. The following four queries give a fair example of the ground on which the trinitarians took their stand:

"Whether the Doctor need have cited 300 Texts, wide of the purpose, to prove what no Body denies, namely a *Subordination*, in some Sense, of the *Son* to the Father; could he have found but one plain Text against his *Eternity* or *Consubstantiality*, the points in Question?" (Query XX.)

"Whether he be not forc'd to supply his want of Scripture-proof by very strain'd and remote Inferences, and very uncertain Reasonings from the Nature of a thing, confessedly, Obscure and above Comprehension; and yet not more so than God's *Eternity*, *Ubiquity*, *Prescience*, or other Attributes, which yet we are obliged to acknowledge for certain Truths?" (Query XXI.)

"Whether the Doctor did not equivocate or prevaricate strangely in saying 'the generality of Writers before the Council of Nice, were, in the whole, clearly on his side': when it is manifest, they were, in the general, no further on his side, than the allowing of a *Subordination* amounts to; no further than our own Church is on his side, while in the main points of difference, the *Eternity* and *Consubstantiality*, they are clearly against him? That is, they were on his side, so far as we acknowledge him to be right, but no further." (Query XXVI.)

"Whether private Reasoning, in a matter above our Comprehension, be a safer Rule to go by, than the general Sense and Judgment of the primitive Church, in the first 300 years; or, supposing

[1] *Defence*, p. 6.   [2] Cambridge and London, 1719.

it doubtful, what the Sense of the Church was within that time, whether what was determin'd by a Council of 300 Bishops soon after, with the greatest Care and Deliberation, and has satisfied Men of the greatest Sense, Piety and Learning, all over the Christian World, for 1400 Years since, may not satisfy wise and good Men now?" (Query XXIX.)

These quotations should be enough to give a general picture of the issues raised and discussed and to show why these controversies, in spite of their importance in the history of British Christianity, have not been given a place in my lectures. Both parties assumed ideas of revelation and of the Bible which in my first lecture I have argued to be untenable, and both consequently ignored the fact that the revelation of God in Christ, properly appreciated as revelation in act, involved a revision of the conception of unity which would ultimately relieve trinitarianism from the necessity of seeking to preserve the divine unity by any form of subordinationism. Hence from the point of view of my lectures these controversies had nothing to contribute to the exposition of the doctrine which it was my aim to present.

The impression which they leave on my mind is that *on the basis of argument which both sides held in common*, the unitarians had the better case. They could counter their opponents' biblical exegesis with interpretations equally, if not more, convincing, and such passages as the following found a weak spot in their armour:

"If the Father be really first in rank and order, and the fountain of the divinity, it necessarily follows that he is the one supreme God, and from him is derived all the divinity ascribed to Christ. But it is beyond my imagination to conceive, how you can make this consistent with the avowed plan of your answer, which is to prove that the Son and Holy Spirit are equally divine with the Father, and have the same essential perfections. This reduced to plain sense and language, conveys an evident contradiction: the Son and Holy Spirit are equally supreme with the Father, excepting that they must be allowed to be inferior."[1]

The trinitarians, on the other hand, I believe to have been standing for the truth, but unable to make good their case for want of revision of their premises.

It was not the first time that this had happened in the history of the Church. In the christological controversies of the fifth century the orthodox theologians were hampered by assuming with their

[1] *Defence*, p. 53.

opponents a conception of God inconsistent with the Nicene doctrine of direct creation. Hence there was more of truth in their inconsistencies than in the more logically coherent teaching of Nestorius and Eutyches.[1] I have argued in the lectures that the place of the divine revelation in human thought is that of empirical evidence, the recognition of which for what it is requires the revision of human ideas of God, of unity, and of revelation itself. In both the christological controversies of the fifth century, and the trinitarian controversies of the seventeenth and eighteenth, we see the dynamite of the empirical evidence exploding the unrevised ideas. The difficulties of the orthodox exhibited the incapacity of their existing conceptions to assimilate the revealed truth. The reason why those controversies have not been discussed in these lectures is that the lectures as a whole are an attempt to learn the lesson they have to teach, which lesson is that further discussion of the question on their lines is unnecessary and unprofitable.

[1] On this see my contribution to Rawlinson: *Essays on the Trinity and Incarnation* (London, 1928), pp. 376–92.

NOTES ON SOME RECENT CONTRIBUTIONS TO THE THEOLOGY OF THE TRINITY

IN his Gifford Lectures for 1918 on *God and Personality*, Dr. C. C. J. Webb broke new ground in his discussion of the doctrine of the Trinity, and laid all subsequent theologians under a debt of obligation to his work. He recalled to mind two truths which at that time were often overlooked: (i) that in orthodox Christian theology God is not a person, so that it is more accurate to speak of personality *in* than *of* God, and (ii) that the unitarian doctrine of the personality *of* God is logically connected with the doctrine of the necessity of the created universe to the being of God.

The revolt against the idealist metaphysic was due to insistence on the necessity of interpreting empirical facts and not explaining them away. Dr. Webb's lectures played a notable part in that revolt by their insistence that full weight should be given to the evidence provided by religious experience. This requires us to account for a consciousness both of distinction and of community of nature between man and God, on which he said:

"The description and mutual reconciliation of those facts of religious experience which I have described as at first sight mutually inconsistent and so requiring to be harmonised by the help of this conception of a Mediator will, I think, be found to involve, when worked out into a theological doctrine, the recognition of a twofold Personality in the Divine Nature." (P. 182.)

But in his discussion of the philosophical importance of the idea of a Mediator, Dr. Webb seems to me to underestimate that of the distinction between myth and history. He rightly, I think, holds that the place of myth is in the presentation of empirical events for which historical evidence is lacking, and that truth in the case of myths means correspondence with those standing truths which are the subject-matter of philosophy. But he omits to notice that these standing truths are themselves arrived at by the philosophical interpretation of what is empirically given, *i.e.* of history. He is content to leave open the question whether the incarnation is myth or history, and to treat St. Paul's account of the Christian experience of adoptive kinship with God as illustrative of an element in religious experience generally. In this he reflects the outlook of the idealism which in other ways he is undermining. The doctrine of the Trinity is left, so to speak, in the air unless the experience on which it is based is experience of a definite, concrete, self-revelation of God in history.

With regard to the doctrine of the Holy Spirit, Dr. Webb follows in general what he takes to be the Augustinian idea of the *vinculum*, and regards the "personality" of the Spirit as intended to assert something less than I have maintained is required by the evidence. He writes:

"The intention of the theological phraseology to which I have referred I take to be no other than this—to claim for the life of mutual knowledge and love which, in the intercourse of Religion, the worshipper, so far as he realises his sonship, enjoys with the Supreme, and in enjoying it recognises to be no other than the very life itself of the Supreme—to claim for that life a complete concrete reality, in no respect less than that of those who share in it and have their being in it." (P. 275.)

Dr. Webb does not base this conclusion on any supposed requirement of the nature of unity, on the argument that to admit a plurality of persons in the full sense of the word necessitates tritheism. On the contrary. He insists that the unity of the Godhead must be thought of in such a way as to allow of personal relations between the Father and the Son. As I have suggested in my fourth lecture, it looks as though the reason why the Spirit is in this respect treated differently from the Son is that Dr. Webb has treated the patristic theology as the source of orthodox doctrine rather than the evidence of the New Testament. So far as I can see, Dr. Webb's conception of the divine unity would not be altered but enriched by that evidence as I have interpreted it in these lectures.

Ten years later this conception of the divine unity was definitely rejected by Dr. H. Wheeler Robinson in *The Christian Experience of the Holy Spirit*.[1] As the title of his book shows, Dr. Wheeler Robinson resembles Dr. Webb in that his theology is based on an analysis of religious experience. But his conclusion is very different.

"We cannot possibly make sense of the classical doctrine of the Trinity without deliberately eliminating the full and rich content of the term "person" which fifteen centuries have bequeathed to us. . . .

The fourth-century doctrine in its historical interpretation is much more intelligible than some of the modern attempts to defend

[1] London, 1928.

it. It safeguards the values of Christian experience by relating them to the ultimate being of God, and it declares that God is for ever in Himself that which we have found Him to be in our experience of Him. It asks us to think of Him as eternally existent in three forms of being beyond our experience of being, but it does not ask us to ascribe to each of those forms of existence a conception of personality which belongs rather to the *unity* of the Godhead. Personality, as we so far know it, exhibits the approximation of a developing self-consciousness towards unity. Its true analogy, therefore (incompleteness apart), would be with the *ousia* rather than with the hypostases of the Godhead." (Pp. 254–5.)

How is it that Dr. Wheeler Robinson comes to interpret Christian experience so differently from Dr. Webb and myself? A careful reading of his book shows that his thought is throughout controlled by an idealist metaphysic of the type maintained by Pringle-Pattison. "Spirit" is fundamentally the medium through which God realises Himself in the universe.

"In our survey of the work of the Holy Spirit we have so far seen that in Jesus Christ the Spirit of God revealed through Nature and history finds a unique and adequate vehicle in terms of human personality. This new centre of "realised revelation" or "revealing realisation" expands into the corporate personality of the Church, as the Body of Christ." (Pp. 199.)

Hence the typical expression of Christian experience is found in Eph. ii. 18, "Through Him (Christ) we both have our access in one Spirit unto the Father," interpreted in such a way as to be consistent with the idealist metaphysic and not with that of an ultimate tripersonality in God. The extent to which the idealist metaphysic had come to dominate the theological mind may be seen when he writes: "This unity of the Godhead in the Christian experience of the New Testament is of primary importance, and remains true for all unsophisticated reproduction of that experience"(p. 231).[1]

In 1930 Dr. W. R. Matthews (now Dean of St. Paul's) published his *God in Christian Experience*, in which he refers to both the above books. His judgment is cautious and balanced. He points out that historically theology has attempted to conceive of the Trinity by analogy both from the individual soul and from society. In the end he tends to follow Webb rather than Wheeler Robinson and to favour the social analogy. He speaks of "the conception of a reciprocal relatedness of active and conscious centres" and of "the possibility that, in the case of the Godhead, the relation between the First and

[1] On this see Appendix VIII below.

Second Persons may itself be Personal" (pp. 194, 198). And, further, he says:

"The New Testament evidence for the personal conception of the Holy Spirit is mixed, and I cannot resist the conclusion that, in many cases, the Holy Spirit is thought of as the power, influence, or presence of God through Christ. I am sure that the normal attitude of most Christians towards the Holy Spirit is of this character, and the idea of personal relations with the Spirit is very little prominent in the life of devotion. Perhaps this state of things is the mark of imperfection. . . . At least there is some support in the New Testament and in the Christian consciousness for the belief that the Spirit is a divine Person, and the Catholic Church has decided that the doctrine is part of the Christian faith. To the present writer this last fact, though not finally decisive, is of very great moment. I should be very slow to recognise that, in a matter of this fundamental importance, the mind of the Church has been mistaken, and should prefer to hold, even if there were less to be said in support of the dogma than there is, that the inability to make the belief real to myself was due to defect of spiritual insight or understanding." (P. 196.)

Working on entirely different lines from any of the above, Father Lionel Thornton of the Community of the Resurrection produced *The Incarnate Lord* in 1928. This is in my opinion the greatest theological work that has appeared in my lifetime. I believe that if it had been originally written in German or Russian, British theologians would have been falling over each other in their eagerness to expound it to their fellow-countrymen; as it was the work of an Englishman writing in English they could not be bothered to wrestle with its unfamiliar and, at first sight, uncongenial terminology. In it Father Thornton set out to expound the Christian doctrine of God in terms of the philosophy of A. N. Whitehead. In doing so, he never fell into the temptation to assimilate the historic revelation to the demands of the philosophical system, as so many of the idealistic theologians had done. On the contrary, he brought into the philosophy from the Christian revelation what it needed to make that system work, to save it from the necessity of postulating pan-psychism in order to account for the movement in the universe. I have referred in my third lecture to his thorough-going investigation of the New Testament teaching about the relation between the Spirit and the risen Christ, and its convincing demonstration of the distinction between them.[1] I can say no more

[1] Above, p. 83, and Appendix IV.

about this book here beyond expressing my very great indebtedness
to it, an indebtedness which speaks from almost every page of these
lectures.

More recently, and very surprisingly, Professor Karl Barth has
come out as an advocate of the view that the Persons of the Trinity
are not to be regarded as Persons in the full sense of the word, but
that it is to "the one single essence of God . . . that there also belongs
what we call to-day the 'personality' of God."[1] He urges that what
are commonly called "Persons" would better be called three "modes
of existence" of the one God. I call this "surprising," because
Professor Barth is not, like Dr. Wheeler Robinson, a professed
adherent of Pringle-Pattisonian, or any other, philosophy. He
claims to be a biblical theologian, expounding biblical doctrine.
And yet his theology seems to me in flat contradiction to the biblical
evidence. The ground of his assertion appears to be the conviction
that the other view necessarily involves tritheism. If this be so, then
it would seem that his thought is governed by considerations which
are essentially rationalistic rather than biblical. Instead of allowing
the empirical evidence of the biblical revelation to revise his idea
of unity, he insists on making that evidence conform to the requirements of his *a priori* conception of unity. For this reason I must
emphatically dissent from the judgment of his English translator
who finds in his work the greatest contribution to the exposition
of the doctrine of the Trinity in modern theology.

I should not omit to notice the "sophiological" works of the Russian
Orthodox theologian, Father Sergius Bulgakov. Most of them,
however, are written in Russian and thus inaccessible to those who,
like myself, cannot read that language. But in 1937 he published
in English a summary of his thought in a book entitled *The Wisdom
of God*.[2] From this it appears that Fr. Bulgakov represents that type
of theology which in my discussion of St. Augustine, St. Thomas and
Calvin I have rejected as unprofitable. His thought is based on
the twin foundations of *a priori* metaphysical assumptions and the
acceptance of the Bible as giving revelation in the form of propositions concerning the inner mysteries of the Godhead. On these
foundations he builds a system in which the Wisdom of the Hebrew
Wisdom literature is identified with the substance of patristic
trinitarian theology and differently hypostatised in the different

---

[1] *The Doctrine of the Word of God*. English translation by G. T. Thomson
(Edinburgh, 1936), p. 403.
[2] New York, the Paisley Press; London, Williams & Norgate.

persons of the Trinity. Then the problem of creation is solved by regarding this Wisdom as existing in two modes, as the uncreated substance of the divine Trinity and as the created substance of the universe in process of becoming. Through this double functioning of His Wisdom-substance God is enabled to be both the Absolute and the Creator.

Fr. Bulgakov clearly thinks that in this way he has succeeded in finding a satisfactory metaphysical solution to the problems both of the unity of the divine Trinity and of creation. I am not convinced, however, that the success is more than verbal. And in any case, of this whole method of thinking I can only say what I have already said of it in connection with the classical theologians, that while to some minds it may be helpful as an aid to devotion, I can see no grounds on which it is possible to discuss the question of its truth.

If Miss Dorothy Sayers' fascinating little book, *The Mind of the Maker*,[1] were to be regarded as an exposition of the doctrine of the Trinity it might be thought to fall under the condemnation of those which confuse the begetting of the Son with the creation of the universe. Indeed, there is one passage which seems to suggest this: "It may be more fruitful to consider time as a part of creation, or perhaps time is necessarily associated with Being in activity— that is, not with God the Father but with God the Son" (p. 80). But pp. 31–32 show clearly that this is not the intention of the authoress. What she is concerned to do is to point out that the threefoldness involved in human creative activity suggests an analogous threefold- ness in the Divine Creator, and not to maintain that the created universe is in any sense internal or necessary to the being of God. In my third lecture I have argued that the three elements in human personality suggest the probability that in God there is a similar but *eminent* threefoldness—eminent in the sense of unifying elements each more fully personal than those which constitute the human self. In a like vein, I take it, Miss Sayers is arguing that the threefoldness essential to human creativity suggests the probability that in the Divine Creator there is a similar but eminent threefoldness. In this case, the Divine Threefoldness is thought of as wholly characterising the Creator; Father, Son and Spirit are all to be thought of as constituting the Creator as over against the created. Read in this way the book is a very illuminating aid to the understanding of the faith.

[1] London, 1941.

I welcome most heartily a remarkable article by Canon Phythian-Adams of Carlisle, entitled "Gospel and Creed," published in the *Church Quarterly Review* for January–March 1941. It came to my notice at an advanced stage in the composition of these lectures, and its interpretation of the New Testament is so similar to that which I had been working out at greater length that it is worth while remarking here that neither of us has plagiarised from the other. Neither of us had any idea that the other was thinking along these lines at all.

THE PERSONALITY OF THE SPIRIT IN CHRISTIAN
DEVOTION

AMONG the passages quoted from Dr. Wheeler Robinson in the previous appendix are two which suggest that to ascribe "he-ness" to the Holy Spirit, as I have done in the lectures, is to teach a doctrine which is untrue to the main current of Christian devotion:

"The fourth century doctrine . . . asks us to think of Him [*i.e.* God] as eternally existent in three forms of being beyond our experience of being, but it does not ask us to ascribe to each of these forms of existence a conception of personality which belongs rather to the *unity* of the Godhead."
"This unity of the Godhead in the Christian experience of the New Testament is of primary importance, and remains true for all unsophisticated reproduction of that experience."[1]

Now it is true that, so far as I know, there is extant no instance of hymns or prayers addressed to the Holy Spirit that is certainly earlier than the tenth century. It is also true that the standard form of Christian worship is worship offered by the Christian to the Father in union with the Son through the Spirit. But that this worship was ever felt to be incompatible with the doctrine of the "heness" of the Spirit seems to me to be unlikely from the fact that the Paraclete passages in the Fourth Gospel were an integral part of the liturgical scriptures of the Church.

In the fourth century St. Basil of Caesarea devoted a great deal of his treatise *De Spiritu Sancto* to a defence of that form of the *Gloria* which treated the Spirit as parallel to the Father and the Son in the conglorification of the Persons of the Trinity. In § 73 he says that this form was traditional, and had been used in the previous century by Origen and by Julius Africanus. A similar strain is found in § 14 of the second century document describing the martyrdom of St. Polycarp. This same parallelism is preserved in the "Nicene" creed of 381.

When, therefore, from the tenth century onwards, the Church began to use devotions directly addressed to the Holy Spirit, it was

[1] *Op. cit.*, pp. 254, 231.

enriching its prayer life by realising more fully the potentialities
of its traditional doctrine of God.

Of six hymns addressed to the Holy Spirit in the *English Hymnal*,
two are ascribed to the tenth century or earlier: βαδιλεῦ οὐράνιε,
παράκλητε (No. 454) and *Veni Creator Spiritus* (No. 344). One is
ascribed to the thirteenth: *Veni sancte Spiritus* (No. 345). The
seventeenth and eighteenth centuries produced Bishop Cosin's
adaptation of the *Veni Creator Spiritus* (No. 153), Dryden's "Creator
Spirit, by whose aid" (No. 156) and Coffin's "O holy Spirit, Lord
of grace" (No. 453). A book of devotions published at this same period
contains four offices of the Holy Ghost. The first opens thus:

Invitatory
> *Come let's Adore our God that sanctifies us*
> *Come let's Adore our God that sanctifies us.*

Come, let us humbly first implore his Grace, to make us worthy
to adore our Sanctifier, who from the Father and the Son eternally
proceeds, and with the Father and the Son is equally glorified.

> *Come let's Adore our God that sanctifies us.*

He infuseth into us the Breath of Life and brings us forth into
our Second Birth, a Birth that makes us Heirs of Heaven, and gives
us a Title to everlasting Happiness.

> *Come let's Adore our God that sanctifies us.*

Let us prepare our Understandings to assent to his Truths, and
our Will to follow his Divine Inspirations; let us fill our Memories
with his innumerable Mercies and our whole Soul with the Glory
of His Attributes.

> *Come let's adore our God that sanctifies us.*

Let us confidently address to him our Petitions, who promises
to help the Infirmity of our Prayers; let us not doubt the Bounty
of his Goodness, but hope he will grant what himself inspires to ask.

> *Come, let's adore our God that sanctifies us*
> *Glory be to the Father, etc.*
> *As it was in the beginning, etc.*
> *Come, let's Adore, etc.*
> *Come let's Adore, etc.*

Then follows a hymn addressed to the Holy Spirit, and later on
are such prayers as these:

Govern, O blessed Spirit, the Church thou so wonderfully hast
established; govern it with thy special Grace, and always preserve
it in Obedience to thee, and us in Obedience to it.

Quicken us by thy Grace, O Holy Spirit, that we may thoroughly mortifie the Works of the Flesh.[1]

When writing of the Litany in the *Book of Common Prayer* Procter and Frere quote a Latin version dating from the Anglo-Saxon Church of the eleventh century, which opens:

> Kyrie eleison. Christe eleison. Christe audi nos.
> Pater de coelis Deus, Miserere nobis.
> Fili Redemptor mundi Deus, Miserere nobis.
> Spiritus sancte Deus, Miserere nobis.
> Sancta Trinitas unus Deus, Miserere nobis.[2]

It would seem, therefore, that what Dr. Wheeler Robinson calls the "unsophisticated reproduction" of the New Testament Christian experience of God is not that which finds expression in the common prayer of the Christian Church. That prayer bears witness to a religious life which combines (1) the worship of the Father through the Spirit by those who know themselves to be adopted to share the sonship of Christ, (2) devotions addressed to each Person of the Trinity, and (3) devotions addressed to the Trinity as a whole. It implies the theology set forth in these lectures and not that of Dr. Wheeler Robinson's book.

[1] *From Devotions in the Ancient Way of Offices*, pp. 392, 408, 428. Reformed by a Person of Quality and published by George Hickes, D.D. Third Edition, London, 1706.

[2] *A New History of the Book of Common Prayer* (London, 1908), p. 411.

INDEX